CW00924261

THE SWIMSUIT

THIS IS A CARLTON BOOK
This edition published in 2007 by Carlton Books Limited,
20 Mortimer Street, London W1T 3JW

A CIP catalogue record of this book is available from the British Library.

ISBN: 978 1 84442 079 7

Printed and bound in Dubai

Executive Editor: Lisa Dyer
Senior Art Editor: Lucy Coley
Designer: Barbara Zuñiga
Illustrations: Adam Wright
Copy Editor: Nicky Gyopari
Picture Researcher: Jenny Lord
Production: Caroline Alberti
Special Photography: Russell Porter

THE SWIMSUIT

CARLTON
BOOKS

CONTENTS

introduction 6

chapter one: FROM BRIGHTON TO BIARRITZ 12

chapter two: THE ST TROPEZ SET 32

chapter three: STAR QUALITY 62

THE BEAUTY PAGEANT 90

chapter four: THE RETURN OF THE HOURGLASS 100

THE BIRTH OF THE BIKINI 134

chapter five: THE FABULOUS FIFTIES 144

chapter six: FAR-OUT GROOVES 178

chapter seven: THE BEACH BABE REVOLUTION 204

CALENDAR GIRLS AND PIN-UPS 228

chapter eight: LET'S GET PHYSICAL 236

chapter nine: NEW-LUXE NINETIES 256

chapter ten: POST-MILLENNIUM TRENDS 278

designers and brands 294

index 297

acknowledgements 303

Introduction

During the past 200 years, no single item of clothing has evolved as dramatically as the swimsuit. Only the aeroplane and space rockets have taken off faster, and if any part of their inventing process had involved ladies showing their ankles, we would all still be rowing between London and New York and the moon would be a big, but distant star.

From murderous Victorian crinolines to barely-there wisps of fabric, the swimsuit has acted as a clothing barometer of our times. It was more than pure coincidence that the monokini arrived along with the contraceptive pill, or that the voluptuous hourglass-corset costume returned after the frugal hardships of wartime. Skinnier models than ever may be scaring us on the catwalks but on the beaches, real women still look fabulous in their swimsuits. We can't help but be inspired by the sirens of the past. Images of the great 1940s and 1950s pin-ups are as deeply entrenched in western culture as national flags and tea or coffee. Rita Hayworth, Marilyn Monroe, Brigitte Bardot, Ursula Andress – all still conjure up the glorious golden years of the swimsuit and bikini. Even further back in time, early seaside postcards of 'Bathing Belles' seem comical to us, but to society, they were the beginnings of something radically different. The bathing beauties in their multi-layered, knee-length swimsuits heralded the arrival of a new young woman who, along with her swimsuit, would only ever keep striding forward.

From the manufacturers who worked with artificial fibres to invent fabrics strong and waterproof enough for swimming, to the women who wore their early designs and shivered on the beaches, so many elements have played a part in the swimsuit's sensational history. Lastex, the stretch fibre developed by US Rubber in the late 1920s, along with DuPont's Lycra fibres, helped transform the soggy, knitted costumes of yesteryear into the sleek, super-comfortable body-clingers women wear today.

Sportswear manufacturers, such as Speedo, Jantzen and Catalina began by producing athletic swimming costumes, but nothing brought greater change for the swimsuit than its passage from practicality to style. When fashion got hold of swimwear, there was no turning back. All the great fashion players of the twentieth century had a hand, from Coco Chanel and her boyish shapes to Christian Dior and the return of the hourglass figure. One factor, however, has driven swimsuit design further through the ages than any other, and that's the beach holiday: nothing feels nicer than sand between the toes and sun on the skin. Despite what we now know about all the risks associated with a trip to the beach, most of us are still willing to take that chance at any opportunity. Strip away all the gloss of the modern spa holiday or the deluxe resort retreat and what are you left with? Water and the opportunity to go in it – from this fundamental fun-factor all swimsuits were born.

The Swimsuit Timeline

1910s

1907: Australian swimmer and 'underwater ballerina' Annette Kellerman is arrested in Boston, Massachusetts, for indecent exposure; she was wearing a one-piece bathing suit in public.

1913: Jantzen introduces the first rib-stitch bathing costume for the Portland Rowing Club in Oregon.

1916: The first annual Bathing Suit Day, a fashion show of the latest designs, is held at Madison Square Gardens, New York.

1920s

1921: The first Miss America pageant is held in Atlantic City, New Jersey, under the title of the Inter-City Beauty Contest.

1925: Lastex, a trade name for an elastic latex rubber, is invented by the American Rubber Company and incorporated into bathing suits. Mabs of Hollywood use it in their designs, while Cole of California use a version they patented as Matletex.

1928: The term 'maillot', first used to describe tight-fitting one-piece jersey suits, enters the English dictionary.

1928: The Australian MacRae Knitting Mills renames itself Speedo on the back of the launch of its racerback swimsuit design and the slogan 'Speed on in Your Speedos'.

1930s

1930: French fashion designer Elsa Schiaparelli patents a backless swimsuit with a built-in bra to promote strap-free tanning.

1935: American designer Claire McCardell creates a cut-out maillot that's seen as the forerunner of the bikini; her 'diaper' swimsuit is first introduced in this decade.

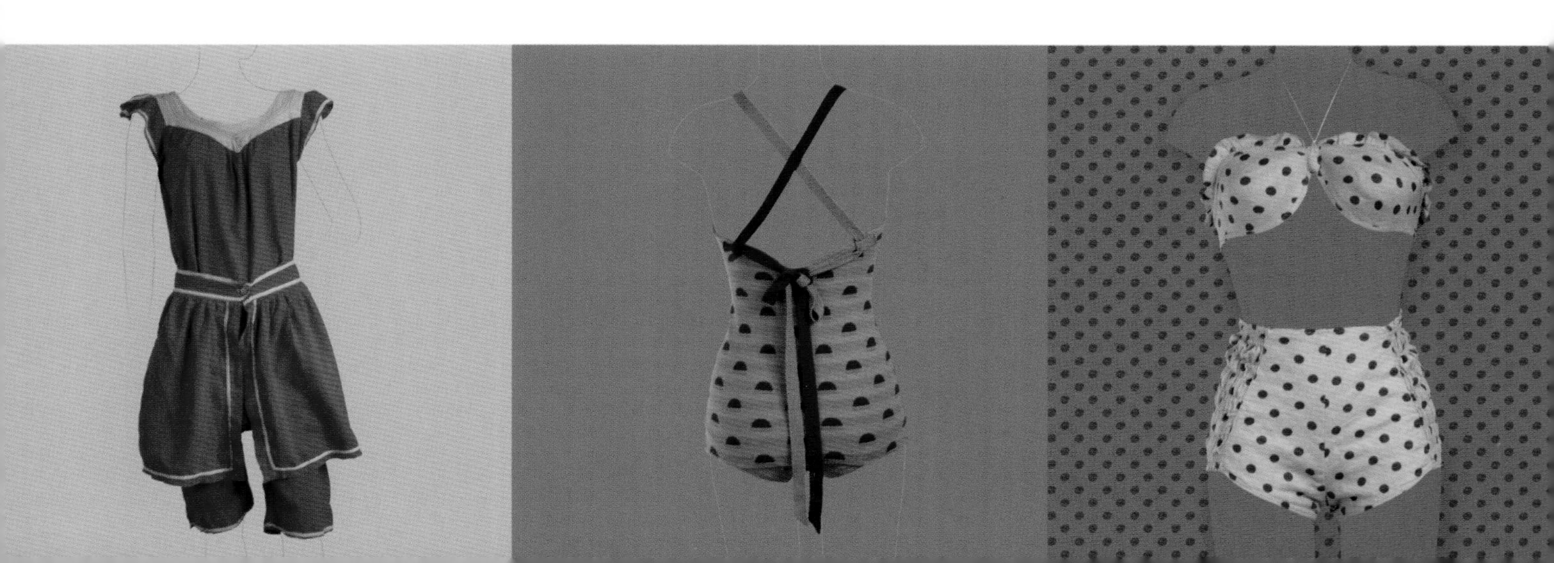

1936: Margit Fellegi, the Hollywood costumer, begins collaborating with Cole of California, producing glamorous swimwear for the stars.

1940s

1940: British Nylon Spinners begin production of their version of nylon, Bri-Nylon. Their promotion campaigns run for years, peaking in 1961.

1946: Louis Réard and Jacques Heim simultaneously launch the 'first' bikini.

1947: Christian Dior debuts his New Look couture collection, starting the trend for hourglass silhouettes in swimwear.

1950s

1950: Cole of California signs swimming star of the screen Esther Williams to a merchandizing and design contract.

1951: Bikinis are banned from the Miss World Contest, following the crowning of Miss Sweden in a bikini.

1952: Catalina starts the Miss Universe beauty contest, having withdrawn from sponsoring Miss America in 1951 after the winner, Yolande Betbeze, refuses to wear a Catalina suit in the traditional tour.

1953: *Vogue* celebrates swimsuits with its Coronation Issue, featuring jewel-coloured suits in velvets, taffeta and faille.

1953: Designers, such as Bob and Bill Meistrell of Body Glove and Robert and Jack O'Neill of the surf brand O'Neill, begin experimenting with neoprene in wetsuits and swimwear.

1955: English actress and sex symbol Diana Dors appears at the Venice film festival in a mink bikini, showing that bikinis were more about glamour than swimming.

1955: Christian Dior brings out a collection of swimwear for Cole of California.

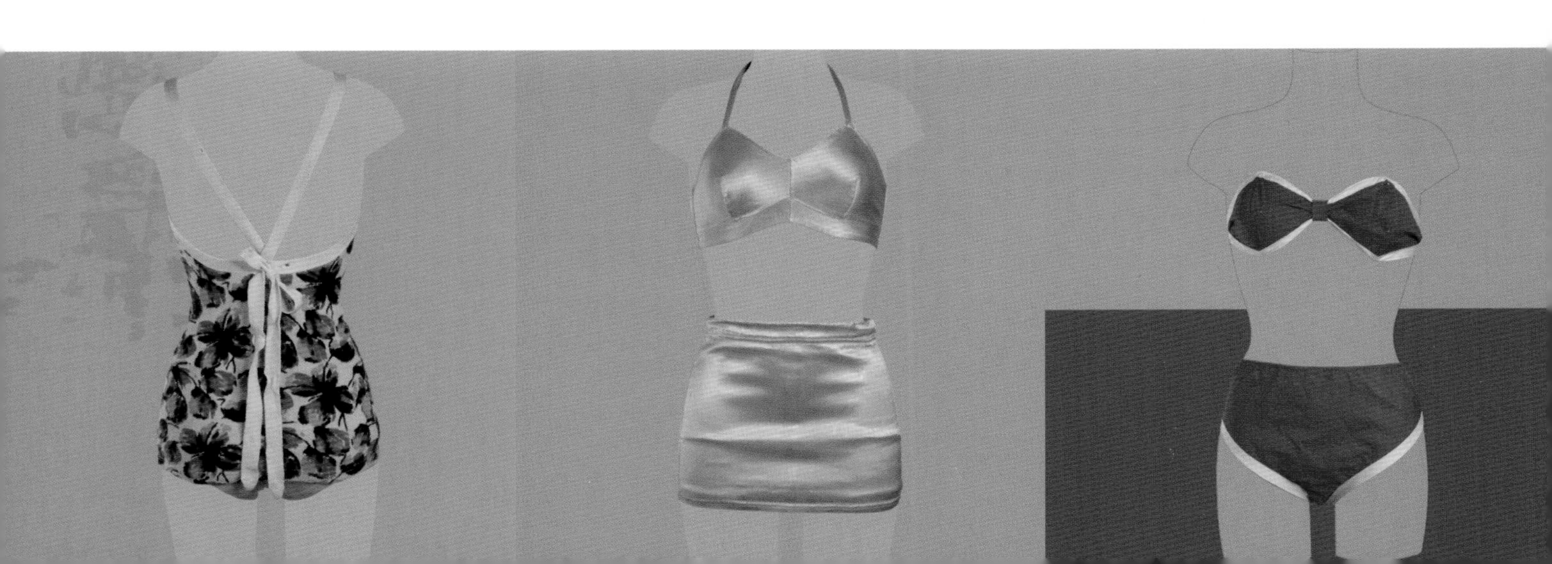

1956: Brigitte Bardot appears in gingham two-piece in the film *And God Created Woman*, kickstarting a fad for the fabric.

1956: Speedo produces a nylon swimsuit for the Melbourne Olympics; previously competitors wore heavy wool and cotton swimwear.

1959: DuPont invents Lycra spandex/elastane, marketed as a replacement for rubber latex in swimsuits and foundation garments.

1960s

1960: Brian Hyland's pop song 'Itsy Bitsy Teenie Weenie Yellow Polka Dot Bikini' becomes a hit, fuelling the desire for bikini fashions.

1964: Rudi Gernreich introduces the scandalous monokini, the world's first 'topless' bikini.

1964: The first Swimsuit edition of *Sports Illustrated* is published, and ever since has showcased new swimsuit styles from international brands on the bodies of the most beautiful girls in the world. *The Pirelli Calendar* is launched the same year.

1964: Cole of California introduces the Scandal swimsuit, a conservatively cut but see-through design constructed of black netting.

1968: The trikini is introduced – literally a three-piece set consisting of bottoms and separate stick-on bra cups.

1970s

1975: Christie Brinkley appears in a tanga by Giorgio di Sant'Angelo for *Sports Illustrated*, setting a benchmark for skimpy swimwear, which she manages to surpass in 1981's *SI* wearing an X-back by OMO Norma Kamali.

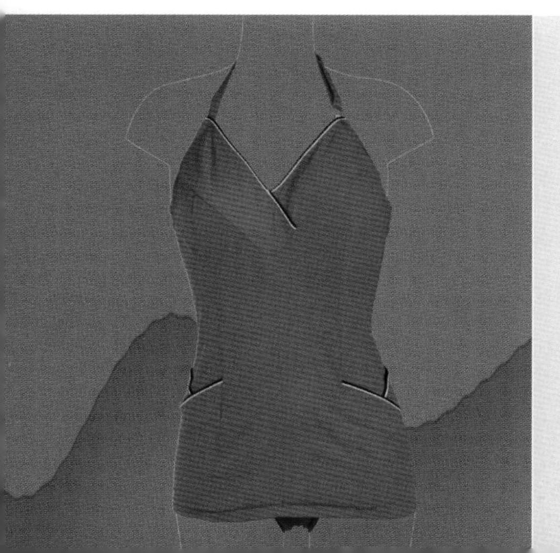

1976: Speedo is the official swimwear licensee for the Montreal Olympics, where 52 out of 54 countries wear the company's swimsuits.

1977: Rudi Gernreich introduces his thong bikini, featuring a narrow strap of fabric on the rear bottom.

1980s

1984: The iconic image of the female bodybuilder Lisa Lyons in a Liza Bruce cut-away swimsuit, photographed by Robert Mapplethorpe, is published.

1990s

1992: Cole of California launches their Top Secret swimsuit, which inflates the breasts via a tiny air pump.

1996: Speedo invents the Aquablade, a water-repellent, drag-reducing, half-leg, sleeveless torso suit.

1996: Beach volleyball becomes an Olympic sport; female athletes are officially required to wear two-pieces. Sports star Gabrielle Reece helps popularize the halterneck bikini.

1997: Jantzen develops the SwimFit website, which allows women to experiment with their swimwear styles without entering a store.

2000s

2000: Arena develops Powerskin for swim competitors at the Olympic Games in Sydney – because it absorbs 15% less water than regular swimwear and is super-light, it never gets significantly heavier in the pool.

2000: Speedo develops Fastskin, another milestone in performance-enhancing swimwear.

2005: Gottex unveils the most expensive swimsuit to date – an $18 million-dollar diamond design.

chapter one

FROM BRIGHTON TO BIARRITZ

FROM THE MID-NINETEENTH CENTURY, THE RAILWAYS OPENED UP A ROUTE TO THE FRESH AIR OF THE SEASIDE ON BOTH SIDES OF THE ATLANTIC. IN ENGLAND, GEORGE IV HAD BESTOWED ROYAL PATRONAGE AND FASHIONABLE FAVOUR ON BRIGHTON. He rebuilt the Royal Pavilion between 1815 and 1823, and by Victorian times the town was the country's leading bathing resort. The pebble beach was dotted with changing machines and the chilly English Channel was the most dipped-in of England's coastal waters. In the USA, the Atlantic coast from New Jersey down to Florida, and coastlines in California, were busy with locals taking to the waters.

PAGE 12: A bathing beauty poses on a breakwater in a knitted swimsuit dress over tights in 1920. The dress would have been attached to the tights at the waist to prevent it riding up. Rubber pumps were worn to keep the tights in place and the sand out.

BELOW: An American beach scene from the early 1900s. Dark-coloured swimwear protected modesty by remaining opaque when wet. Men fared better in baggy shorts and long, vest-like T-shirts made from wool. They were similar to underwear, but being dark in colour prevented too many anatomical details being revealed when wet.

RIGHT: A sunny day on Brighton beach, England, in 1913 where only the men seem to be swimming. The ladies are well dressed in informal summer outfits and may or may not have been swimming, as wet clothes at this time were still seldom seen out of the water. Women entered and left the sea from changing cabins.

The actual act of swimming was almost impossible for women in those days. The cumbersome outfits they were obliged to wear for modesty's sake were heavy and restricted movement. Instead of abandoning swimming to the men, they fearlessly waded into the water dressed, as some nineteenth-century diarists remarked, in more clothes than they would wear on dry land. The modesty and decency laws of the day cost them dear and women were known to drown in the simple act of trying to take a swim. They could only watch enviously as their menfolk, clad in woollen combinations, frolicked at the other end of the beach.

It took the First World War to shake off Victorian attitudes to swimwear, and by far the biggest changes came from the chic French. The Atlantic resorts of Deauville and Biarritz with their combination of fresh, sunny weather and fashionably dressed, wealthy visitors put seaside holidays on the society pages. French women wore more daring versions of English swimming outfits, slashing their bloomers and skirt lengths to more manageable proportions. Yet modesty was still a hard taskmistress and fabrics were cumbersome and unwieldy in the water. Pioneering American knitwear manufacturers investigated knitted, ribbed fabrics for swimwear and by the 1920s the French fashion designers Gabrielle 'Coco' Chanel and Jean Patou were working with lingerie-weight jersey knits to bring a new, sleek style to the beach. Pretty soon sportswear, suntans and, most of all, swimsuits were the height of fashion.

The Queen Is Not Amused

The health benefits of taking to the waters have been driving us into the drink for centuries. Even Elizabeth I, who was famed for the pungency of her court, enjoyed the occasional trip to the Roman baths in Bath. In fact, she was so keen on her visits to this famous spa town that in 1591 she granted Bath a Royal Charter to maintain the baths for future generations. The Queen entered the waters completely clothed with gaggles of courtiers looking on and the scene was set. After the Romans had retreated, immersing one's body in water had been considered a recipe for disease and death. Once the Queen had endorsed it, however, it became fashionable once again. Bathing was seen as a way of cleansing and toning the skin, boosting the circulation and metabolism, improving lung functions and generally increasing one's sense of wellbeing.

BELOW: Despite their innocent poses, these two 1900 beauties are modern glamour-model prototypes. Both are demonstrating extreme daring for the times by exposing bare legs, and a deep cleavage in the case of the girl on the right. This was far more flesh than would ever have been seen on beaches at the time.

ABOVE: These nautically striped ensembles, from 1915, feature the new, daring Princess cut – a shorter-skirted dress worn over matching breeches or stockings. To keep the legs covered, two pairs of stockings, one pulled up over the ankles and another pair worn beneath them, were sometimes necessary, as seen here.

ABOVE: The elaborate pintucking and tie-waist create a feminine shape on this 1918 swimsuit. The unflattering, helmet-style hat is designed to keep the sun off the face and the hairstyle in place – the suntan had yet to become fashionable.

After the opening of the Bath Assembly Rooms in 1771, the town was the hub of the English social scene. No one actually swam; they simply entered the water and bobbed around. Jane Austen spent time in Bath in the early 1800s, basing scenes from her novel *Persuasion* there. Young women sported white muslin shifts to bathe in, which became fetchingly transparent when wet. This fashion was so popular that many kept their muslins wet for evening entertainments, to the delight, no doubt, of their male companions. There was no notion of the bathing costume until well into the middle of the nineteenth century, when the sensible Victorians came along and ended all the fun.

No single ruler before or since has inflicted so many rules of propriety on society as Victoria. By the end of the century, women were floundering around in the water in voluminous, full-skirted dresses with matching ankle-length bloomers. Such outfits were made from heavy serge, cotton drill and wool and were usually handmade by a lady's dressmaker. The skirts were weighted down with shot to prevent them floating upwards, and stockings were worn beneath the bloomers for extra modesty. Bathing garments were not to be found for sale in clothing outfitters because swimming was still not considered fully decent as a public activity.

A suntan was frowned upon as being a sign of a hard-working, field-slogging peasant background, so ladies were also swathed in bonnets, scarves and

ABOVE: Euro-bathers enjoy a dip in the Danube in 1910. The men's knitted unitards were forerunners of the female versions, which would become fashionable ten years later. Here, the women are making do with cotton serge creations with attached knee-length bloomers. These were fine when dry, but the fabric puffed up and sagged when it got wet, as seen on the right.

caps. Shoes were made of leather and laced up over the ankle and the bottoms of their bloomers to prevent them ballooning with water and coming off. History is vague, but it is a wonder that nineteenth-century beaches were not peppered with the corpses of drowned but modestly clad ladies. Changing cabins were wheeled down to the water's edge and women hopped on and off the steps straight into the water.

Changing cabins were small wooden huts mounted on to high iron wheels with steps that unfurled from the door down into the water. For a few farthings local boys were paid to haul the cabins to and from the water's edge so that bathing ladies could descend into the sea privately. Inside, the more deluxe versions had a small carpeted area for dry changing, holes in the floor for drainage, a mirror and shelf for hairbrushes and hooks to hang clothes.

ABOVE: These two happy swimmers lounge on the bathing platform and tow bar of their changing cabin off a French beach in 1900. European swimming styles were way ahead of those in the USA – the uncovered cleavage area of this young lady's unitard would have been considered highly immodest at the time.

LEFT: St Leonards-on-Sea, on the very fashionable East Sussex coastline of the UK, 1895. In the foreground the gentlemen's changing cabins can be seen at the water's edge and at least 183 metres (200 yards) away from the ladies' cabins, beyond the next jetty. The male swimmers would all swim over to the ladies' side.

BELOW: Pablo Picasso was much taken with the sea and the fashion of sea-bathing and promenading. His painting *The Bathers, Biarritz* (1918) shows where his interest lay, in the carefully outlined contours of his luscious bathing beauties – even the boulders and shading in the sand show erotic curves and mounds.

Most beaches had male and female bathing areas, and cabins could be hired for a penny a day from local councils or they were loaned to patrons by the bigger hotels. Ladies who bathed commonly had servants to help them disrobe owing to the amount of fastenings on corsets and underwear that had to be negotiated before the actual changing could take place. Even though men swam in woollen combinations, women were unable to do anything else but bob around, just as they had done at Bath two centuries before.

The French, however, shunned the heavy serge and cotton ankle-length dresses, pantaloons, stockings and hats of the English and wore much shorter, skimpier versions. Although paintings from around 1870 by Claude Monet and Eugène Boudin of the beaches at Trouville and its close neighbour Deauville show fully dressed characters, reports at the time spoke of bathers dressed in 'expensive but dainty creations of Charles Worth [the great Parisian dressmaker] worn on the sands. In fact, the daily bathing festivals are mere show parades.'

RIGHT: British swimming enthusiast Agnes Beckwith fought long, hard battles with the British authorities for the right to wear less restrictive, lightweight swimming garments. Supported by the ASA (Amateur Swimming Association), she forged a new path for swimming as a legitimate way for women to keep fit. In this poster the early glamour of the swimsuit is revealed.

Brave Souls

Towards the end of the century, persevering female swimmers took to the waters and proved what women could do. Eliza Bennet swam the Hudson River in 1877, and Agnes Beckwith swam 9.6 km (6 miles) from London Bridge to Greenwich in 1875. Both women wore pared-down versions of the old swimming outfits, precursors of the 'Princess' suits that came about thanks to the lingerie designer Amelia Bloomer. She pioneered the Rational Clothing movement in the 1880s, designing and manufacturing lightweight pantaloons similar to those worn by men on the Indian subcontinent. Bloomer and her female friends tried to introduce a more comfortable mode of female clothing featuring shorter, less elaborately corseted dresses worn over the top of the pantaloons. These fashions did not catch on, thanks largely to the male establishment of the time, but they were adapted for bathing clothes. By the 1890s, such outfits were common for female bathers and were known as Princess suits.

Made from the same heavy cottons and serge as earlier numbers, Princess suits were slightly less cumbersome by nineteenth-century standards.

THE BLOOMER POLKA
COMPOSED & INSCRIBED TO
MRS. COLONEL BLOOMER
BY
J. J. BLOCKLEY.
AUTHOR OF THE OBERON POLKA
LONDON ADDISON & HOLLIER, 210. REGENT ST

RIGHT: This portrait of Amelia Bloomer shows her wearing one of her own designs – a comfortable, loose-fitting coat dress worn over pantaloons, which were soon to be known as 'bloomers' after Amelia herself. She may look modest to modern eyes, but at the time such outfits created a scandal and caused Amelia and her friends to be thrown out of hotels and banned from many public places.

ABOVE: Beach belles emerging from their cabin, from the cover of the 1895 *Illustrated London News*, illustrated by Amédée Forestier. In a bid to entice hopeful 'belle-spotters' to the coast, the young lady on the steps is actually far more outrageously attired than the average female swimmer of that time would have been.

Featuring a dress worn over pantaloons, or a one-piece with a gathered skirt worn over the top, the dress or skirt was usually knee- or calf-length, allowing for greater movement of the legs. Elbow-length or even slightly shorter sleeves, a button-up back, and shorter matching bloomers made for a more modern look. They always came in dark colours, so that onlookers would find it hard to tell if the wearer was wet or not, and special, slightly less cumbersome underpants, corsets and vests were available to be worn beneath. Some came with sailor-style white edging or gathered necklines pulled and tied with a piece of ribbon, but all were extremely modest by modern standards. Princess suits could also be purchased from clothing and department stores by the turn of the century, rather than having to be hand made. This made them more available to all and the inevitable popularity of sea bathing grew.

However, the world was still not ready for such displays of the female form. Women could be arrested for revealing too many inches of calf, and modesty wardens patrolled the beaches of Europe and the USA to ensure laws were adhered to. Armed with tape measures, the wardens would stop women on the beach and measure the space between the ankle and the bottom of their bathing pantaloons. The legal space allowed varied from place to place and depended on the height of the woman. Fines were enforced for those who flouted the modesty laws.

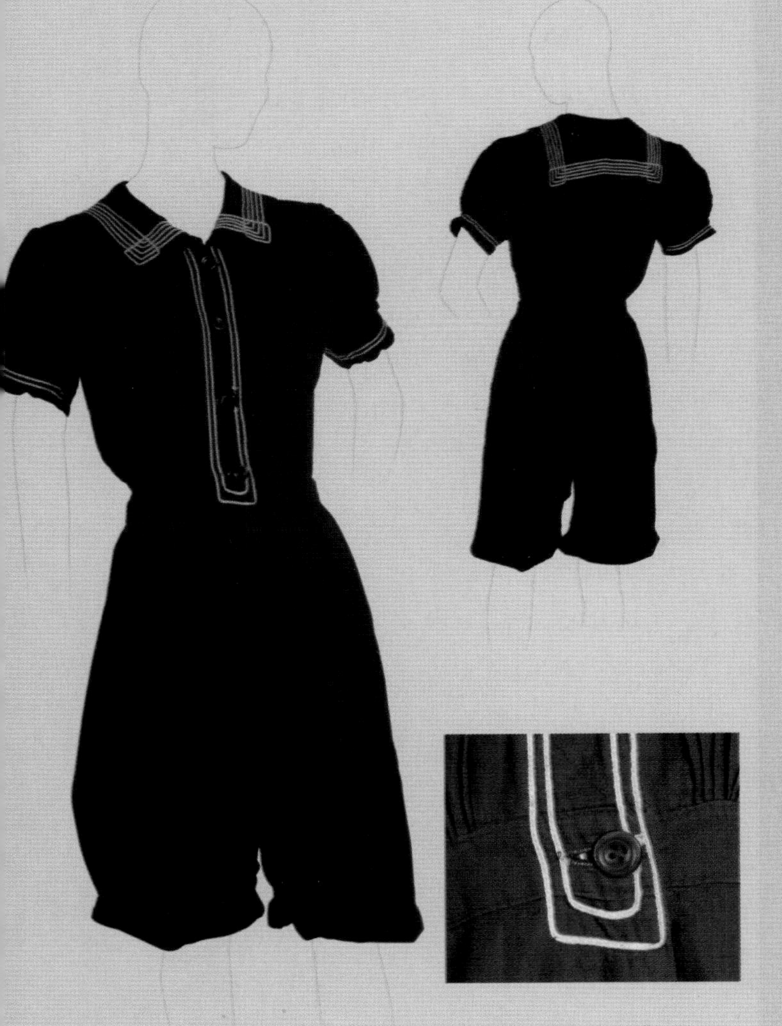

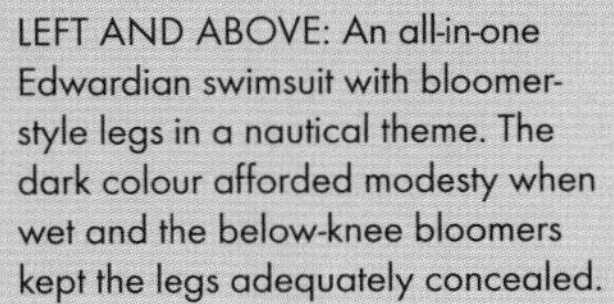

LEFT AND ABOVE: An all-in-one Edwardian swimsuit with bloomer-style legs in a nautical theme. The dark colour afforded modesty when wet and the below-knee bloomers kept the legs adequately concealed.

ABOVE: An Edwardian-era red wool Princess suit with the Fosporter label, consisting of a dress worn over bloomers. Very similar to Victorian styles, these had shorter sleeves or were sleeveless and exhibited more leg, though they were worn with stockings and laced shoes.

New Freedom

After Victoria's death in 1901, many women breathed a huge sigh of relief, shook off their bloomers, went to work and eventually got the vote. Careers in retail, clerical offices, finance and education opened up. Swimming became more popular and leisure time for the new working classes was spent by the sea or at the nearest lake or river. Swimming became a fitness phenomenon alongside the traditional health custom of 'taking to the waters'.

Due to their cumbersome outfits, most women found it impossible to swim very far. Yet ridiculously, this was put down to a natural female fear of the water, rather than a fear of the swimming outfits, which genuinely claimed lives. Princess suits hindered the wearer with restricting seams and waistbands. Arms could barely be moved above shoulder-height and broad movements were impossible, according to Australian professional swimmer Annette Kellerman. She balked at the 'awful water overcoats – those awkward, unnecessary, lumpy, bathing suits' that women had to wear. Kellerman was also the first to bring up swimming safety issues for women in public, by claiming that such suits 'have caused more deaths by drowning than cramps'.

Kellerman came to Europe in 1905 as a novelty act, completing successful swims across the Danube and the Seine, although failing to complete her two attempts at swimming the English Channel. As her reputation grew, so did her daring. In order to improve her diving routines, she began to make up her own swimming outfits. Knitted one-piece suits for swimming with scoop necks, short sleeves and shorts-style legs were already being worn by men. Kellerman reputedly took a boy's black all-in-one vest and underpants combination and sewed her own black wool stockings to the legs, creating a unitard. When she first appeared in this outfit in public she caused a sensation. Nothing of her body shape was left to the imagination and she quickly became a pin-up as well as a personality.

Kellerman demonstrated her diving and swimming skills in a huge glass tank as part of a touring show, which she took to the USA in 1907. While on tour, she was arrested at Revere Beach near Boston for indecent exposure. Her crime was taking to the waters in a one-piece self-made swimsuit cut away mid-thigh. The judge showed leniency when Kellerman claimed the suit was necessary for streamlined swimming. She went on to enjoy even more fame starring in movies such as *Siren of the Sea* (1911) and *Mermaid* (1911) and wowing cinema audiences as the first major star to appear nude on screen in the three-hour epic *Daughter of the Gods* (1916). Esther Williams starred in the 1952 screen version of Kellerman's life, *Million Dollar Mermaid*.

LEFT: Feisty female Annette Kellerman being arrested for indecent exposure, along with a friend, in Boston, Massachusetts, in 1910. Both are probably sporting boy's swimming unitards, or Annette's homemade version with rolled-up stockings and a long vest top. Kellerman fought hard for women to be able to wear safer garments in the water.

ABOVE: Early versions of the California beach babe posse, wearing their 'racy' knitted swimsuits. Decency laws were more relaxed on the West Coast, where the burgeoning Hollywood economy was starting to gain influence. Lucrative advertising featuring such 'babes' boosted local businesses and by 1915 these scantily clad females were becoming commonplace.

The Swimsuit Is Born

Knitting mills traditionally produced lingerie, hosiery and men's underwear alongside woollen outer garments. Before synthetic fibres came into use in the 1930s, the mills were at the core of the fabric industry, wielding enormous power and dictating the price of wool worldwide.

Portland Knitting Company in Oregon, USA, were producing knitted goods when they were asked to create a woollen suit for the Portland Rowing Club to use in cold weather. This was a pure virgin wool one-piece garment in a rib-stitch knit that stretched. It became so popular that the company began offering 'bathing suits' in their 1915 catalogue, and went on to change their name to Jantzen Knitting Mills. It wasn't until 1921 that Jantzen began advertising the garments as 'swimming suits'. Other knitting mills cashed in and became famous swimwear companies, such as Cole of California, Mabs of Hollywood, Catalina and Speedo in Australia. The wool industry was to enjoy a 20-year boom before the arrival of stretch rubber thread.

The Australian company Speedo was originally known as MacRae Knitting Mills. This Sydney-based company began producing hosiery and experimenting with swimwear in 1914. In the mid 1920s MacRae branched out and held a staff competition to find a winning slogan for their newly developed swimwear line. A staff member came up with the words 'Speed on in your SPEEDOs' and the world's most famous sporting swimwear brand was born. Speedo specialized in garments for competitive swimmers, becoming the official Olympic brand.

The new knitted bathing suits became known more simply as 'swimsuits'. Worn by both sexes, these garments featured vest or short sleeve-style tops with built-in legs. Women sometimes wore matching knee-length tights beneath.

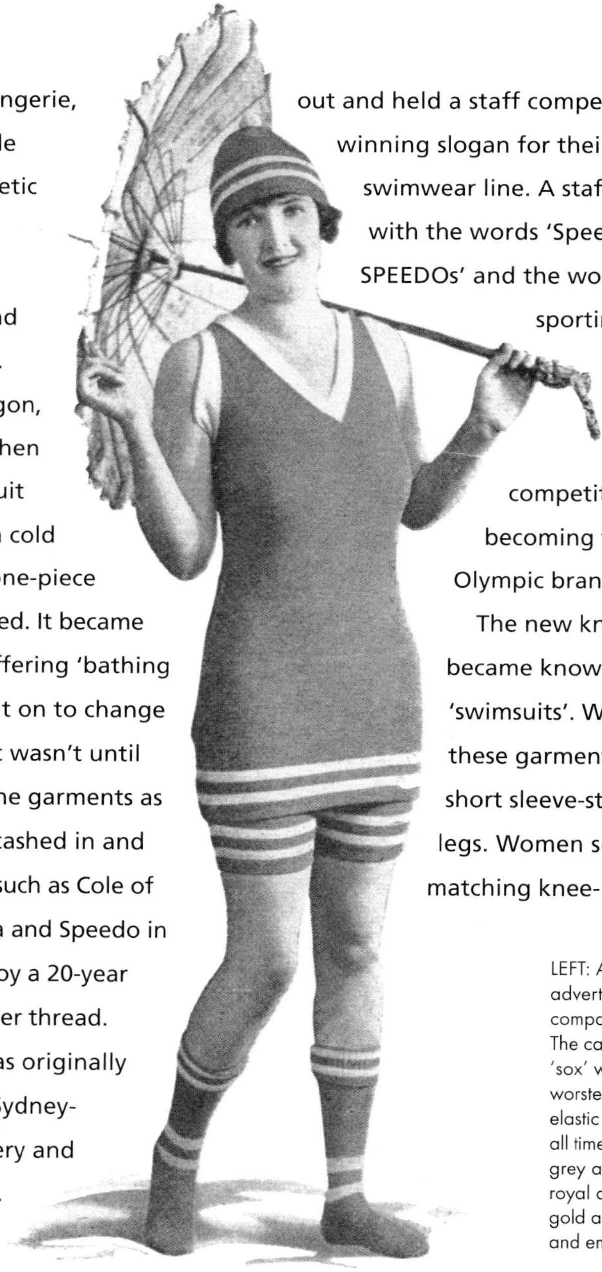

LEFT: A 1918–9 Jantzen knitwear advertisement for one of the company's first female 'bathing' suits. The cap, bathing suit and bathing 'sox' were all knitted from fine worsted yarn in the 'classic Jantzen elastic rib stitch, which fits the body at all times'. The available colours were grey and green, black and gold, royal and white, green and white, gold and white, and olive drab and emerald.

Female versions had longer bodies that pulled down, T-shirt-style, over the crotch area or had short skirts attached for modesty. Available only in dark colours to prevent transparency or discoloration, some suits featured horizontal stripes around the neck and knees, or simple decorations like buttons on shoulders or tie-belts on the waist. The new swimsuits resembled a modern, knitted 'skinny rib' style sweater, but made of natural wool, they became heavy when wet. However, when dry they looked fantastic to a world that had been buttoned up for so long.

ABOVE: Three winners from the 1912 Women's 100-metre freestyle Olympic swimming championship. They are all dressed in knitted swimsuits from the Australian company that would later become Speedo. Women's competitive swimming took a couple of decades to become as acceptable as the male version of the sport in Britain and the eastern USA, where decency laws still rendered it taboo.

LEFT: Mildred June was not the most famous of Mack Sennett's 'Bathing Belles' – that honour belonged to Mabel Normand, who with Mack Sennett became so notorious that a musical was written about their life. Here, Mildred poses in a satin Princess swimsuit, with shorts instead of bloomers, stockings and a scooped-out, revealing neckline.

RIGHT: In this 1918 still from one of Sennett's earliest films, *College*, a fine selection of bathing costumes are being modelled by the background Belles. Despite bare arms and knees (and, unusually, in the case of Bebe Daniels at the front of the line, thighs), ankles remain covered for decency's sake. Gloria Swanson is on the rock and gets the best bathing bonnet. Such outfits were considered coy and very saucy back then.

Girls, Girls, Girls

The Wild West – California to be precise – became the hub of the swimsuit industry from around 1918 until the early 1920s thanks to three core components: beaches, girls and the movie industry. With slightly less rigid law enforcement than Europe and the eastern USA, girls took to the beaches of California in their swimsuits inspired by stills from films starring Annette Kellerman, Theda Bara and Mary Pickford. The California look was slightly curvier than the sophisticated, stick-thin profile of the flapper stalking the eastern seaboard and Europe. In the early 1920s there was a profusion of Hollywood films set in jungles or focusing on showgirls or scantily clad queens. Theda Bara's Cleopatra remains a classic example.

Showbiz impresarios such as Mack Sennet hired 'Bathing Belles' to promote their work and cash in on the new voyeurism – men liked looking at women in bathing suits. Sennet produced the Keystone Kops movies and took his Bathing Belles on promotional tours. Foxtone News also used girls dressed in Jantzen swimsuits to promote film reels. By the 1920s, swimsuit companies had contracts with most of the big studios. Sennet staged dancing reviews featuring naked girls, another French idea taking hold of popular culture, and during one memorable New York run a real cop ran on stage and tried to arrest the star as she danced. The audience roared, thinking it was a Keystone Kop sketch, and Sennet shows grew more popular than ever.

chapter two

THE ST TROPEZ SET

THE 1920S SAW THE FIRST BIG DIVIDE IN EUROPEAN VERSUS AMERICAN STYLE. SPORTY, PRACTICAL AND AIMED AT EVERYONE, THE MODERN AMERICAN LOOK WAS ALREADY TAKING SHAPE. In contrast, the Europeans went for a darker-edged, sleeker style, with fashions more closely cut to the body and distinct class differences. The swimsuit epitomized the difference perfectly. Both sides of the Atlantic favoured the practical one-piece knitted 'maillot', but in France the costume's legs were shorter in length, the knitted ribwork was more finely woven and decoration was kept to a minimum.

Beach holidays were the height of fashion and there were two main factors involved. The first was a rise in the popularity of sporting pursuits among the wealthy and aristocratic, while the second was the suntan. A tan suggested prowess at outdoor sports and proved that someone was wealthy enough to enjoy sport and travelling to exotic destinations.

Golf, tennis and swimming were pursued in the upmarket beach resorts of Biarritz, Deauville and the Riviera in France. Since the eighteenth century Biarritz had been known for the therapeutic value of its waters with pilgrims flocking there for cures to their ailments, but when Empress Eugenie, the wife of Napoleon III, built her palace on the beach in 1854, it became a hotspot for European royalty and high society. With its casino and nightlife the town was a favoured leisure destination for aristocrats, politicians and socialites in the 1920s. Resorts along the French Riviera – such as Antibe, Cap Ferrat, Nice, Cannes, St Tropez and Monte Carlo – were first noted as winter resorts for northern Europeans and later as summer playgrounds for the rich and famous. Favoured residences for royalty and the wealthy, they also attracted the world's artists, writers and intelligentsia.

Free Guide from
Municipal Enquiry
Bureau, Brighton.
BRIGHTON
Frequent S.R.
Expresses 1 hour
from London.

LEFT: By the 1920s, the British seaside resort of Brighton, on the Sussex coast, was enjoying a heyday. This railway advertisement, by celebrated artist Henry George Gawthorn, has all the colour and light of the French Riviera. This style was closely mirrored by many of the great British seaside promenades.

PAGE 32: Jean Patou was the first of the great sportswear designers of the twentieth century, and his use of a logo became a fashion tradition. Here, the JP logo is incorporated into the front panel of this knitted one-piece swimsuit. The shorts are attached beneath the skirt and the belt is made from rubber to match the model's superstylish (for 1928) swimming cap.

RIGHT: A poster from the 1920s depicting the seafront at Antibes on the French Riviera. Here, the blue sea occupies much of the image, rather than the buildings and promenade that are seen in the Brighton poster opposite. The Mediterranean was the ultimate holiday destination, offering months of sun, sea and sand.

LEFT: Wealthy tourists from nearby Philadelphia and New York flocked to Atlantic City to see the pageants, fairs and exhibitions held along the boardwalk and piers. The city's first tavern, Aunt Millie's Boarding House, opened in 1838, starting a 'good time' era that would last a hundred years until the Second World War.

RIGHT: No doubt these bathing beauties, photographed by Atlantic City's famous boardwalk in the early 1920s, were hoping to be noticed by a passing talent scout. The photographer describes their outfits as 'Two beautiful bathing suits of the Annette Kellerman style of silk and knit creation'. Both wear stockings for modesty, though the white stockings on the right have a somewhat surgical look to them. Such beauties were sadly more likely to attract one of the hordes of visiting mobsters, for which the town was famous, than Hollywood scouts.

Long Island in New York and Palm Beach in Florida enjoyed a similar clientele in the USA, while Atlantic City, New Jersey, became the world's most notorious seaside resort. The town's beaches were dotted with daytrippers from Philadelphia and New York and members of their underworld gangs. Gangsters loved the place because of its proximity to the Italian neighbourhoods in the big cities, and even held a convention there in 1929.

The differences between European and American resorts broadened in the early part of the twentieth century. Some of these differences were weather driven, others were commercial. The Côte d'Azur resorts did not need to provide floor shows, piers stretching out into the ocean or constant parades and entertainments because the hot beaches full of scantily clad bathing beauties, the blue skies and seas and the fabulous mountain scenery rendered anything else unnecessary. In northern Europe and East Coast USA, the crowds flocking to the coast required spectacles and entertainments to take their minds off the chilly breezes and occasionally unfriendly seas.

American resorts were the focal point for different kinds of parades to which the bathing beauty element became a central and crucial part of seaside life. Parades were often held weekly in the summer to draw changing clientele and to capitalize on the assets offered by the young women in swimsuits. Atlantic City catered for the mass market with a pier, boardwalk and various different entertainments designed to wow the crowds. The Steel Pier's high-diving horse attraction was established in 1924. Several times a day a horse and its swimsuit-clad female rider would leap from an 18-metre (60-foot) tower into a pool of water. Amazingly, one of the most famous – Sonora Carver – was blind. Harry Houdini, the great escape artist, and Annette Kellerman also performed in Atlantic City, where excess ruled until the outbreak of the war.

Rules and Regulations

Swimsuits held an allure that captured the common imagination. The emergence of the female form into public view after centuries of long skirts had an enormous and transformational effect on society. This was mostly good, affording as it did greater access for women to sporting pursuits. The only downside was the issue of sexuality.

In the UK the Amateur Swimming Association plunged into the heated debate on women's swimming costumes as early as 1901, and by the late 1920s it had approved a knitted maillot style that was virtually indistinguishable from the male version.

Debates raged in the British press about the decency of female swimming garments and repressed males from all walks of the establishment struggled violently with their inner turmoil regarding the Venuses of every shape and size now frolicking with near abandon on the beaches. One by one the seaside town councils of England were forced to accept the growing numbers of female swimmers, who in the 1920s outnumbered men on the beaches by four to one, owing to the losses in the First World War.

As late as 1922 female bathers were still being arrested in Chicago for flouting modesty laws and revealing too much thigh at a public park in their swimsuits. Nine inches or less of leg showing above the ankle was all that was legally permitted in public in the USA at that time; any more was considered indecent. Few legal authorities bothered to impose such restrictions, though, realizing they were fighting a losing battle. Chicago was unusual because a crimewave in 1922 meant that the authorities were cracking down on transgressions of every kind. It should also be said that, although readily available, one-pieces with their 'revealing' form-fitting shape were still considered an immodest step too far in Middle America.

LEFT TOP AND BOTTOM: An illustration from a 1920s Jaeger brochure, *Bathing Suits for Men, Women, Boys and Girls; Pure Wool Suits*. The catalogue shows styles for sale and lists Jaeger's American branches and the addresses: New York, Boston, Philadelphia, Chicago and San Francisco. It states: 'Jaeger, a recognized specialist in wool, offers suits of the best quality, and whether in fresh or salt water Jaeger suits retain their original color.'

RIGHT: The name of this particular ensemble from July 1922 was 'Neptune's Daughter'. It consisted of a one-piece suit with a 'body and knickers of navy blue and a full pleated skirt, disclosing Roman stripes to give a festive air. The cute little bowtie, with Roman striped ends at the V-neck, catches the eye immediately'. The knitted fabric was said to give 'the utmost freedom of motion and protection from chill winds'.

LEFT: Pictures and illustrations tended to exaggerate the real glamour quotient of the average woman's swimming attire, as this front cover from the June 1927 edition of the British magazine, *The Bystander*, proves. The thin straps, deep necklines and clearly visible nipples and body contours in the illustration by William Barribal were far removed from the actual outfits seen on Britain's beaches.

RIGHT: French fashions, particularly those from Paris, were considered more chic and stylish than their British counterparts. This advertisement for *callottes de bain* appeared in a June 1930 issue of *The Bystander*.

FAR RIGHT: This 1924 advertisement for Gorringes department store in London, which appeared in *Sketch* magazine, shows the height of swimwear fashions at the time. Taffeta seems a particularly surprising choice for swimwear to modern minds, but its water-repelling qualities made it a common choice. The sheen was also flattering to the wearer and provided a lighter contrast to the heavy wool serge fabric that was often worn.

Costumes et Calottes de Bain—

—As Worn To-day in Paris-by-the-Sea

THERE is all the difference in the world between a lady's bathing costume designed for swimming and that for the plage and the shallows of the surf. Dainty examples of both kinds are here shown, and from the two models portrayed it is obvious that a useful swimming suit can be as delightful to look upon as one of the more elaborate type

IN NAVY-BLUE SERGE
Trimmed with white braid

IN NAVY TAFFETA
With a double skirt

IN GREY TAFFETA
Trimmed with dark blue taffeta

IN GREEN TAFFETA
Scalloped with navy-blue satin

IN BLACK SERGE
Trimmed with pale blue braid

Models, Leon Hellé
Photographs, Henri Manuel

Exclusive to THE BYSTANDER

GORRINGES
By Appointment.
By Appointment.
Newest Designs in Bathing Dresses
Post Orders should be accompanied by remittance or leading business house reference.
Postal Orders and Treasury Notes should be registered. Carriage paid in the United Kingdom.
N 809. Dainty BATHING COSTUME in Black Celanese Artificial Silk, trimmed Royal Blue Braid. Combination and Over-tunic are attached, giving double thickness. W's. 55/9
O.S. 59/6
Pretty Rubber BATHING CAP in large variety of colours, with narrow bands and rosettes with ends in white or contrasting colours 5/11
N 615. BATHING COSTUME in good Woollen Stockinette, separate Knickers and Tunic, trimmed White border at neck and hem, with embroidered design in mixed colourings. Colours: Navy, Saxe, Black, Almond, Rust, All sizes 37/6
Dainty Rubber BATHING CAP in all colours, trimmed ruche in White rubber and rubber flowers 3/11
N 812. BATHING COSTUME in Black Celanese Artificial Silk; Tunic and Knickers attached, double throughout, ensuring invisibility, trimmed deep points of colour in fancy Artificial Silk. Black / Turquoise, Black/Red. W.'s 45/9
O.S. 49/6
Rubber CAP trimmed cluster of self colour and White or contrastting shade 2/11
N 808. Effective and practical BATHING COSTUME in Black Silk Taffeta. Tunic and separate knickers, trimmed on hips with self frills edged scalloped narrow coloured Ribbon, neck and sleeves trimmed to match. Black / Royal, Black / Orange, Black / Self. W.'s 79/6
O.S. 87/6
BATHING CAP in coloured rubber, trimmed contrasting colour or White 3/6
FREDERICK GORRINGE, Ltd., Buckingham Palace Road, London, S.W.1.

Fashion Meets Sportswear

By the 1920s, swimwear combination outfits, two-pieces and all-in-ones in a variety of fabrics including silk stockinette, jersey (a wool knit that was ribbed on only one side), plain wool, cotton drill and serge were worn by women worldwide. Such early swimsuit prototypes came with problems. They were still not much use when wet, elongating, sagging and revealing rather more of the wearers than was probably intended. Serious swimmers dived in, did their thing and then changed again quickly afterwards. The average woman who had survived the hardships of war and witnessed huge economic and social change began to demand more than mere practicality from her swimming garments. She took her cue from the elite ladies and heiresses in the society magazines, who demanded a new concept from their bathing and beachwear – namely, fashion.

Manufacturers experimented with other materials besides fabric for bathing suits in a quest to share the enormous growth and profits of the wool mills. The most extraordinary of these was the wooden swimsuit of 1929. Featuring thin slats fashioned into two barrel shapes connected to a waistband, one above and one below, it looked as uncomfortable as it presumably felt for the wearer. Wool was the only fabric that worked in terms of flexibility, so the market was left to the mill owners to develop as their own. Fred Cole, who founded the famous Cole of California label from his family firm, West Coast Knitting Mills, took it upon himself to create the 'first fashion swimsuit' in the USA in the late 1920s. Cole called it the 'Prohibition Swimsuit' because of its extremely skimpy cut for the times – a deep, U-shaped neckline, dropped waist and tiny skirt over the shortest shorts.

Jantzen
Swimming Suits

THESE Champions wear and endorse Jantzens:
UKE KAHANAMOKU, Honolulu, World's Champion at 100 yds. Olympic Games 1920.
ORMAN ROSS, Illinois Athletic Club, World's Champion at 220, 440, 880 yds. Olympic Games 1920.
EWIS (Happy) KUEHN, World's Champion Diver, Olympic Games 1920.
VM. (Buddy) WALLEN, Illinois Athletic Club, National Mile Champion.

SPARKLE of blue water—tang of salt breeze—gulls wheeling down to ride the waves—splashes of gay color on the beach.

Isn't it good to be alive—to dive into clear, cool water and feel every muscle active—stroke after stroke as you swim! Then to float back lazily.

Those who really enjoy water sports find the Jantzen the logical bathing suit. Practical because it permits the utmost freedom of action in the water. Beautiful because it fits perfectly and holds its shape permanently. The Jantzen stitch made these features possible. It's elastic—*never binds, never sags.*

Jantzens are made in exquisite colors—plain or striped. The good shops in your city are showing new models for *men, women and children.* Or, if you do not find them, write to us.

Jantzen Knitting Mills
PORTLAND, OREGON
Creators of the Elastic-Stitch Swimming Suit

Jantzens at Catalina Islands

LEFT: The first national advertisement promoting Jantzen's 'swimming suits' with their rib-knit stitch ran in *Vogue* and *Life* magazines in 1921. The illustration, by Ruth Eastman, shows female bathers in alluring knitted pieces twirling parasols in front of a hunky beach boy. The knitted swimming bobble hats were intended to keep hairstyles in place.

RIGHT: This 1925 Jantzen advertisement depicting the famous Diving Girl as illustrated by Frank Clark features the iconic slogan: 'The suit that changed bathing to swimming'. The illustrations of swimming strokes and sea and poolside views create a happy, healthy image of the female swimmer and promote swimming as a sport. Jantzen also won customers through its emphasis on comfort, after women had suffered from years of heavy and dangerous discomfort in the water.

While the fledgling Hollywood movie industry grasped the swimsuit with glee, in Europe it was to form a new range of design possibilities for the Parisian fashion houses. Beach pyjamas began as a style idea from Gabrielle 'Coco' Chanel. Inspired by the nautical colours used by the navy and wide-legged sailor pants, Chanel created the first beach pyjamas in the 1920s. Other designers quickly caught on. Chanel, Jean Patou and Jeanne Lanvin were also producing 'sportswear', ranges of matching separates that could be worn for playing golf or tennis. In fact, these ranges were just as likely to be worn by the society dolls and flappers for watching such pursuits rather than actually playing them, but what the hell, sporty was trendy, end of story.

Swimwear posed a bigger problem, and scope was limited. The one-piece or 'maillot', as it was known, was still considered risqué on European beaches until the middle of the decade, owing to the way the knitted fabric fitted around body contours. Although women were enjoying new freedoms in terms of streamlined dresses and corset-free undies, they were still wearing dresses and knickerbocker-combos on the beach.

FAR LEFT: By the end of the 1920s beach – or 'lounging' – pyjamas were all the rage, worn by starlets and the stylish. Here, Marcel Rochas versions show the relaxed, masculine style of trouser shapes in his Lido collection for 1930; the wide-legged 'palazzo' design became the height of daywear fashion in the years that followed.

LEFT: These beach pyjamas with a small bolero jacket were made some time during the late 1920s or early 1930s. The bright, splashed fruit print is representative of the artistic colours and patterns that were fashionable at the time. This fabric may originally have been a beach wrap or robe that the owner refashioned into beach pyjamas.

LEFT: This wide-legged pantsuit, from the late 1920s, would have been worn after a day on the beach for late afternoon cocktails or for a dressier lunch. Graphic prints were stylish at the time, as was black, which had been strictly reserved for mourning or far more formal wear in previous generations.

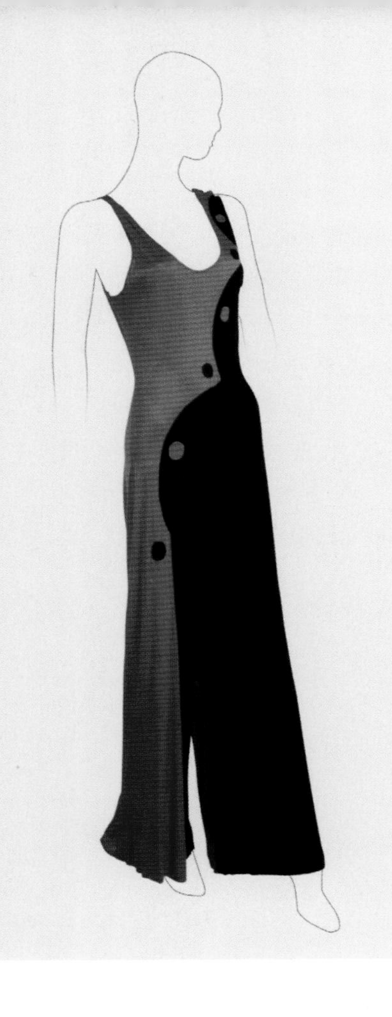

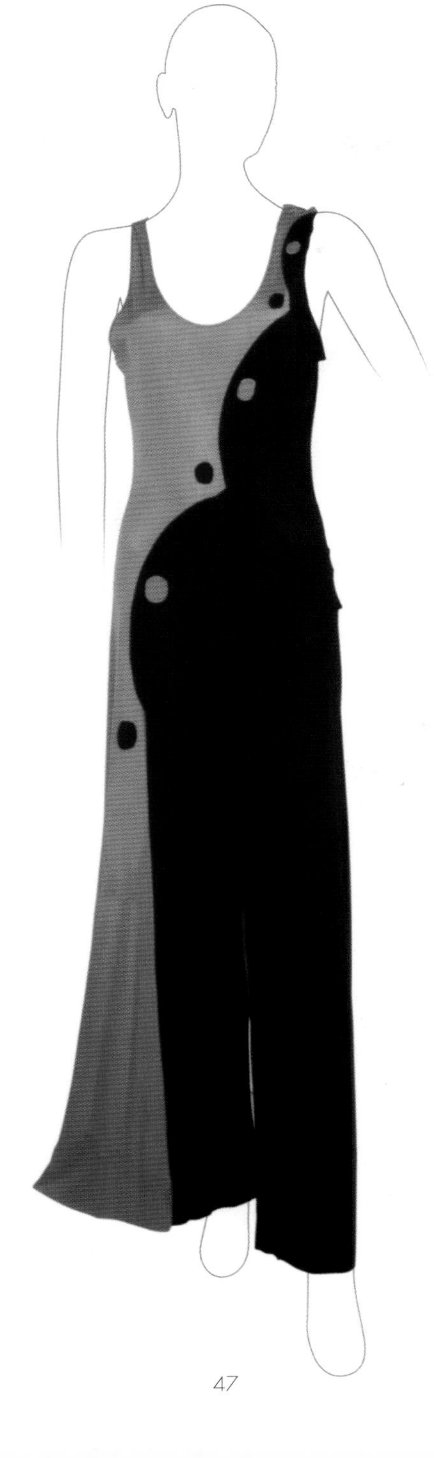

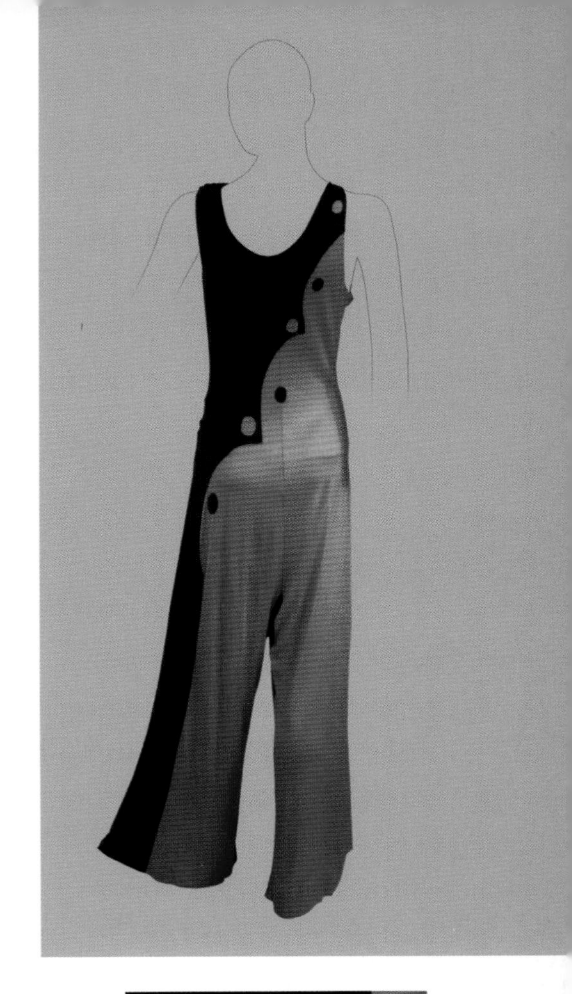

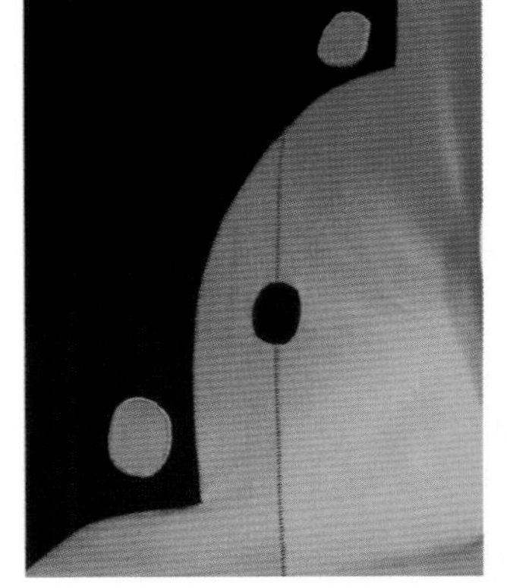

ABOVE AND RIGHT: A harlequin-style all-in-one pantsuit from the early 1930s. The French Pierrot character, the comedy clown nursing a broken heart, who often wore a black-and-white outfit, detailed with contrasting buttons, inspired this highly unusual print. Pierrot was a much-used image of French artists in Paris around the turn of the century.

Artistic Leanings

Coco Chanel was instrumental in pulling the one-piece swimsuit off the taboo list and into fashion. She opened a millinery shop in Paris before the First World War, followed afterwards with boutiques in Paris and Deauville. Her speciality was jersey knitwear, previously used in the main as an underwear fabric. Chanel experimented with different weaves to find the closest, most comfortable jersey knits to suit her groundbreaking designs, and her signature style was smart-casual with elegant, streamlined shapes. She loved navy blue, white stripes and wide sailor trousers, which she reinvented for her summer clientele, and her influence on fashion was far-reaching. She helped pioneer the boyish haircuts, chunky accessories and straight-up-and-down silhouettes that have become associated with the 1920s.

Fashion and art crossed over for the first time when Chanel turned her attention to the swimsuit after designing a series of costumes for Sergei Diaghilev's ballet *Le Train Bleu*, staged in Paris in 1925. The ballet, named after the famous train that took the Riviera-bound glitterati on their summer breaks, celebrated everything that was trendy about the seaside at the time. Set on the beaches of the Côte d'Azur, the ballet was a collaboration by Paris's coolest artists including contributions from Jean Cocteau (libretto) and Pablo Picasso (set painting). Chanel's maillot costumes and

RIGHT: Dancers from Paris's fashionable ballet of 1925, *Le Train Bleu*, wearing early swimsuit designs by Gabrielle 'Coco' Chanel. The dancers performed Sergei Diaghilev's ballet to modern moves, choreographed by Nijinsky, in celebration of the annual migration of chic Parisians to the Côte d'Azur.

all-in-one costumes woven from a knitted bouclé fabric were almost unisex and just risqué enough to shock and entice audiences at the same time. The shapes were translated into saleable versions for the Chanel boutiques and promptly sold out.

Jean Patou had already opened boutiques in Deauville and Biarritz and was soon to follow with shops in Venice and Monte Carlo. Patou was known as the best sportswear designer of the time. Although he began his career creating gowns for Hollywood movie stars, including Louise Brooks, from his Paris salon in 1919, he found his niche with sportswear. The tennis star Suzanne Lenglen was his muse, wearing Patou on and off the courts. He also dressed notorious showgirls the Dolly Sisters. These identical twins took 200 changes of clothing on an American tour in 1925, all by Patou. The Dolly Sisters loved the French Riviera and regularly broke the bank at the casino in Cannes, spending their own cash or coaxing it out of their wealthy male prey.

LA BAULE LES PINS
SON CLIMAT MERVEILLEUX
SES TERRAINS BOISÉS - SA PLAGE
Société Générale Foncière
FACILITÉS DE PAIEMENT
Bureaux de Vente
LA BAULE LES PINS ET
63 BOUL^D MALESHERBES - PARIS

RIGHT: This French poster from 1926 sums up the new sophisticated spirit of French coastal resorts, such as La Baule. Advertisements like these popped up across northern Europe, encouraging the migration south to glamorous resorts, including Juan-les-Pins, St Tropez and Antibes. French advertisements focused more on swimming and sporty pursuits than promenade posing, even though there were plenty of both.

ABOVE: Models in jersey swimwear by Lucien Lelong, 1929. Jersey was popular in the 1920s because of its incredible versatility. Chanel made it her signature fabric, but classic Parisian couturier Lelong, who trained the young Christian Dior, was also a master of swimwear designs. His swimsuits were cut smaller, allowing for slight stretch and therefore a better fit on the female form.

Patou kept an eye on trends with the help of his younger sister Madeleine and through her he picked up on the increasing trend for making sport fashionable. Europe's elite adored tennis, shooting, fishing, cycling, walking and swimming, so Patou obliged by creating lines of clothing not just for playing sports in, but for watching in, too. Patou clothes carried an edge, which distinguished them from those of other designers. Form-fitting and elegant, they were also sexy in a very understated way, so that really only the wearers were aware of the effect. Skirts were slightly shorter or flared in a particularly flirtatious way, cardigan twinsets long and lean in the body, dresses fitted with deep V-necks. He also created a whole look, from clothes to shoes, hats, accessories and lingerie.

Patou's designs were among the first to feature a designer logo, his signature JP. This appeared on the front of fine-knit maillots or on the breast pockets of beach cover-ups and cardigans, signifying that the wearer knew her fashion onions. At the forefront of the fashion-and-sports craze, Patou named his shops Sports Corner, with different sections for tennis, golf and swimming. He set the trends for resortwear in the South of France and others quickly followed. Patou swimsuits always featured a long body, with the lower hemline going straight across the top of the legs, with or without matching shorts beneath. He also returned to the natural waist with his slimline belts, marking a departure from the low waists of flapper fashions.

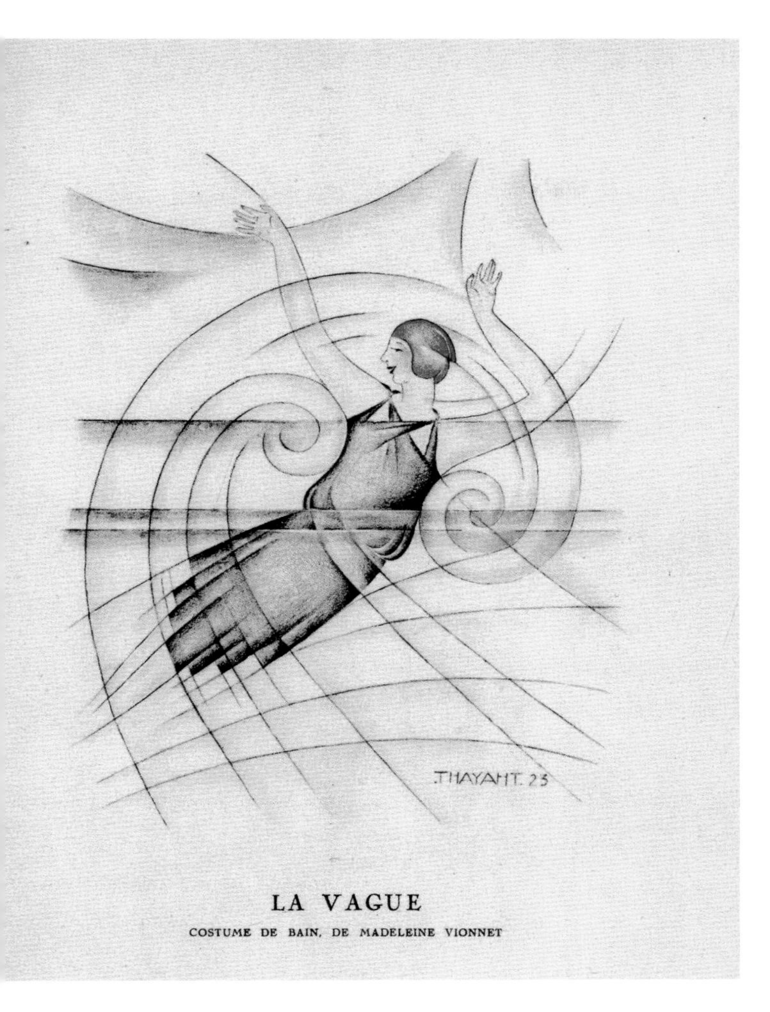

THAYAHT 23
LA VAGUE
COSTUME DE BAIN, DE MADELEINE VIONNET

ABOVE: An illustrated colour plate from a 1923 edition of the *Gazette du Bon Ton* – an early fashion magazine. The Fauves-inspired illustrations of the day's top graphic designers, published by Lucien Vogel and Georges Lapape, became iconic 1920s fashion images. Here, a swimmer wearing a suit by Madeleine Vionnet floats in an abstract decorative landscape.

RIGHT: Diving summed up the sporting spirit of the 1920s and the image of the female diver, shown here modelling a Jean Patou swimsuit, was highly influential at the time. It was a new age for Western society, and women in particular – this fashionably clad diver from 1929 could vote, drive a car and even forge her own career.

LEFT: Chanel's great rival Elsa Schiaparelli enjoyed great success with her swimwear lines. This 1928 Schiaparelli two-piece bathing suit, with matching socks in mad stripes, summed up the boyish fashions of the day. Note the model's bobbed hair and mannish pose.

ABOVE: A graphic geometric print from a 1920s beach wrap. It was common to find strong, art-inspired prints on beachwear, in contrast to the stark boyishness of swimsuits in the 1920s. The art of Pablo Picasso and Salvador Dalí as well as the Modernist themes that appeared in design and architecture inspired fabric manufacturers at this time.

Cubism and modern art began to be reflected in the design of swimsuits. Elsa Schiaparelli, Jean Patou and Sonia Delaunay all incorporated graphic prints inspired by Cubism into their designs for beach capes and wraps. Delaunay produced her prints for the textile company Bianchini-Ferier, which was an important fabric supplier to the Parisian fashion houses. By 1927, the Riviera had overtaken Deauville and Biarritz as the place to go, thanks to higher sunshine guarantees. Swimsuits were sold in the boutiques of Chanel, Schiaparelli, Poiret, Molyneux and Lanvin in Cannes. These suits came in dark, flattering combinations of black and cream or navy and white, sometimes with white or red buttons on shoulder flaps or breast-pocket details. Necklines were either scooped or square, and pant-legs varied from a straight, slashed 'over-vest' look across the top of the thigh, to a longer, mid-thigh length. Small matching belts were looped through waistbands, fastening with a simple square buckle. Horizontal stripes, motifs like the JP logo or a small anchor or mock sailing club badge featured occasionally and decoration was always stark and graphic, in keeping with the design 'feel' of the age.

RIGHT: Lady Edwina Mountbatten was at the forefront of the British aristocratic beach set. Famously fit, she enjoyed swimming and keep-fit instruction at Deauville (as seen here in 1924) and on the Riviera. The graphic print on her beachrobe is typical of the time, as are her fully made-up face and earrings.

Beauty and the Beach

The suntan was the perfect beauty accessory for the designer swimsuits now being produced by other big fashion names including Edward Molyneux and Helene Yrande. Chanel loved the feeling of freedom of being by the sea at Deauville. An early portrait from 1916 shows her there dressed in a nautical-style swimming ensemble, probably of her own design. Later, she was to be photographed on the same beach with a suntan, a truly ground-breaking move that cemented her cult status as a trendsetter equal to Patou. Instead of shunning such an outrageous look, her society clientele embraced it as a sign of a healthy outdoor life. Not to mention the fact that a suntan could be extremely flattering.

Up and coming starlets including Gloria Swanson and Joan Crawford loved to pose with their suntans darkening their faces and so accentuating their bone structure. In 1928 Patou manufactured the first suncream to aid the skin-tanning process, called Huile de Caldée, a simple concoction of perfumed oils. Girls in the know had already been spied on beaches rubbing coconut oil into their skin to help achieve a more golden tan.

Dresses were designed to show off tanned skin on summer evenings with features including low, scooped-out backs, deep V-necks and no sleeves. Society girls did not only wear their swimsuits for swimming. Keeping fit was all the rage along the Riviera, with several society ladies hiring their own personal trainers to take them through rudimentary gymnastic routines. The hourglass figure was laid to rest for the time being and replaced by the slender frame. Cleavages were very definitely 'out' thanks to the tubular fashion shapes pushed by Paris. The maillot swimsuits reflected this with scoop necks that finished above the breastline and seamless contours.

TOP LEFT: This stylish beach bag and parasol set would not look out of place in modern resortwear collection. The nautical navy and yellow stripes were a common theme, almost uniform in fact, when it came to beachwear accessories of the 1920s. The bag's bone handle is also a classic design feature of the period.

BOTTOM LEFT: A finely crafted, wooden-handled parasol from the 1920s, in a botanical print reminiscent of the textiles of William Morris.

RIGHT: A 1925 shot showing models posing in a typical beach scene. The outfit on the right features ruffles around the waist and an Art Deco tulip print on the swimming hat and the satin beach robe. Matching details pulled together the designer swimwear look of the 1920s, giving the Riviera set a glamorous edge over the ordinary beachgoers of the day.

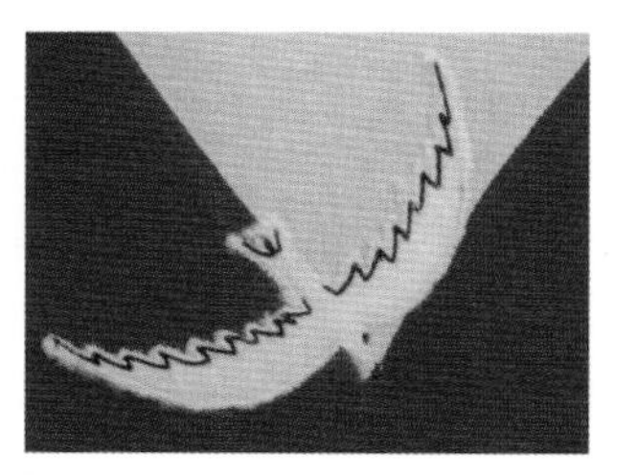

ABOVE AND RIGHT: This 1920s chevron-striped swimsuit with the Cortesca label would have been worn with a belt in a contrasting colour. Based on early-century men's sleeveless tanksuits, women's styles were androgenous and athletic-looking. Abstract patterns and stripes – as here, accented with a dove motif on the front and back – were the only sparse decoration.

LEFT: An illustration by Joyce Dennys from the September 1929 issue of *Sketch* magazine offers a humorous example of the streamlining of swimwear fashions, from the modest Princess suit to the cutaway maillot. It is entitled 'It's Good Cut that Counts – Even in Swimming Suits'.

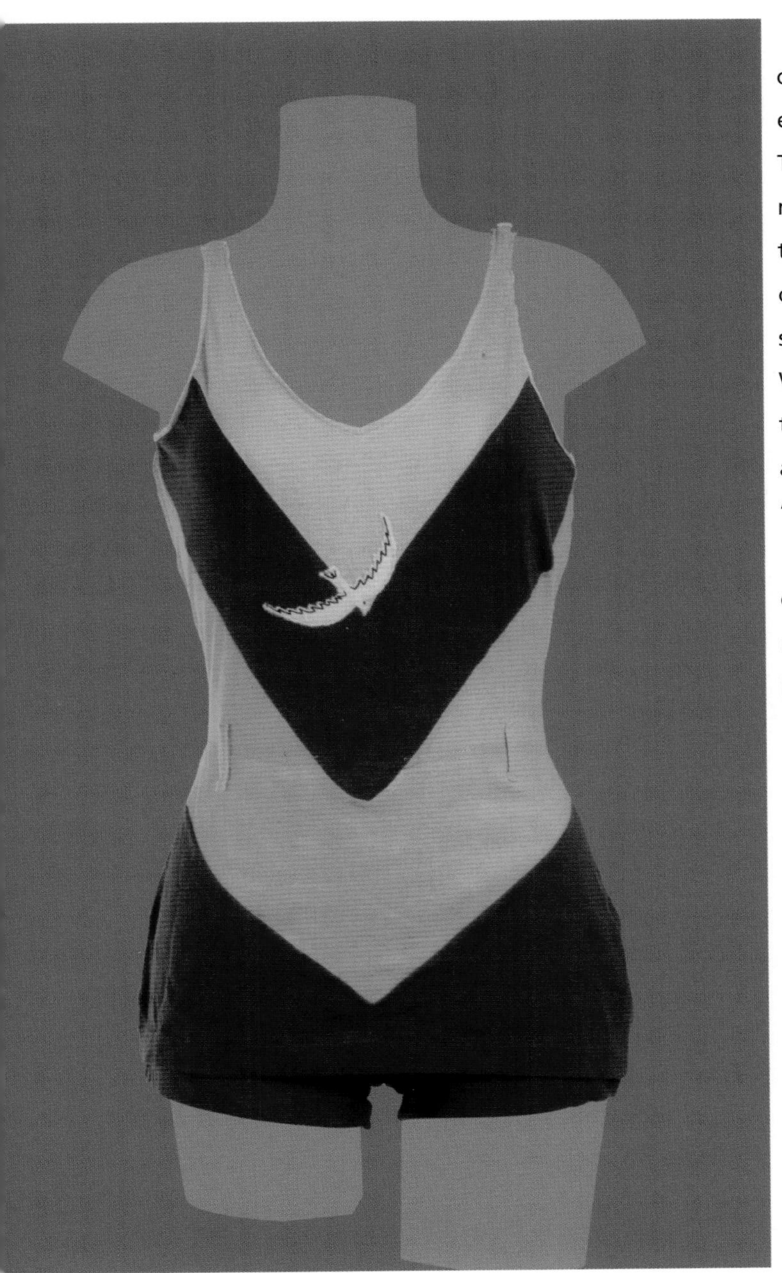

The new body shape was part of the political climate, indirectly representing the growing emancipation of women in many areas of their lives. The corset was cast aside for more comfortable silk, rayon (the new artificial silk) and fine jersey underwear, though not without protest. The corset manufacturers of the USA in particular decried the new, boyish body shape, claiming that women simply looked 'saggy'. Women wore simple tie-fastening 'flattening' bras to enhance the slender look or shunned underwear altogether in the case of some of the most outrageous 'flappers' of the time, such as dancer Josephine Baker.

This was the decade that saw the arrival of two controversial beauty aids still causing argument today, namely the sunlamp and the diet pill. The fashion for being slim and tanned was totally revolutionary, yet it took hold with an eternal grip. This was because, unlike the previously fashionable plump, pink and pale look, which required a good diet and a cossetted existence to achieve, anyone could look 'with it' in the 1920s. With a boyish, skinny, tanned body, fashionably cropped or bobbed hair, pouty lips and kohled eyes, any girl could hope to waltz in to any party and grab the best guys. Social class boundaries disintegrated as never before because beauty, talent, creativity and eccentricity were the new social requirements.

LEFT AND ABOVE: A knitted, ribbed swimsuit from the late 1920s shows the direction in which swimwear was heading. Note the cut-away back for extra tanning and the tight, form-fitting shape, accentuated by contoured ribbing. Breasts were making a fashion comeback after the flattened-down fashions earlier in the decade and the V-shape floral decoration accentuates this.

RIGHT AND ABOVE: This Modernist-inspired design is in an interesting colour combination of orange, grey and deep red. The crossover back straps became a fashionable swimsuit detail that has lasted to the present day. The knitted fabric is plain, but closely woven to give a stretch similar to that of the ribbed version. The square-cut hem provided a modesty skirt.

The Cult of the Lido

Beaches were not the only places for topping up a tan. Public swimming pools began to appear in answer to the demand for places to swim. Most towns had a bath-house and, where possible, councils incorporated swimming pools alongside. In Europe the lido, named after a stretch of beach known for its glamorous swimmers and sunbathers near Venice, was born. The most famous, the Piscine Molitar in Paris, was a huge Art Deco arena surrounding a pool where Parisians could go to take the summer sun. Soon, lidos popped up all along the coasts of Britain and France and by the 1930s most major towns boasted one. Lidos featured high diving-board towers that would never have made it past modern health and safety regulations, and provided the perfect backdrop to the seaside beauty contests of the mid-twentieth century.

Like everything associated with swimming, lidos came in for much criticism from certain prudish portions of society. In 1920 the British newspaper the *Daily Mail* reported on an incident in Tonbridge, Kent, in which an elderly lady had mounted the high diving platform at the local outdoor pool to make a speech against mixed bathing, using her umbrella for emphasis. In the end, someone pushed her in and she had to be rescued. Like King Canute, she could not stem the tide.

More lidos were built, but the debate on mixed public bathing raged on both sides of the Atlantic. Men were accused of being afflicted by 'lido libido' in 1934 when they were photographed rolling the tops of their swimsuits down for all-over chest-tanning purposes.

LEFT: *At the Lido*, by Georges Barbier, 1920, is an enticing image of recreational swimmers enjoying their leisure in the sunshine. Lido became the term for outdoor swimming and sunbathing areas – the name came from the Venice Lido, Italy's most fashionable beach at the turn of the twentieth century.

BELOW: Parisiens enjoying the Champs Elysées lido in 1930. Here, the rich and beautiful could swim and also enjoy a cocktail or two. Notice the unshaven armpits of the lady in the foreground – it wasn't until the 1940s that Hollywood's hairless beauties set a new trend that women would follow.

Young women were still being hounded for sporting swimsuits in mixed public bathing areas by straitlaced societies and the more prudish factions in the press. But just as the First World War had forged new boundaries for women with respect to their right to vote and to have careers, so the Second World War, thanks to their vigorous and equal war effort, was to liberate women from the moralistic oppression they had suffered during the 1920s and 1930s. After the war, people were so grateful to have survived that they wanted to celebrate by going to the closest beach or jumping in the nearest lido.

chapter three

STAR QUALITY

DESPITE THE DARING BREAKTHROUGHS OF THE AGE, SWIMSUIT STYLES CHANGED LITTLE UNTIL THE 1930S. THE TRUTH IS THAT THE WORLD WAS STILL ACCUSTOMING ITSELF TO THE SIGHT OF LADIES' LEGS. Daring though the duchesses, princesses and countesses of the Riviera were, many of them were dependent upon family wealth or rich husbands for their income. While it was one thing to cut one's hair into a bob and dance the Rag, it was quite another to reveal too much of one's anatomy. Knitted swimsuits became heavy and cumbersome when wet so they had to be changed out of pretty quickly after a swim. It wasn't until the very end of the decade that one-piece maillots were finally accepted into public view. Tops remained modestly cut with vest-like sleeveless or short-sleeved, T-shirt styles predominating.

The biggest change of all was the fabric revolution. New fibres burst into the clothing market with stretchy, shiny and semi-water-resistant qualities. For those who could afford it, this was the end of the knitted swimsuit, though mothers and grannies continued churning out their knitted versions for many years to come, and they hung around until well into the 1950s.

Hollywood's influence on the swimwear industry was huge. The biggest female stars had their own swimwear contracts with manufacturers, with cheaper versions available to buy across the counters of the growing department store chains. Retailing grew slowly – despite the after-effects of the Wall Street Crash and the onset of the Depression on both sides

PAGE 62: Models sunbathing on a beach in 1930, with the men in Jantzen trunks. The model on the left wears a two-piece jersey bathing suit by Patou; the centre model, lying face down, appears in a one-piece wool suit by Helene Yrande; and the top model, on her back with legs crossed, wears a one-piece tricot bathing suit with white jersey stripes by Molyneux.

ABOVE: The photographer George Hoyningen-Huene created spectacular swimwear shots for *Vogue* in the 1920s and 1930s. Here, models demonstrate their toned physiques and aristocratic profiles. The swimsuits, by Jean d'Ahetze (left and centre) and Jane Regny (right), show the sensible styles that remained popular on beaches until the end of the decade.

of the Atlantic. Those who had any cash took refuge from the hard times at the cinemas and theatres when they could afford it and occasionally splashed out on the cheaper products that were mass produced for the large stores.

On both sides of the Atlantic, fashionable body shapes changed, with the demise of the flapper and the boyish look of the 1920s. Curls and curves returned, though the cleavage stayed firmly in the future. Filmmakers were subject to the Hays Code, introduced in 1930 as a form of censorship. Films had been becoming increasingly wild and so the code was introduced to curb violence, immorality and nudity in the industry. Nudes were banned completely, as was the act of undressing unless strictly necessary to the plot. Lingerie on screen became pretty much taboo, but swimsuits were still allowed, so the filmmakers explored this route instead.

BELOW: The swimwear department of Jaeger, around the mid 1930s, showing customers and models discussing designs for the beach. Jaeger knitted swimsuits remained the garment of choice for more mature women in the UK, who liked the long bodyline, thick knitted fabric and high necklines.

LEFT: Clara Bow models a knitted silk swimsuit in an early Hollywood publicity shot from 1930. The glamour imbued by swimsuits added another dimension to the average starlet's repertoire and newer fabrics allowed for even more glamorous styling. Although Ms Bow's suit retains the classic shape, the fabric is clearly finer, with a sheen not found on wool suits.

RIGHT: MGM 'feature player' Florine McKinney was one of hundreds of girls payrolled by the studio in the 1930s and groomed for stardom. Some made it as big stars, others remained mere eye-candy. Here, Florine is surrounded by three other wannabe starlets (left to right), Muriel Evans, Martha Sleeper and Kay English. Note the softer, more feminine design of their swimsuits and the new fashion for fuller, curlier hair.

Do Put Your Daughter on the Stage, Mrs Worthington

Contrary to the Noel Coward refrain, a career in showbiz gained in respectability by the end of the 1920s. The birth of the film industry, despite being run by characters shadier than many a silver-screen villain, made it legitimate for nice girls to work in entertainment. The words 'actress' or 'dancer' were no longer synonymous with the word 'prostitute'. Acting in films became a real career choice for a chosen few. Audiences thrilled to each new release and picture houses were packed. Stage acting also became a legitimate profession and even society ladies, including Lady Diana Cooper, went on the London stage.

The upshot of this surge in respectability was a huge influx of cash from willing audiences and a desensitization towards swimsuits and skimpy attire. Entertainment was suddenly a part of everyone's daily life. People on both sides of the Atlantic visited the cinema once a week if they could afford it. Male stars set women's hearts fluttering but the female stars had a strong influence on the way women looked. Joan Crawford, Marlene Dietrich and Greta Garbo became icons. Their on-screen wardrobes set fashion trends, and, more crucially, their body shapes were emulated. Broad shoulders, a natural breast outline and a long, sleek line from waist to ankle was the ideal. On a different level, stars such as Deanna Durbin and Ginger Rogers offered a more wholesome, girl-next-door glamour, which had great appeal in the USA. The flat flapper chest gave way to more audience-friendly, naturally shaped breasts. The greased-down bob made way for face-framing curls. Womanly looks, rather than boyish skinny styles, grew in favour.

Hollywood was a powerful advertising tool for the swimwear industry. Jantzen, Cole of California and Catalina all had their own stars attached to their label. Jantzen's included Loretta Young, Joan Blondell and

Ginger Rogers. Marlene Dietrich was reputedly so taken with one particular swimsuit that she rushed off to the Hollywood store where it could be bought and ordered one in every colour. Barbara Barondess, Lillian Bond and Martha Sleeper were Columbia Studio signings who modelled the latest line in rubber bathing suits from US Rubber. Bond looked so good in a swimsuit that she also modelled in one for Shredded Wheat ads. Catalina included their designer, Mary Ann DeWeese, in their ads as a stylish face to 'front' its business and persuade more women to buy.

The costume designer Edith Head navigated the Hays Code inventively for *The Jungle Princess*, a 1936 film starring Dorothy Lamour. Head dressed the starlet in fetching sarongs and swimsuit-style short dresses with just enough draping and coverage to count as 'proper' garments. There was an unofficial 'tally' of the number of swimsuit/lingerie scenes that could appear in any one film. The rule was, if there seemed to be too many, there were too many! Negligees came into style as filmmakers scratched around for ways of showing even slightly seductive imagery. The one-piece finally became acceptable, body contours and all. Every woman owned a swimsuit and gradually the modesty police patrols on the beaches of the USA and Europe hung up their batons.

ABOVE: A 1932 shot of the young Myrna Loy, posing by a Hollywood pool in a suit made from the new Lastex fibre, which allowed for the cut-away strap design of her swimsuit. Lastex did not bag or sag when wet, so strappy designs could keep their shape even after a dip, meaning that a new range of more daring and revealing swimsuit shapes could be created.

RIGHT: Dorothy Lamour perches on a craggy fibreglass rock in a still from *The Jungle Princess* (1936). Her sarong-style swimsuit, in a stretchy fabric with an exotic print, cleverly bypasses the Hays Code decency laws. Lamour went on to star in the *Road To...* movie series starring Bing Crosby and Bob Hope.

ABOVE: Only a Jantzen fits so perfectly. This 1934 advertisement from the *Saturday Evening Post* by artist Willard Cox was for the Jantzen Molded-Fit swimsuits, which afforded movement in all directions; for the first time Jantzen offered the Bra-Lift swimsuit, a defining improvement of the flat construction swimsuits worn by both sexes at the time.

All in the Fabric

A huge leap forward came originally from the Dunlop rubber company, in the form of Lastex. A very fine elastic yarn made from latex rubber covered with thread, Lastex hit the market in 1931. With a wonderful stretchy quality that could be woven into many different types of fabric, Lastex was great news for the swimwear and lingerie industries. Soon the American companies Jantzen, Mabs, Cole, Catalina and BVC in California had all produced their own versions of the new wonder-fabric.

California became the hub of the swimsuit industry thanks to the new yarns. Luscious new fabrics with names including Suedette, Velva-Lure and Satin-Knit, an artificial stretchy velvet were introduced. Lastex worked well on artificial fibres; when combined with rayon (artificial silk), the result was the most gorgeous, shiny and stretchy fabric imaginable. A much broader spectrum of colours and prints were available than had been suitable for knitted swimsuits. Exotic, floral jungle-style prints were popular, as were stripes that met in an upward- or downward-facing V flatteringly placed along the centre seam.

ABOVE: Another Jantzen advertisement by George Petty, which bore the caption 'Running improves my figure? Silly, it's just my Jantzen!'. By the late 1930s, fuller chests and rounded breast shapes had returned to fashion, though the emphasis was on modest, perfectly natural, covered-up curves.

Jantzen introduced their Molded-Fit swimsuits, which were luxuriously soft and made of Lastex, promoted as the 'miracle yarn'. The suits stretched in all directions to mould and shape the body as if the wearer was bathing nude. Traditional knitted swimsuits tended to flatten the breasts in a straight line from breastbone to waist, sagging unattractively when wet. But swimwear manufacturers were developing new moulded versions to fit in a far more flattering way, creating a curved line from neck to waist that remained shaped even when wet. BVC, another Californian company, was the first to incorporate built-in brassieres, but pretty soon most swimsuits in the new stretch fabrics also featured interior structuring of some kind. The 'floating bra' by Gantner-Mattern (swimwear designers) could be detached from the outer lining. These garments must have felt fantastic for their wearers, and a twenty-first-century woman might well envy her 1930s counterparts for such flattering beachwear. Bumps and bulges were ironed out and breasts were accentuated, but all in a very covered-up, ladylike manner.

LEFT: Slender starlet Evelyn Greig poses in a photograph by Horst P. Horst from 1934. Her Lastex swimsuit is by Jantzen. The daring cut-out design has a modern flavour, and the top fastens on to the shorts with big buttons, so the shorts can be worn separately. Horst created some of the greatest fashion photographs of the age.

RIGHT: This illustration by Frank Clark is from an Italian advertisement for the Jantzen Sun-suit, which featured in a 1930 edition of *L'Illustrazione*. Made for sunbathing and active swimming, the Sun-suit was cut-away to promote the popular tanning trends and has a modesty panel overskirt that conceals the shorts.

LEFT AND ABOVE: This French-designed knitted swimsuit with the Atlantic French label features an exotic flower print on a navy blue background. Note the adjustable straps and conical-shaped breast moulds – this would have given the wearer a feminine shape, though the V-neckline remains high-cut for modesty. The 'adjustable strap' technology of a small plastic hoop and a metal adjuster on the strap has stayed virtually the same since its invention in the 1930s.

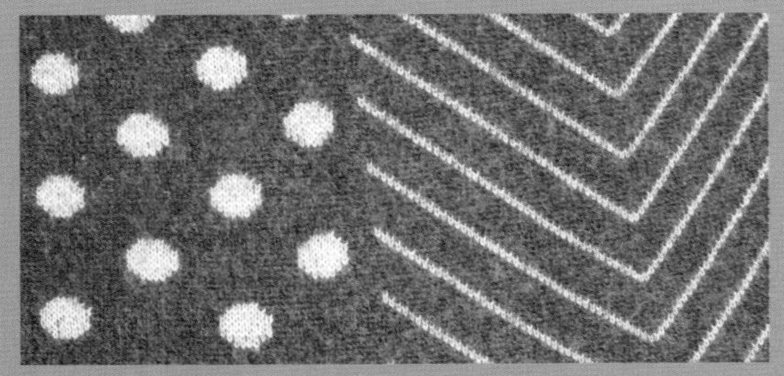

LEFT AND ABOVE: This swimsuit is by the British wool brand Wolsey Knits. Swimsuits were largely available only at large department stores in major cities, so most British women knitted their own sensible 'swimmies'. The fine knit on this version shows that it is factory-made, but there would have been a Wolsey yarn pattern for something very similar to be knitted at home.

KEEP TRIM KEEP FIT SWIM
The Shouldaire •
typically Jantzen in its individuality
The Vogue of the Sun has swept the Shouldaire into instant popularity. Its complete modesty and practicability has kept it there. On the beach a jaunty, voguish sun-suit—an ingenious tie enabling you to drop shoulder straps for an even coat of shoulder tan. Every inch a Jantzen in the water—fitting smoothly, perfectly, comfortably, the elasticity of its famous Jantzen-stitch giving with every movement of the body. Like all Jantzens, smart and distinguished on the beach, in colors that are new and alluring; but above all, you will find it really is easier to swim in a Jantzen. You'll find the famous red Diving Girl on every genuine Jantzen. Your weight is your size. Jantzen Knitting Mills, Portland, Oregon; Vancouver, Canada; London, Eng.; Sydney, Australia.
Jantzen
The suit that changed bathing to swimming
JANTZEN KNITTING MILLS, (Dept. 113), Portland, Oregon
Please send me style folder in colors featuring 1931 models. Womens Mens
Name Address
This advertisement appears in Collier's issue of June 13th in two colors

The main types of swimsuit were the two-piece, maillot and dressmaker. The two-piece was a precursor of the bikini, featuring large waist-to-thigh bottoms and a top that came down to just above the waist, revealing no more than three inches of in-between flesh. The maillot evolved into having a slightly shapelier neckline and narrower shoulder straps, but remained a pretty simple-shaped garment. Dressmakers were the most common style, featuring top halves that followed the daywear fashions of the day built into a swimsuit design. Dressmaker styles often had short skirts attached, which could be pleated and sometimes had side splits to enable greater ease of movement. Halternecks, narrow ties, button-down straps and even stay-up styles came into vogue. Jantzen introduced the Shouldaire, a swimsuit with an internal drawstring above the bustline, which allowed the straps to be tucked inside the top of the suit for strapless tanning.

LEFT: A simple but clever concept by Jantzen, the Shouldaire was a suit that would stay up even with the straps rolled down, thanks to an inner drawstring above the bustline. Suntans were all the rage in the 1930s, and this design promoted strap-free tanning. The advertisement, from 1931, was illustrated by artist Frank Clark.

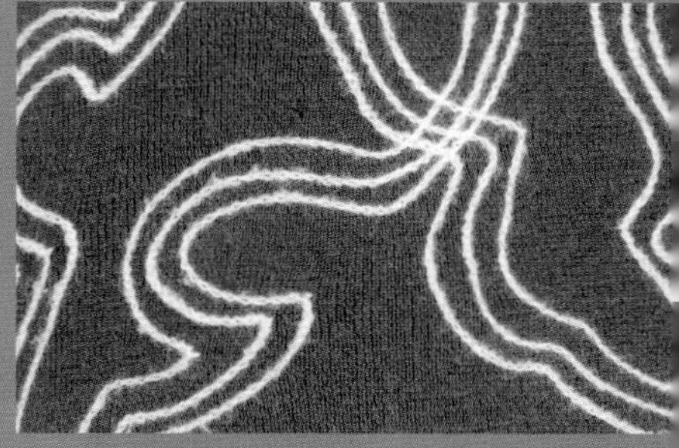

LEFT AND ABOVE: A knitted Forma label swimsuit with a white chainstitched embroidered design in a favourite 1930s colour, bottle green. The tie-back straps allow for better shaping of the top half of the suit. Forma swimsuits specialized in strong, simple shapes in closely knitted yarn, but such suits were falling out of fashion by the mid1930s due to the arrival of artificial fabrics.

LEFT: A 1934 front cover illustration from *Tatler*, by Lewis Baumer, showing a swimsuited beauty bouncing on a beach ball. Large rubber balls, such as the one pictured here, were the latest craze for exercise classes. Rubber itself was a relatively new concept and was used for the manufacture of everything from clothes to children's toys.

BELOW AND RIGHT: A 1938 hand-illustrated Jaeger catalogue entitled *Swimwear, Shorts and Slacks* shows the season's latest swimsuit and sportswear fashions. The brochure opens up to form one large leaflet, the opposite side of which appears on page 80.

JAEGER
C.115. Uplift front, adjustable sun back. Patterned with numbers. Several colours, 25/9
C.143. Square pattern and neck. Patch pockets. Straps tying round waist . . . 29/6
C.130. Heavy blue wool, scattered with ships. Adjustable sun back, 21/9

Seaside Style

Shorts, halterneck tops, playsuits and beach pyjamas all complemented the new swimsuits, which were not only worn for swimming. Loving the new styles, women wore them as tops with wide sailor-style trousers for the newer beach-side games including bowls, pitch and putt and croquet. Designers including Chanel, Molyneux, Patou and Schiaparelli continued their swimwear lines, adding in accessories such as rubber shoes, matching hats, beach bags and wraps. 'Schiap', as she was known, loved the new fashion shape, making the broad masculine shoulders, narrow waist and flattened-down hip-to-knee line her own. Scorned by Coco Chanel, who called her 'that Italian' – for her love of embroidery and colourful adornment, hers

were Hollywood's most sought-after gowns. Schiaparelli's swimwear was simple, but she loved new colours like shocking pink and also pioneered the use of a new fastening invention, the zip. Emphasizing the return of the bosom, Schiaparelli even designed a swimsuit with the pointed bra cups on the outside. She also used unusual fabrics such as upholstery and towelling (terrycloth) for beachwear.

JAEGER
JAEGER
1. C.132. Romper swim-suit. Various colours. 21/9
2. C.155. Sun top, thick ribbed wool . 10/6
T.11. Worsted slacks, concealed zipp fasteners at sides 35/6
3. C.114. Halter-neck swim-suit with seagull pattern. Various colours 21/9
4. C.120. Trunks and top, in gay stripes. Various colours 25/9
5. C.104. Stripy trunks and top. In mixed bright colours 16/9
6. C.149. Romper swim-suit, brassiere top. Adjustable shoulder straps, and belted, 21/9
7. C.123. Two-piece romper suit. In pink, blue, and light shades 21/9
8. C.129. Trunks and tiny top, fancy edging. In gay colours 16/9
9. C.135. Three-piece swim-suit. Trunks with ribbed elastic waist band, uplift brassiere, square necked coat 39/6

The ongoing love of all things long and lean led to a boom in the beauty industry and much more body awareness among cinema-going, magazine-buying women. Early versions of diet pills containing narcotic

LEFT: A beach scene showing the 1938 styles that could be ordered from the Jaegar catalogue. The brochure introduced the collection with the words: 'Jaeger believe that chic by the sea cannot be divorced from comfort... All these Jaeger sea clothes have actually been tried in use, we have dived in our swimsuits and lounged very sportingly in our sun numbers.'

RIGHT: This model is wearing a ladies' beach suit at the summer fashion show at London's Oxford Street branch of Jaeger in the 1930s. Life-size, white wood-carved figures, imitating mannequins, are seen in the background. The model is wearing a beach suit in myrtle green jerseyette.

LEFT, BELOW AND BELOW RIGHT: A late 1930s corset-style shorts playsuit with a matching long jacket is an example of early cruisewear, perfectly suitable for lounging on the deck of a ship. The short puffed sleeves on the jacket are typical of the period; structure in the form of padded shoulders was introduced at this time – the strong, broad shoulder flattering the narrow waistline. The totem motif in the print represented a fascination with ethnic influences, while the corsetry served as a styling detail rather than a form of support.

substances that supposedly suppressed the appetite or speeded the metabolism caused users to lose the power of sleep completely. Many a Hollywood star's distant gaze and aloof manners could probably be ascribed to a drugged-out trance than to her health and vitality.

Dancers such as Ginger Rogers were cutting a dash through the new Hollywood musicals including *Roberta* (1935) and *Swing Time* (1936). Ginger was run ragged by her partner Fred Astaire yet she maintained a feminine shape that cinema-going women wanted to emulate. The fitness craze continued and fresh-air pursuits from cycling to hiking attracted fashionable folk. In the USA and Europe, open-air swimming pools and lidos were social hotspots, with swimming and diving clubs opening up everywhere. Magazines featured models in fitness poses, running, performing jumping jacks or limbering up before entering a pool. The designer Helene Yrande specialized in sporty American swimsuits with striped panels, high necklines and matching shorts for wearing during exercise, while another American, Tom Brigance, designed sportswear for Jaeger and Simpson's of Piccadilly in London during the 1930s.

Sensible Swimmies

The swimsuit market thrived in the USA, but had less hold in the UK. Glamour was equally popular, with women taking their cue from Hollywood films and the increasing number of British productions, but less sunshine meant that beach life was strictly for holidays or very warm summer weekends.

British women bought their swimsuits from department stores such as Army & Navy or Bourne & Hollingsworth in London. The British market was conservative and knitted swimsuits stayed popular among young career women. On small salaries, Hollywood-style Lastex swimsuits were out of reach for most women. Glamour was achieved through fashionable hairstyles and make-up; lipsticks, nail varnish, powder and grease paint were bought in beauty salons or at Woolworths and used sparingly. By contrast, the French led the way with several innovative styles, introducing halters as early as 1933 and exotic two-pieces that revealed an expanse of skin.

THIS PAGE: Illustrations from the 1938 edition of the *Ladies' Jaeger Swim and Sun Suits* catalogue, showing styles to order. Top right is the Art Deco-style front cover image of the catalogue.

LEFT: A 1930 photograph by Horst P. Horst of a male and female model in Izod swimsuits. The unisex aspect of sport and fitness brought a new equality of the sexes. Sporty swimwear followed the same clean lines on both men and women.

At the end of the 1930s companies including Kleinert and US Rubber began producing swimsuits. By the end of the decade, these more affordable versions arrived in British stores and took over from woollen styles. British manufacturers experimented with other cheaper fabrics including cotton seersucker, a quilted fabric with a puffy appearance that kept its shape when wet.

The new swimsuit fabrics could not provide all the answers. Rubber suits looked pretty good on the wearer for the first few outings and kept their shape better than knitted versions but they were uncomfortable and fragile. The rubber was easily ripped and would also dry out and crack after swimming. Rashes and chapping were caused by the intense heat generated beneath the suits. Rubber was a temporary solution to the problem of finding a form-fitting, non-saggy swimsuit fabric, but the manufacturers were looking for something more. Lastex and similar fibres were better, but the rubber in the Lastex perished after a while, giving only a limited lifespan to swimsuits.

LEFT: Underwater photography, filmed dance sequences, and swimmers in glass tanks all formed part of popular entertainment in the 1930s. This image from 1939 shows a model floating underwater in the Oceanarium at Marineland, Florida. She is wearing a ballet-style bathing suit in white Celanese jersey by Tom Brigance, with a wide satin waistband and ruffled top.

RIGHT: An uncomfortable-looking bathing suit from 1935, suitable only for the slenderest of frames. This suit is made from perforated dark rubber, a fabric used for about a decade in swimsuit manufacturing. The holes enabled the skin to breathe and stopped condensation from building up, which would eventually rot the suit. Rope detailing on the neck adds contrast.

Later in the decade, the DuPont company introduced the first commercial version of nylon in 1938, a huge leap forward. DuPont started out as a gunpowder milling company, but began research into nitrocellulose and the manufacture of artificial silk in 1902. In 1920 the DuPont Fibersilk Company formed and began producing artificial silk known as rayon. Research continued into a durable, water-and-chemical-resistant completely artificial fibre. In February 1935 the first successful nylon fabric was produced. In 1937 the company began experimenting by swapping the silk threads in hosiery with nylon for greater stretch and durability and in 1940 the first nylon stockings hit the shops. DuPont went on to pioneer other artificial fibres for use in swimwear manufacture, including Dacron and, later, Lycra. Swimwear enjoyed a close relationship with lingerie and nylon was to become a crucial element of both. These new fabrics and fibres were every bit as much the stars of the decade as the Hollywood sirens who wore the cutting-edge swimsuits.

ABOVE AND RIGHT: Two cotton sateen bathing suits from1936–40, by Bimba, probably manufactured in the UK. The direction of swimsuits towards the end of the 1930s was becoming more glamorous and detailed. Built-in underwear, frills and bows made for a prettier, less practical look, while ruching around the waist added a flattering curve.

RIGHT: An advertisement for Kestos lingerie, which ran in the July 1932 issue of *The Tatler* in the UK. Although the idea of underwear to be worn beneath your swimwear was short-lived, it demonstrated how clothing manufacturers at the time were wrestling with the growing desire of every woman for a shaped body on the beach. Knitted sensible but shapeless swimsuits were left for the very old and the very young and swimwear took on a dramatic new look.

The Beauty Pageant

The first 'bathing belle' parades began in the USA at the turn of the twentieth century, with California's Floral Parade of 1905 being one of the first recorded events. At these precursors of modern beauty contests there was little actual competing. Such events were mainly staged so that audiences could legally look at girls parading around in their bathing costumes with various hat and accessory adornments. Parades quickly spread in popularity, culminating in the Annual Bathing Suit Day first held at Madison Square Garden in New York in May 1916.

Bathing beauty parades in California were a way for girls to be spotted by revue promoters, such as Mack Sennet who was always on the lookout for 'babes' for his Bathing Belles group and semi-naked theatre shows (see also pages 30–1). 'Revues', 'follies' and 'cabarets' were all euphemistic terms for shows involving naked girls, big business in the Roaring Twenties. Beauty parades were soon swamped with would-be paraders and it became evident to organizers that contests would have to be held to reduce the numbers. Meanwhile, the Miss America

LEFT: Miss America contestants from the final held on 9 September 1927 pose in the home of the contest, Atlantic City, New Jersey. Beauties representing their home cities and states sport sashes over their one-piece swimsuits. Some wore stockings but the more adventurous went without.

RIGHT: A 1937 composite image of selected winners of the Miss America Beauty Pageant from 1921 to 1937, entitled 'The Evolution of the Bathing Beauty', shows how the face of American glamour changed so dramatically over that 16-year period. Notice the knee-stockings and Princess suit on the 1921 model, compared to the form-fitting, sheer fabric of the 1936 winner, Rose Veronica Coyle.

contest was born out of the annual Atlantic City 'Fall Frolic' festival, which attracted bathing belles from all over the USA. The first Miss America was crowned there in 1921 and although the swimsuit section was the contest clincher, contestants also took part in musical variety shows and parades of evening gowns.

A historical archive for the town of Elgin, Illinois, records the 1925 local heat for the Miss America contest, won by Miss Lucille Burns, a sales associate from a local department store. Miss Burns won the contest after judges could not decide on a winner from the final four. A dentist was called in to examine the contestants' teeth, just as happened in horse sales, and Miss Burns was declared the winner thanks to her outstanding oral health. She was subsequently snubbed at the celebration dance by her fellow contestants, who felt that her victory was unfair because measurements were not taken of their vital statistics. Had they been measured, presumably some other paragon of physical perfection might have been chosen. Miss Burns and her mother went off to the Miss America final in Atlantic City, where they were relieved to discover that judges were not allowed within five feet of the swimsuit-wearing competitors, so a degree of decorum was upheld.

Although fashions changed, the swimsuit category remained. Nervousness about being seen in a swimsuit was not the way to win Miss America, as the victor was expected to be pictured all over the world in her winning bathing ensemble. In these early days such immodesty was regarded with suspicion as the parades seemed to attract the kind of women who were not held back by strict family values or moral guardians. The reputation of the contests as unsavoury events for women of looseish morals grew, and as a result the contests failed to take off elsewhere in the world until after the Second World War.

Swimsuits Please!

After the Second World War and, ironically, increasing female emancipation, the commercial possibilities of beauty pageants were realized. Big companies launched beauty contests to find girls who could help promote products. Nothing guaranteed a front page faster than a picture of a pretty girl in a bathing suit. Long Beach authorities carried on with an International Festival of Beauty. Instead of swimsuits, they had a 'playsuit' section to cater for entrants from cultures dictating female modesty. Playsuits were essentially swimsuits with miniskirts attached. However, poor Miss Austria complained that they were fine for girls with slim legs, but not so flattering for those who

The California-based swimsuit manufacturer Catalina recognized the potential, sponsoring and dressing entrants to the Miss Universe contest. This was held in Long Beach, California, for nine years before breaking away from that particular borough and going international. When Catalina pulled out, the relied on the full view from ankle to hip to make a leg-lengthening impression. Playsuits lacked the necessary pizzazz for the pageants, and the swimsuit section remained the highlight of every other beauty contest.

The heyday of English seaside holidays from the 1940s to the 1960s saw the arrival of pageants at all the big resorts around the UK. The first to gain recognition was Morecambe's Bathing Beauty Queen, which began in 1945. The winner won seven guineas and a new swimsuit, but the 'paltry' (according to the local paper) prize did not put other contestants off in the following year. By the end of the 1940s, every town had a contest and Miss Great Britain was

launched in Morcambe in 1952. Girls were judged on their physiques and personalities, but it was their swimsuits that clinched the deal. The suits of the time featured much in the way of hidden corsetry and underwiring, giving lucky girls who could afford the best styles an extra edge.

ABOVE: A full-length portrait of the swimsuit-clad contestants at another Atlantic City Beauty Pageant in 1937. The Inter City Beauties Showmen's Variety Jubilee Pageant, held in front of the famous Steel Pier on the boardwalk, was one of many contests designed purely for the purpose of parading women in swimsuits. There were less rigorous entry requirements for these contests than those for the virginal Miss America pageant, so married women, for instance, and women of all ages, with good enough legs, could enter.

ABOVE: A 1946 'fun' shot from the Miss America Pageant. The contestants laughingly pull judge Ken Murray to the ground for a bit of roughing up. Wearing a variety of one-piece and two-piece swimsuits, the girls were all the very best of friends. Of course.

The most famous international contests were Miss World and Miss Universe. Miss World was launched by Eric Morley after the Festival of Britain in 1951 as a gala for bikini-clad beauties: 50 per cent of judging was based on form, 20 per cent on facial beauty, 20 per cent on poise and 10 per cent on audience acclaim. Yet the passing of time complicated what had been a fairly simple competitive process. In the first two-thirds of the twentieth century, the winners were chosen according to how they looked in a swimsuit. Most contests also featured a clothed heat of some kind involving daywear or evening gowns, but the bottom line was quite literally, the bottom line. By the mid 1950s, however, bikinis were banned from many contests. It was thought that those contestants sporting something teeny-weeny might gain an unfair advantage, so one-pieces remained the staple.

The demise of the British seaside was one of the contributing factors to the dwindling popularity of the beauty contest in the UK from the 1970s. Sponsorship was never really taken up by suntan cream companies as had happened in the USA with Coppertone and Hawaiian Tropic, so there was little commercial support. Simultaneously, feminists were finally winning their arguments about the swimsuit parade – why should a woman be judged on her body shape, they argued. A few pageants have survived, with contestants trying to prove their worth as individuals through interviews and video clips, without having to be seen in swimsuits at all. Few of the women ever crowned

LEFT: The final of the Miss World contest, 1951. 'The prettiest girl in Sweden', 22-year-old Kerstin 'Kiki' Hakansson won the contest at London's Lyceum ballroom. Her scanty bikini and perfect curves no doubt helped. Two-pieces were banned shortly afterwards as it was felt that they gave their wearers an unfair advantage.

as beauty queens went on to achieve fame and fortune later in life. Like glamour models today, beauty queens of yesteryear believed the people around them who promised that great things would come from posing in the almost-buff. But then, as now, looking great in a swimsuit would not pay the bills for ever.

The contestants were expected to parade around in swimsuits displaying their bodies in as sexy a way as possible, yet lead exemplary private lives. It was too unrealistic and scandals plagued the contests. Helen Morgan, the British winner of Miss World in 1973, was forced to resign her title after four days when it was discovered she had a child, and in 1984 the first black Miss America, Vanessa Williams, famously stepped down after pornographic pictures of her, taken years before, were released. Beneath the euphemisms, the perfect beauty queen supposedly needed a virginal image.

LEFT AND BELOW: Miss World in 1968 was Miss Australia, Penelope Plummer. Compare her modest outfit with that of Miss Venezuela, 1979's winner. Her cut-away disco-style swimsuit reveals more than it actually covers and was highly fashionable at the time.

LEFT: Another Swedish winner, Eva Ruber-Staier, is crowned Miss World at the peak of the contest's popularity in 1969. She was the quintessential blonde beauty queen and one of a string of Swedish Miss Worlds.

Beauty contests, however, were still great news for the swimsuit industry. The contests showcased fashionable trends such as the halterneck, lace-up fronts, mesh cutouts, string bikinis, and hoop or buckle details attaching whole suits together. If Miss World or Miss America wore a certain style of swimsuit, it would be sure to be copied for the department stores.

LEFT: Three contestants in the finals of the Miss United Kingdom contest, 25 August, 1981. Posing by the Serpentine in London are Georgina Kearney of Scotland, Lyn Coombs of Arun, and Nikki Wright of Swanage. By the 1980s, beauty contests were going out of fashion in the UK. Contestants generally did not want to go into glamour modelling but did not have the right looks for fashion, so most ended up as catalogue or advertising models.

LEFT: Miss World contestants of 1999 pose for a preview shot in Malta. Iin the 1990s, the bikini was readmitted. If a girl could not carry one off, the contest was no place for her. A few brave souls still chose a one-piece but what is the point of a brutal fitness regime if you can't show off your abs?

BELOW: Five stunning young finalists from the 2005 Miss Tourism Queen International Pageant. Here the girls are posing for the Miss Bikini section of the contest, which also featured tests for personality and movement. They represent, from left, Poland, Mexico, Columbia, Thailand and Estonia.

chapter four

THE RETURN OF THE HOURGLASS

PAGE 100: Fashion and style parted ways with glamour and gaudiness at the end of the 1940s, as this fashion shot by Clifford Coffin from 1949 demonstrates. Sleek bathing caps keep smooth waves under wraps and trim torsos sit cross-legged and demure on the smooth sand dunes. The bare backs of the suits made for a better suntan, and ruching, as seen on the suit in the foreground of the shot, was particularly fashionable.

LEFT: A glamorous blonde poses in what could possibly be a Cole of California swimsuit from 1940. The bustle on the back of the cotton print halterneck builds up the profile of the wearer to hourglass perfection. The basketweave umbrella was a typical beach accessory of the time.

RIGHT: A 1943 Jantzen patriotic billboard by artist Pete Hawley with servicemen and a blonde pin-up beauty wearing a luxurious Velva-Lure swimsuit named Coquette.

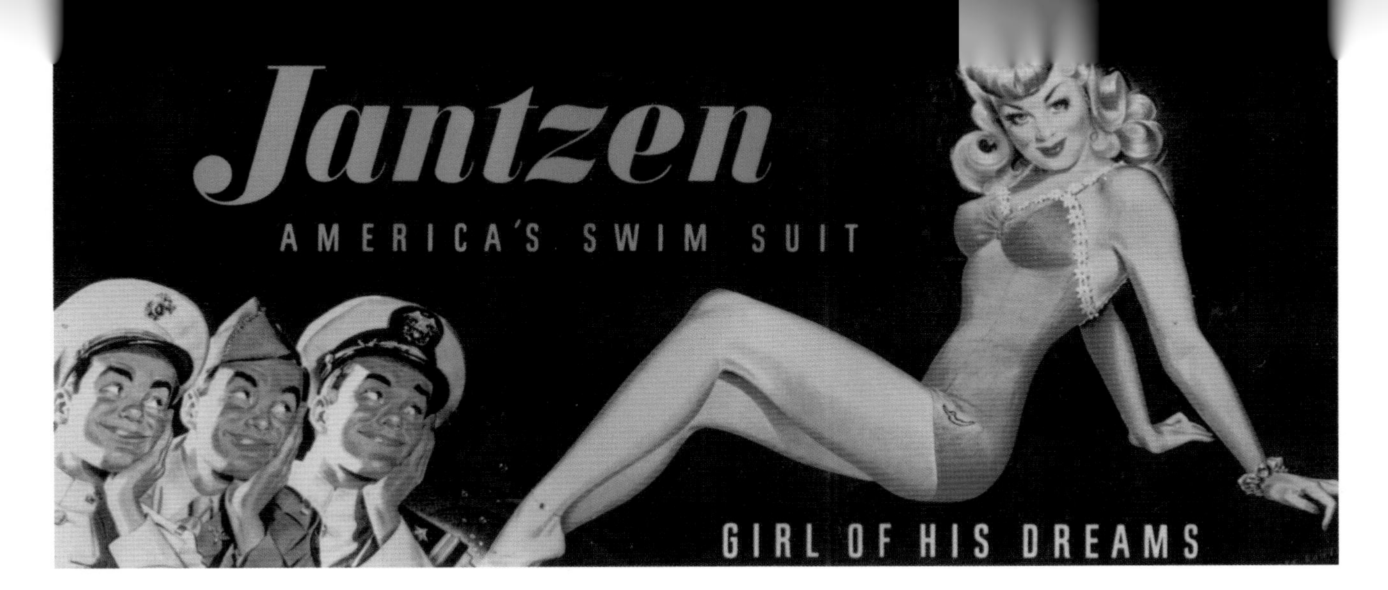

After the outbreak of war in 1939, swimsuits were the last garments on people's minds. Hollywood's famous swimsuit manufacturers were conscripted to make parachutes or army uniforms and nylon was withdrawn for the war effort. Clothes were cut from the minimum of cloth until Christian Dior grasped the postwar mood and launched his 'New Look' on the world in 1947.

In Britain utility clothing and clothing bonds were issued when war broke out. A group of couturiers including Hardy Amies and Edward Molyneux designed a small, spare range of clothes cut to save on fabric and trimmings, to be mass produced for sale in department stores around the country. The British government had to control manufacturing of everything in order to preserve resources during wartime. Across the Atlantic, new designers including Claire McCardell and Tina Leser came on the scene. Their sporty, pared-down outfits suited the mood and became part of a new 'American Look' that heralded the beginning of 'casual' clothing. British women saved their coupons for clothes, stockings and underwear, returned to home-knitted swimsuits and dreamed a few Hollywood dreams.

Despite straitened circumstances, the Hollywood motion-picture machine kept on rolling, churning out war films with victorious endings and musical comedies to keep their audiences cheerful. To help everyone feel even more upbeat, the studios recruited beautiful girls to star in their productions. Lauren Bacall, Betty Grable, Rita Hayworth, Veronica Lake and Virginia Mayo were just some of the new names. All had one thing in common: a figure to die for. Small, pert breasts were replaced by something more substantial, waists became tinier and a new shape emerged. Gently corseted at first because most women were reluctant to return to tightly laced-in waists, the feminine, powerful and sexy hourglass shape returned.

Jitterbugs and Doodlebugs

When war broke out in Europe, the British government became more organized than it had ever been in an effort to guard resources and security. Coupons were issued with which to buy valuable fabric, wool or made-up clothing. In 1941 the average Briton had only 66 clothing coupons for the whole year; in 1942 this was reduced to just 48. When you consider that a coat might cost six, it is easy to understand that swimsuits came near to the bottom of everyone's lists. People could still have fun, but frivolities had to be forfeited.

Luxurious American imports including cosmetics and the newly invented nylon stockings suddenly ceased as cargo space was needed for munitions and food rations. The North Atlantic was too dangerous for ships to be crossing with non-essential items. European women had to make do with gravy browning and other crude leg paints to fake the look of nylon and they had to work harder at looking good under such severely straitened circumstances.

ABOVE: An advertisement for the Jantzen 'Petty Girl' suit of 1940. More curves began appearing in Jantzen advertisements as the 1940s progressed, partly through having enlisted the help of pin-up artist George Petty, who had gained fame as an *Esquire* illustrator and creator of the popular Petty Girl. His girls were healthy, curvy and heavily airbrushed. Artists McClelland Barclay, Pete Hawley and Alberto Vargas were all commissioned by Jantzen over the years.

Paris salons found operating in the war extremely difficult owing to the scarcity of materials. They just about managed to put out collections once a year, but this was always a miracle, with all the different houses helping each other out. Coco Chanel went to Switzerland and manufacture of her famous sportswear ceased. In the USA Stanley Marcus of the famous Neiman Marcus department stores was placed in charge of clothes and fabric conservation for the government. He did a fantastic job, managing to convince the whole nation that closely cut, made-to-last clothes could be fashionable. For the long term he worked to maintain this style, preventing fashion from moving on during the war and thus rendering old clothes out of date. He kept the whole nation feeling stylish in the same old clothes for five years.

ABOVE AND FAR RIGHT: This orange-and-black floral one-piece in wool with crossover back straps is possibly a Carolyn Schnurer printed suit from the early 1940s. Made of wool and with a modesty panel, the suit would have been chiefly worn for swimming, as sun-lounging wear was becoming more decorative and constructed.

RIGHT DETAIL: Stitching on the bodice and waist show the emphasis on the curvy female form in the 1940s, which contrasted with 1930s plain sheath designs. The exotic, tropical-style flowers show a Southern Pacific/Hawaiian inspiration, which was important in the decade.

Curves and the Home Front

Despite all the limitations to a woman's life in wartime, one thing survived: glamour. Women made up for their lack of stylish clothes with gorgeous looks. Advertising campaigns by cosmetic companies urged women to make the most of their appearance at all times in order to cheer up their men and defy the enemy. Rolled-back hair and lipstick was worn every day, and a more grown-up, feminine look was the result.

The curvaceous heroines on the big screen helped reinforce this healthy image. Smiling, big-bosomed and with almost homely figures, these women reminded the fighting forces of all the best bits of the women they had left at home. It was no time for slender ice-maidens and Hollywood stars Rita Hayworth, Jane Russell and Lana Turner provided the forces with pin-ups to keep morale high. By 1945, the ideal female silhouette had changed completely compared with the idealized shape of a decade before. Shoulders were less squared and masculine. Extra fabric needed for big shoulder-pads and shapes was too extravagant an indulgence. Breasts were rounder, higher and fuller; the waist was smaller, and hips and tummy were allowed to curve out more naturally instead of the hard, flat look. Thighs and knees were rounder, with dimples and softer outlines.

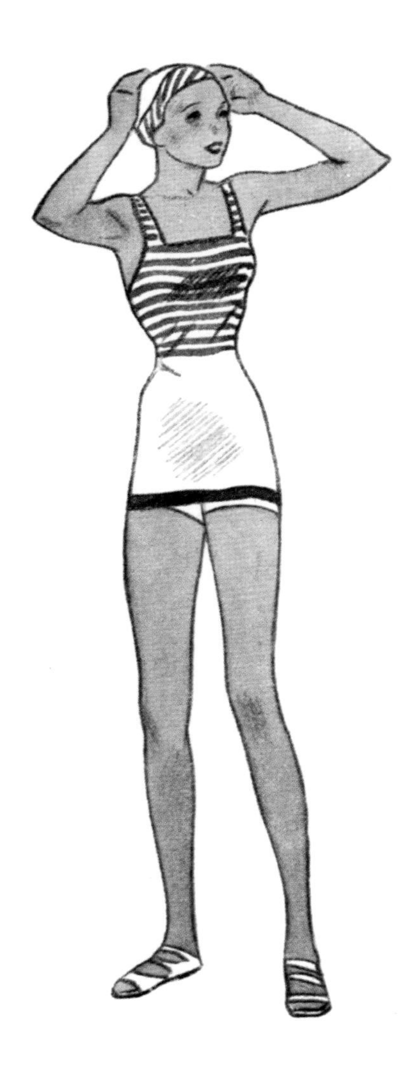

THIS PAGE: Illustrations of crossover shorts-style swimsuits from the same 1943 Jaeger *Beachwear* catalogue.

LEFT: The front cover of the Jaeger *Beachwear* ladies' catalogue from 1943 and a catalogue illustration depicting a halterneck one-piece with a sash-tie belt for ordering.

Rita Hayworth embodied the new female shape in *Cover Girl* (1944) and *Gilda* (1946), clad in curvaceous corseted outfits. Jane Russell had her own bra specially crafted by aeroplane enthusiast Howard Hughes, to help her achieve some magnificent upward thrust in *The Outlaw* (1943). Jane Russell's breasts were so overwhelming a sight on the big screen that the film was banned for seven years until, presumably, the censors felt the public were ready. The 'Sweater Girl' Lana Turner, so-called because her assets looked so amazing in the tight sweaters she wore in *They Won't Forget* (1937) and *Love Finds Andy Hardy* (1938), was the forces ultimate sweetheart but Esther Williams became the swimsuit pin-up. A former USA swimming champion, Williams performed swimming and diving feats both on and off screen. Her graceful, arching body set off her swimsuits to perfection as she went through the moves in *Bathing Beauty* (1944) and *Neptune's Daughter* (1949), and performed one of the most memorable on-screen swimming sequences of all time in *Ziegfeld Follies* (1946). In 1947 Cole of California created the 'Esther Williams' swimsuit, a vampish, strapless affair designed for sunbathing in as much as actually swimming. Williams went on to design her own range of swimming pools and continued starring in films until the 1960s.

LEFT: A young Ava Gardner poses in her polka-dot bikini in 1944. Poised for superstardom, she was one of a perfect posse of hourglass beauties. The daring corset-lacing on the side of her bikini bottoms and on her bandeau top is counterbalanced by her covered navel. Gardner was one of the first girls to be photographed with cleavage, an important new facet of physical glamour.

RIGHT: The starlet swimmer Esther Williams is shown here in 1940 wearing a cotton ruched two-piece, prettily fastened together at the waist with buttons. The midriff is revealed but the strategically positioned bow offers a modest bikini look.

Built to Last

BELOW: A Horst P. Horst photograph from 1940 featuring a model who is far too well dressed for the beach in a pin-stripe two-piece and careful curls. Satin and taffeta were popular fabrics as their sheen was highly flattering to bumps and curves.

RIGHT: The model Lisa Fonssagrieves poses in all the shapes needed to compose the word 'Vogue' for a 1940 advertisement for Brigance swimsuits. Her simple halterneck top and striped shorts were attached at the front and allowed for comfort and movement, as she so ably demonstrates.

The result was a big boost for the underwear industry. Corsets and girdles began a gradual comeback during the 1940s with Warners, Playtex and Berlei the major players. By the end of the decade, the 'waist-cincher' girdle was a requirement in every woman's undie drawer. This had an inevitable knock-on effect for the outlines of the swimsuit as the big American swimsuit companies had to give up Lastex, nylon and silk for the war effort. Cole of California focused on manufacturing parachutes and Jantzen produced fabric for soldier's kits that included tents, clothes, socks and bags. What's more, even though the swimsuit companies were allowed to continue manufacturing their main goods, they had to use 10 per cent less fabric overall in their designs.

Side-stepping wartime fabric restrictions, the American swimwear companies returned to their respective drawing boards, creating swimsuits from what was available. The double-fronted, skirted looks of the 1930s were out, as were turn-over cuffed necklines, matching belts, frills and adornments. Instead of stretch Lastex (or Matletex in Mabs of Hollywood's case), designers built in even more ingenious underwear elements to give swimsuits shape. Boned corseted bodices and lace-up sides, built-in brassieres and button-sided tummy panels all contributed to the redefining of women's bodies through their swimsuits. Jantzen introduced the Double Dare swimsuit, featuring deliberate round cut-outs at the sides on the upper thighs. Such tricks detracted from the temporary absence of Lastex and adjusted the focus to the female body, as opposed to the garment covering it.

After the war ended, colours and patterns grew more elaborate, as did embellishments, with ruching, wrapping, ties and halternecks featuring as the most flattering and popular swimsuit elements. Some suits resembled small waiter's outfits with white front panels and cheeky bowtie prints, while others were boned to stay up on their own, offering a tantalizing taste of what was to come in the next decade.

VOGUE

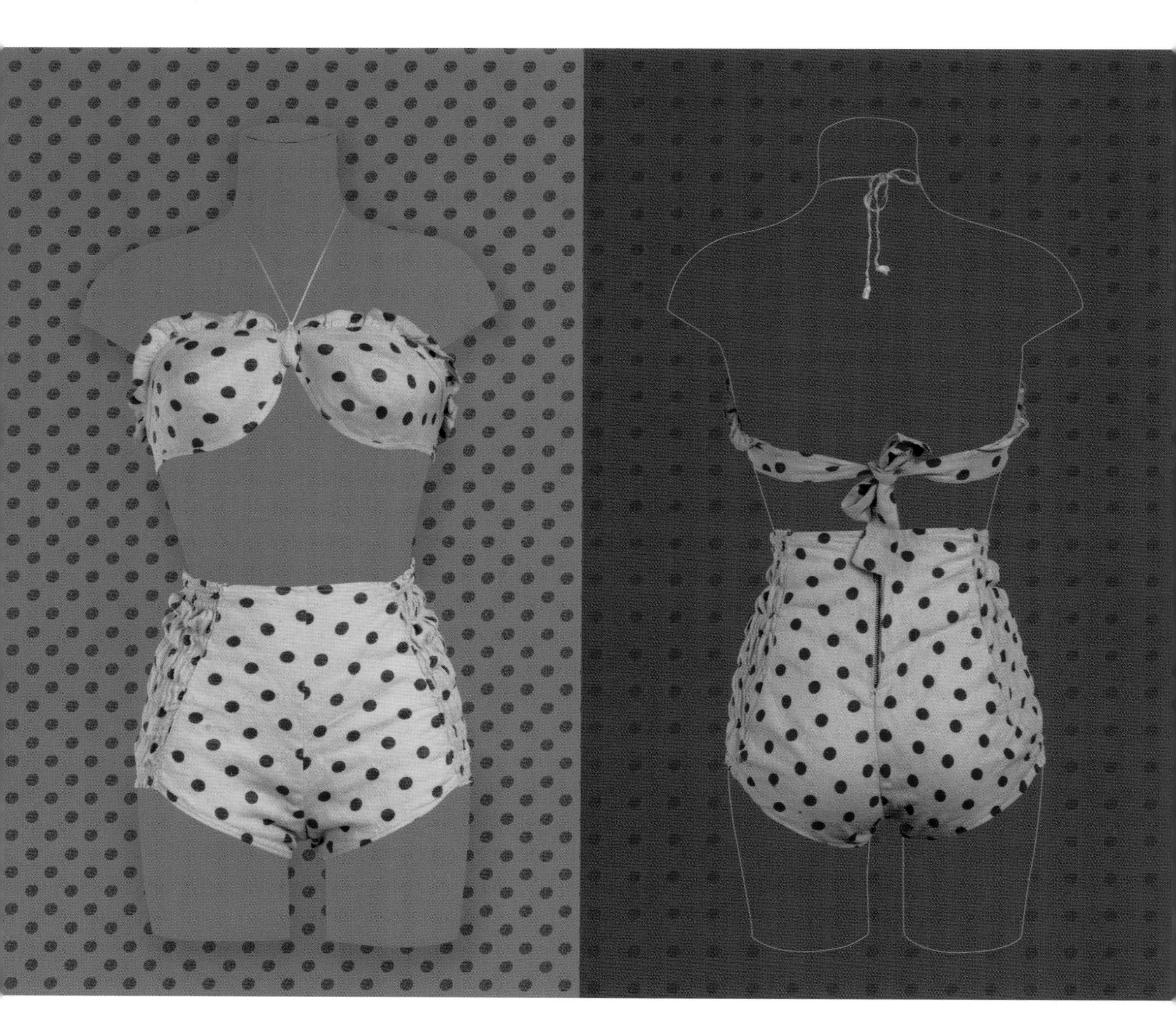

LEFT: A 'Jantzen makes the whole world swim' advertisement from 1948, with the slogan line 'You too can be a "danger" in one of the new Jantzens.' The two-piece bra top was made to be adjustable in three ways. The swimmers are slimmer and less vampy than early 1940s illustrations, and the girl in the foreground has an Elizabeth Taylor look, complete with red lips and black lashes.

LEFT: A polka-dot spot two-piece from the 1940s features a frilled bandeau top that curves around the ribcage. High-waisted bottoms have smocked side panels and a back zip for a form-fitting effect.

The two-piece swimsuit was born in the wartime years, out of fabric-saving necessity rather than the motivation to shock. The unspoken but golden rule was that the navel should always be covered. This was to prove the crucial difference between the two-piece swimsuit and the bikini, which was launched in Paris in 1946 (see also pages 134–43). The bikini, was to cause riots, outrage and worldwide controversy, and the major swimwear brands in the USA avoided it like the hot potato it was for some time. In fact, it was not until the 1960s that the bikini became a permanent fixture on beaches. A staid conservatism still existed at the centre of American society – preachers, politicians and town guilds frowned on undue displays of flesh, which contradicted the strong, sexy image of Hollywood that was evident on screen in every small-town cinema.

BELOW: Ava Gardner lounges in the California sunshine in an elasticated spandex two-piece from 1943. The flattering modesty bottoms were a blessing for the hourglass shape, holding everything in and concealing bulges. In the early 1940s cleavage was coming into style as long as it was firmly wedged in place.

OPPOSITE: The all-American sweetheart Betty Grable poses in a gold two-piece, in 1945. The shaped bodice with its darts and halterneck was a foretaste of swimwear shapes to come. By the 1950s, such outfits could stand up on their own. Grable was considered a bit of a vixen, though she looks demure enough here.

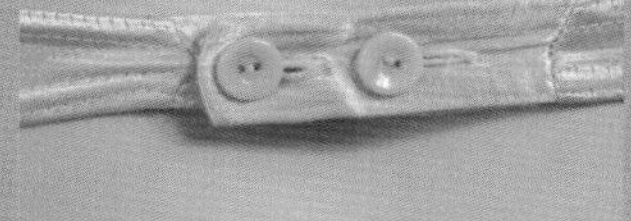

ABOVE DETAIL: Buttons and ties were commonly used for swimwear fastenings, rather than brassiere-type hooks or clasps.

LEFT AND FAR LEFT: These front and back views of a gold satin two-piece show a sheath bottom where a modesty skirt panel appears at the front only and a shelf bra top allows a band of coverage underneath the breasts that also provides support. This style of swimsuit was a favourite of Hollywood stars, such as Ava Gardner and Betty Grable (see pages 114–5), and remained popular into the 1950s.

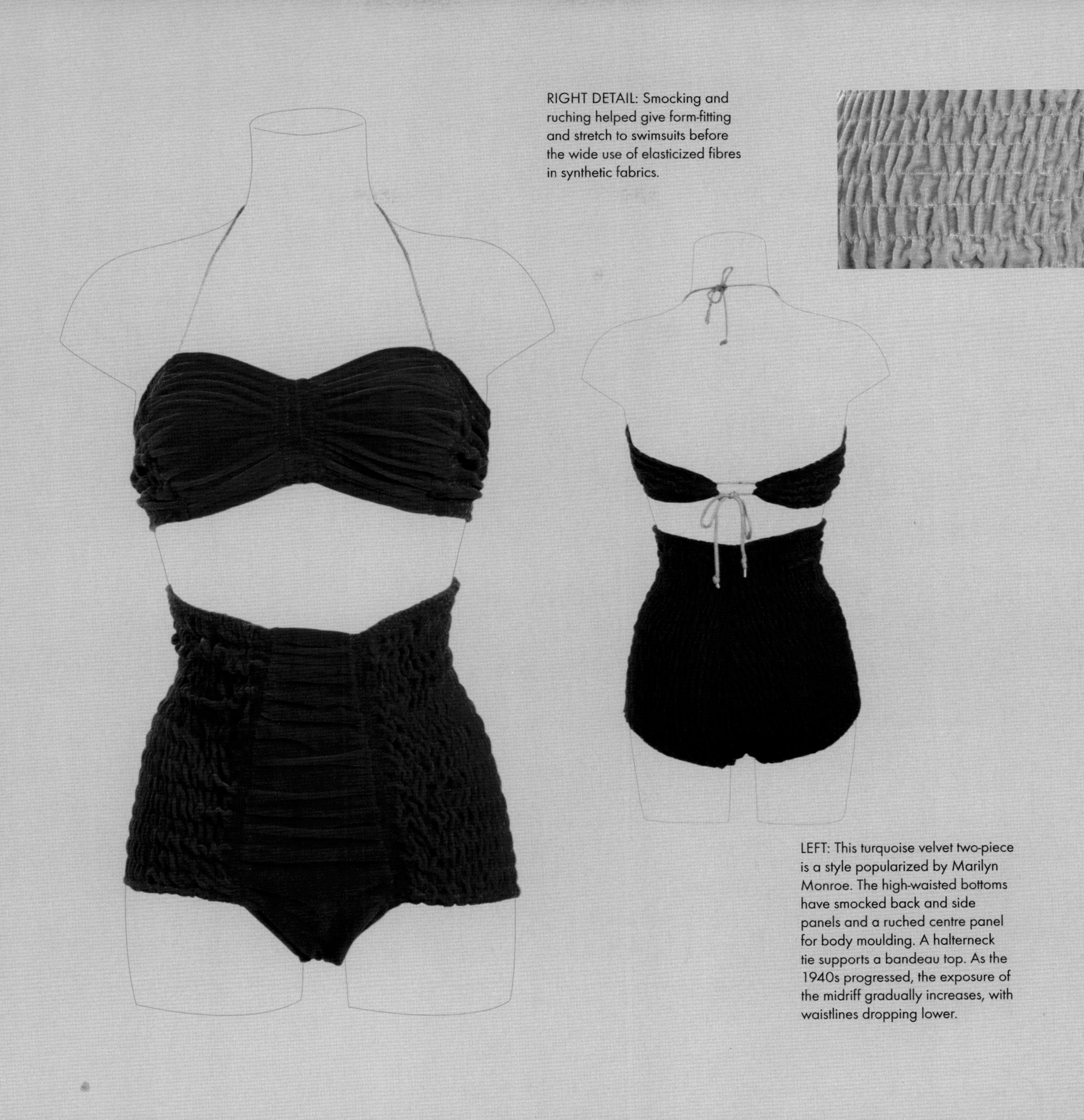

RIGHT DETAIL: Smocking and ruching helped give form-fitting and stretch to swimsuits before the wide use of elasticized fibres in synthetic fabrics.

LEFT: This turquoise velvet two-piece is a style popularized by Marilyn Monroe. The high-waisted bottoms have smocked back and side panels and a ruched centre panel for body moulding. A halterneck tie supports a bandeau top. As the 1940s progressed, the exposure of the midriff gradually increases, with waistlines dropping lower.

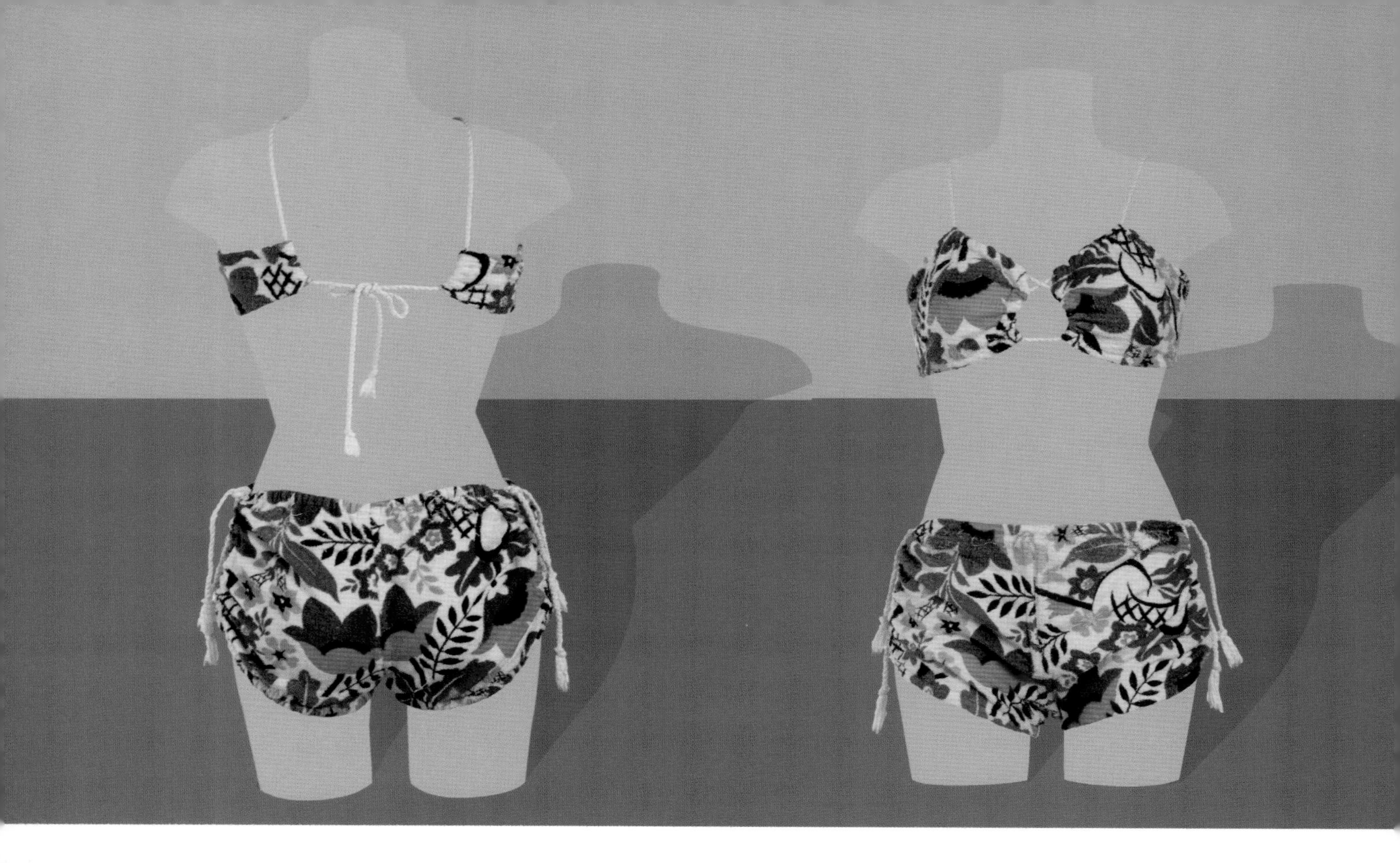

In Britain homemade swimsuits were fashioned from wool and cottons including gingham and seersucker, as there was no swimsuit manufacturing to speak of. Cotton versions featured bibs, button-across front panels and button-down straps at the back. If the buttons perished, you chose others from wherever you could and sewed them on instead, making mismatching buttons a fashion trend that spread to casual tops and sweaters. If fabric faded or wore thin, it was patched. Women thought of ingenious ways to make the best of their swimsuits, sewing handkerchiefs over tears, knitting or crocheting small flower decorations or covering ragged edges with ribbons.

There were few places to display one's swimsuit anyway, particularly in Europe. Some lidos and public pools stayed open during the war years, but people did not have the leisure time to enjoy them and most were closed. The risk of bombing raids, the need to conserve resources including water and the widescale redistribution of the population put the lido lifestyle

ABOVE LEFT: Stretch cotton towelling combined with elastic fibres was just one of many new fabrics to hit the swimwear market in the 1930s and 1940s. Sporty and fun, it held its shape (though it benefited from wringing out in a changing cabin) and dried off quickly in the sun.

ABOVE: A homemade 'diaper' swimsuit – its name reflecting the tied fastening at the front. Constructed from one length of fabric, the swimsuit was hung around the neck with the fabric wrapping through the legs from the front, around the bottom and then tied at the front.

RIGHT DETAIL: This unusual crafted wooden button secures the fabric at the lower back.

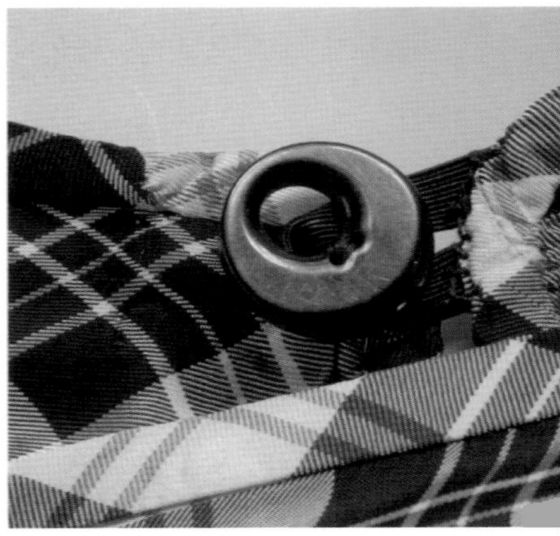

on hold, particularly along the south coast of England; Bournemouth, Brighton and Eastbourne all suffered a dearth of visitors, whose numbers would not pick up again until the war ended.

New Looks and American Names

By the time Christian Dior presented his postwar New Look silhouette at his newly opened Paris boutique in 1947, the hourglass had firmly entrenched itself in the common imagination. Women were more than ready for clothes to enhance their curvy shapes. When the styles finally emerged, everyone went mad for Dior. As raw materials and fabrics filtered back into the fashion markets, the new silhouette crept into all aspects of women's clothing.

Although hugely popular in the USA, the New Look had to compete with another emerging style that was to grow stronger through the decades. The American Look was born through homegrown talent, notably the iconic Claire McCardell. Based on the simple lines laid down by Stanley Marcus, the American Look featured classically shaped pants, skirts, shirts and dresses in strong, natural fibres. Although she became well known for wrap dresses and daywear, McCardell truly shone when it came to swimsuits. Including such designers as Tina Leser and Carolyn Schnurer, the movement was to rival the design houses of Paris when it came to sportswear and swimwear.

LEFT: The model Sabine, left, poses in Claire McCardell's loincloth beachwear of 1946 with working buttons. Deep armholes were used time and again in McCardell designs.

ABOVE: McCardell was interested in classical Grecian draping, as can be seen here in a photograph of her 1946 ivory strapless swimsuit taken by *Vogue* photographer John Rawlings.

McCardell set herself the remit of marrying style and comfort through her designs. She admired the simplicity of Chanel and Parisian designer Vionnet's bias cuts; she experimented with wrap-around and tie-fastenings and incorporated Grecian-style draping and gathering into her designs. Her 'diaper' swimsuit featured cleverly gathered jersey that resembled a baby's nappy and many of her swimsuits featured Greco-Roman styling. One-shouldered tops, tie-waists and softly draped shapes were trademarks that echoes McCardell's revolutionary daywear designs. She aimed to dress ordinary American women in extremely simple designs, which could be mass produced but still look elegant. Her clothes were designed to be worn with simple underwear; tie-belts, wrap-around fastenings and sashes ensured that they always fitted the wearer perfectly. Fond of natural fabrics and cutting edge in her unconventional use of them, she designed simple swimsuits in towelling, seersucker and jersey, as well as raw silk, denim, calico, cotton velvet and different weaves of wool. Not averse to a bit of stretch, McCardell also worked with nylon and stretch fibres woven through wool jersey. There is no surprise that along with strapless swimsuits she originated the elasticated strapless tube top. And as for cut, she brought the cut-away leg, which forms today's basic swimsuit shape, into fashion. In a fashion-forward move in the mid 1930s she also cut out the side panels of a maillot, a design that is widely regarded as a forerunner of the bikini.

LEFT: A 1946 photograph of fashion models Sabine (left, wearing an Emily Wilkens suit) and Janet Stevenson (right, wearing Louella Ballerino) on a breezy beach. Both suits, the knitted one-piece and cotton two-piece, are typical of those worn by ordinary women at the time as they were not expensive or highly glamorous. Similar suits could also be made easily at home.

RIGHT: Models pose in playsuits, the latest thing for beach lounging and sunbathing, in 1941. Instead of sitting around in wet swimsuits, women changed into these racy little shorts-suits, here made from the artificial miracle fabric, rayon. Creaseproof, easy to work with and flattering on the body, 'Celanese rayon jersey' (worn on the model in the foreground) was hot news in the fashion world.

RIGHT: A homemade 1940s ivory unitard-style one piece has crossover back shoulder straps and is made with figure-hugging smocking.

LEFT: A classic Claire McCardell swimsuit in grey jersey photographed in 1945. The unusual choice of fabric for beachwear was a McCardell trademark. This outfit is offset by a red and black polka dot 'Ascot' – a scarf worn to fill in the V-neck area and contrast with the austere fabric. Note the delightful mini-button side fastening – McCardell used buttons for decoration as well as practicality.

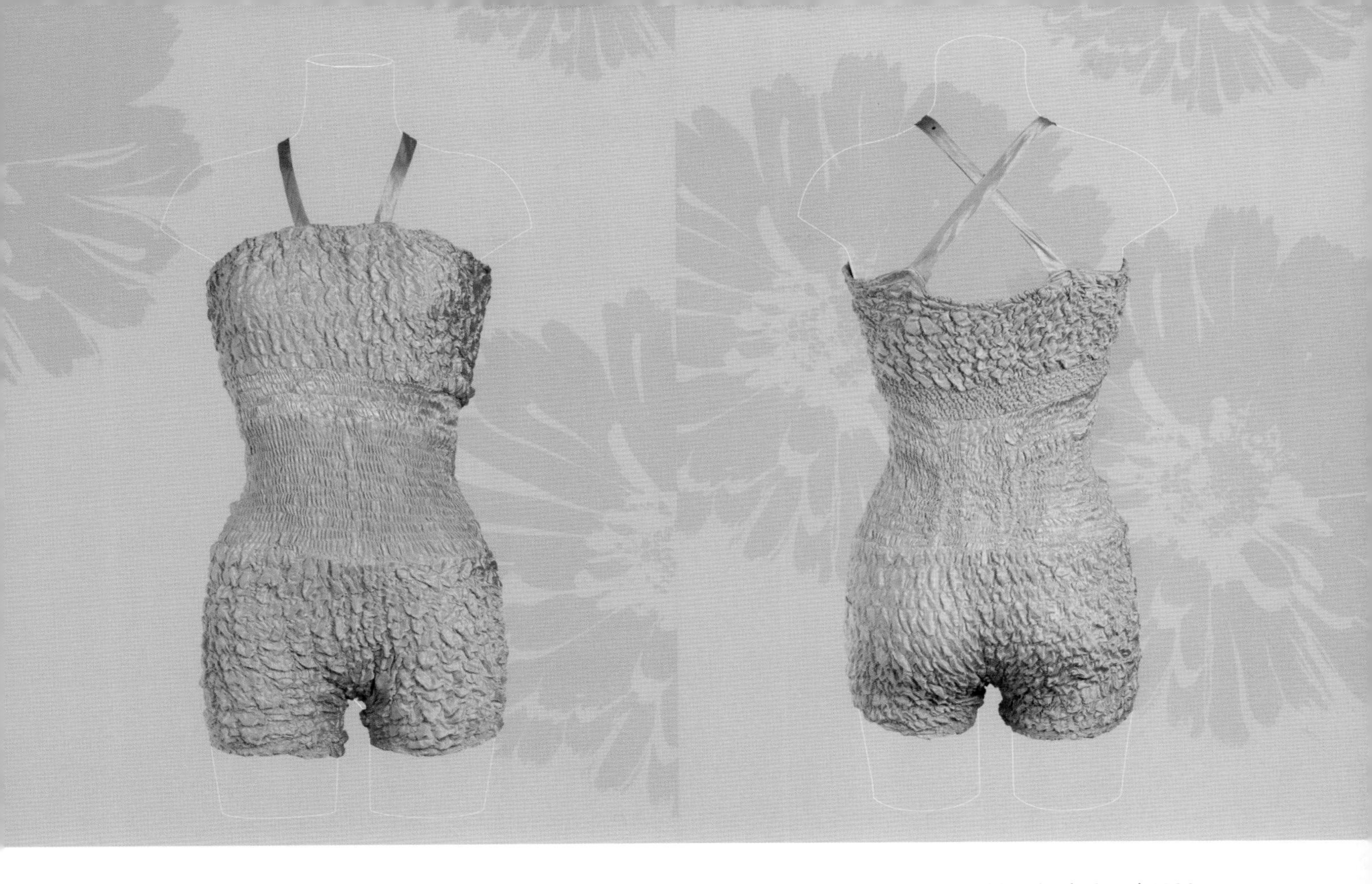

Even after the war, when Lastex, nylon and other artificial fibres returned to the swimwear market, sea water was still a problem for manufacturers. Swimsuits came with instructions for washing out after use to prevent staining and stiffness from salt water; vital rubber fibres soon perished. Most swimsuits were uncomfortable to sit in and drooped when wet. Also, elaborate internal corset-work and construction needed careful handling. Costumes had to be dried out properly, and although they were not like the knitted 1920s versions that required a mad dash up the beach into a changing cubicle because of extreme sagging, women still needed to change after a dip. The solution came in the form of the 'playsuit', essentially a small garment to be worn for sunbathing and pool lounging, but not for swimming. A grey wool playsuit by McCardell, a garment that married beach fun with the kind of fabric you might find in suiting, was a huge hit in 1946.

Tina Leser followed McCardell's lead and introduced bestselling lines of stylish swimsuits with matching cover-ups in cheerful gingham checks, cotton towelling (terrycloth), denim or seersucker. She lived in Honolulu, experiencing beach life first-hand, but she left after the bombing of Pearl Harbor in 1942. Leser took her love of exotic and ethnic-inspired fabrics to the mainland, making strapless dresses from Guatemalan blankets and jackets from Mexican weaves, and Hawaiian prints and shapes remained an important influence in her designs. She produced some of the first wrap skirts and sarongs to come on to the market, and she liked dressy styles – a cotton towelling beach wrap would have jacket-style lapels, for instance, or swimsuits would be crafted from elaborate, evening-style fabrics. Swimsuits, playsuits and beachwear featured in many collections, including a famous one-shouldered Hawaiian print swimsuit from 1943 and a 1947 collection of beachwear and sundresses created in Indian madras plaid. In 1946 she produced a 'complete weekend wardrobe' in jersey aimed at busy working women, making her a forerunner of such modern designers as Donna Karan today.

LEFT: In the 1940s dressier outfits were still favoured at the poolside. Resembling a playsuit, this swimsuit would have been worn at a lido or by a hotel pool rather than at the beach. This type of rayon fabric with a sheen was described as 'sharkskin' and it would have drip-dried nicely in the sun.

RIGHT: A Tina Leser ensemble from 1944 that wouldn't look out of place worn today. Leser travelled widely, seeking inspiration for her tropical colourways and prints. This suit contrasts a sea-green with black, gold and green graphic shapes on the bikini bandeau top and matching sarong.

ABOVE DETAIL: Exotic flower patterns became popular prints for swimsuits and sunwear in the USA, particularly in designs by Tina Leser and Caroline Schnurer.

FAR LEFT AND LEFT: A sarong-style two-piece with decorative brassiere-top tie and crossover back ties that loop through.

Swimwear guru Carolyn Schnurer also loved ethnic prints and colours. Launching her career by designing swimsuits, sundresses and shorts for her husband's swimsuit range, Bert Schnurer Cabana, she travelled the world, gathering inspiration from as far afield as Peru, India, Africa and Japan. She used ethnic details on an essentially western silhouette. Two-pieces became her trademark, though fashion legend has it that after producing the first one for the Schnurer label in 1941, the house model was so shocked that she refused to wear it. Either that particular model relented or another was found, because by the mid 1940s Schnurer's two-pieces, featuring waist-high 'nappy'-style bottoms with ties at the side, matching wrap-around skirts and halterneck tops were top sellers.

LEFT: A two-piece designed by Jane Irwill, worn by model Janet Stevenson in 1943. A famous swimwear model of the 1940s, Stevenson modelled for Clare Potter and Joset Walker as well as McCardell and Schnurer. This two-piece is prettily frilled and seems lingerie-inspired. Jane Irwill was also known for her mid 1940s Baby Bloomer swimwear, a modern take on the early-century Princess costumes, as well as for her 'Knitticisms' knitwear.

During the war, Schnurer worked very hard to build constructed swimsuits from any fabrics that she could obtain. A few nylon and artificial silk threads were available, so these were mixed with the more easily accessible cottons and wools, creating cotton sateen or smoother wool mixes for swimsuits and two-pieces. Schnurer was an expert architect, incorporating uplifting seams, bands, belts and straps to pull in and push out a woman's body in all the right places. This is especially evident in a 1948 advertisement poster for Valvoline Motor Oil, which featured a slick sports car in the background and a glamour girl dressed in a shiny Schnurer swimsuit complete with crisscross bands beneath the torpedo-shaped breasts, a buckled waist belt and button-fastening halterneck. The caption read: 'The Girl wears a faultlessly designed swimsuit by Carolyn Schnurer... Her Car, faultlessly lubricated with Valvoline'.

LEFT: A dark blue Carolyn Schnurer playsuit from 1946. More austere than Schnurer's usual designs, this suit features a Peter Pan collar and small puffed sleeves. Pretty detailing was often contrasted with a vampish edge – note the dark green leather belt tightly cinched at the waist.

RIGHT: The styling on these two-pieces from 1946 is classic Schnurer, with the 'nappy'-style bottoms of a more classical construction than McCardell's versions. Here, a tie-waist fastens one, while a covered hoop forms the centrepiece on the other. The tops are roomy for modesty, yet the bottoms are 'daringly' high cut.

Tighter, Harder, Firmer

In response to the need for water-withstanding swimsuits, US Rubber, a company that had worked on stretch yarns for the swimwear manufacturers, began producing its own suits. These were not terribly comfortable creations, made of rubber that after a few outings began to harden around the edges and lose its colour. Brand new, they looked fantastic, but comfort was not foremost. However, they set the trend for utilitarian swimsuits purely for speedy swimming. US Rubber also introduced a fetching line of hair-protecting swimming hats for women that have stayed popular to this day, despite no improvements in the effect they have on the wearer's appearance.

For all its practicality, rubber alone could not cut it in the glamour stakes. Luckily for the swimsuit manufacturers, the artificial fabric industry moved on in leaps and bounds after the war. Research for the chemical companies freed manufacturers from war materials so they could focus on fashion fabrics, which led to inventions in elastomeric fibres such as Orlon, Matletex, spandex, Dacron and early versions of what was to become Lycra (by DuPont). These fabrics enabled the swimsuit market to update its products constantly, which was a good job, as demand for the swimsuit was growing fast. Mass production of the stretchy, form-fitting and controlling swimsuits available in American stores such as Lord & Taylor and

ABOVE: A 1949 ad by DuPont, demonstrating the versatility of their fabrics, which included rayon. After the war DuPont provided dressmakers, furniture manufacturers and home furnishers with a shiny new solution to silk. Easily washed, yet retaining all its texture and colour, rayon was the wonder fabric of the late 1940s.

ABOVE: An early to mid 1940s photograph, probably from a department store catalogue, showing models enjoying a day at the beach. The classic-design two-pieces are still keeping most of the body covered, and cleavages are also still under wraps. Waistlines, however, are defined, giving an idea of the shape of swimwear to come.

Saks Fifth Avenue spread to the UK through Jaeger, Marks & Spencer, and department stores such as Debenhams & Freebody.

Lana Turner, Rita Hayworth and Jane Russell were part of a Hollywood-inspired craze that would not and could not be halted for at least another two decades. The return of the hourglass was embraced by women all over the world and the men liked it, too. Film stars became screen goddesses. The pin-up was not only born, she had taken over. By 1950, the world was, quite literally, 'all woman'.

The Birth of the Bikini

Two-pieces had been around for at least ten years before engineer-designer Louis Réard pulled off the most famous fashion public-relations scoop of all time and 'invented' the bikini in 1946. Named after the small Bikini atoll island in the South Pacific close to where atom bombs were being tested just four days before the 1946 Paris fashion shows, he no doubt hoped for a similar explosion of interest in his swimsuit. His showmanship outgunned the reserved designer Jacques Heim, who had launched his own version two months earlier, calling it the 'Atome'; both two-pieces claimed the title of the 'world's smallest swimsuit'.

LEFT: Here a still-brunette Marilyn Monroe sports a sexy pose in a bikini, photographed by Andre De Dienes, who took the first beach pictures of her for the Blue Book modelling agency. Marilyn graced dozens of magazine covers in the early 1940s before her first screen test with Twentieth Century Fox in 1946.

RIGHT: The first official outing of the bikini by Louis Réard, modelled by Micheline Bernardini. The suit was so small it could fit in a matchbox and printed in a newspaper pattern that drove home the point that this event was worthy of many column inches of coverage.

Comprising a bra top and two triangles of cotton cloth connected by string, Réard's bikini was the scantiest beachwear outfit ever, came in at a mere 76 cm (30 inches) of fabric – and put the navel centre stage for the first time. It was so small and revealing, in fact, that no Parisian model would wear it. So instead, Réard hired Micheline Bernardini, who had no such reservations as her day job was as a nude dancer at the Casino de Paris. The shots of Bernardini photographed on the official bikini launch day, 5 July 1946, at the Piscine Molitar in Paris, flew down the international news wires at double speed. Her appearance was part of a swimwear fashion show at which the press had been promised something special. She sashayed along suggestively, thanks to her dancer training, and Réard used the publicity to get as many people as possible to notice his product.

Nevertheless, the bikini was not an instant success. American manufacturers, who had long held the majority share of the market for swimwear, did not appreciate the European competition. Jantzen, Cole of California, Mabs of Hollywood and Caltex, among other manufacturers, soon stepped up the pace. Dressing every starlet they could in form-fitting, textured spandex, Lastex and Matletex swimsuits, the Americans outpaced the rather scruffy-looking Bernadini in her shabby cotton bikini. Along with the strength of the American, and in particular Hollywood, model, the bikini was declared to be morally 'indecent', which slowed its chance for market expansion. Unlike the two-pieces available before its launch, the bikini revealed the midriff and navel – a sight previously considered to be about as outrageous as a nipple. It was to be another five years before fully fledged, low-cut bikinis made it on to the beaches of mainstream America. Even in Europe in 1950, one Italian fashion magazine declared that bikinis should be worn purely for sunbathing purposes or on board boats!

RIGHT: Louis Réard, a French automobile engineer, became known as the creator of the bikini, though his design was actually a refinement of the work of couturier Jacques Heim. Here Réard shows off one of his creations in the late 1940s. He had been creating knitted swimwear since 1925 but after the war turned his hand to creations that captured the more lighthearted mood of the time.

How to Stuff a Wild Bikini

Bikinis have enjoyed a colourful life on the silver screen, with some memorable examples during the late 1950s and 1960s. The title of a 1965 film starring Frankie Avalon and Annette Funicello, *How to Stuff a Wild Bikini*, was the last in a string of successful 'beach movies' starring the duo. The cute romantic comedy was a rock 'n' roll teenage concoction of beach parties, bikinis, motorcycles and magic. Annette Funicello played DeDe in the film series, which were glorified excuses for girls with big hair to romp around in bikinis. In fact, the movie was the least wild of the series, mainly because Funicello was pregnant and was thus filmed from above the upper torso only, and Frankie Avalon made only two on-screen appearances as he was elsewhere trying to make it in serious movie roles. Part of a seven-film cycle that included *Beach Party* and *Beach Blanket Bingo*, the movies represented an idealistic moral respectability that was at odds with the current American climate, caught in the tensions of the Cold War and Vietnam War. A slew of films starring Elvis Presley and Sandra Dee followed the same moral template and showcased bikini styles that were likewise innocent and girly, and a million miles from the Hollywood vamp.

The bikini made an impact on cinema screens in 1956 in Roger Vadim's film *And God Created Woman,* starring the young Brigitte Bardot. Naturally leggy and slim with big enough boobs to fill a sexy top, this young French ingenue set a whole new trend for sex symbols. Suddenly, the bleached-out, pumped-up, zipped-in Hollywood queens were old hat. Bardot and

RIGHT: Brigitte Bardot modelling swimwear on the beach at the Cannes Film Festival in 1953. Her 1956 film, *And God Created Woman,* launched Bardot into the spotlight and became the benchmark for bikinis on celluloid. However, Bardot had already appeared on screen many times before, notably in *Manina, la fille sans voile* in 1952, released as *The Girl in the Bikini* in the USA and as *The Lighthouse-Keeper's Daughter* in the UK.

her bikini were where it was collectively 'at'. Ursula Andress briefly stole Bardot's crown in the 1962 Bond film *Dr No*. As Honey Ryder, her emergence from the sea in an ivory number complete with belt and dagger became an iconic cinema scene; the bikini was created by a West Indian dressmaker in Jamaica and was designed to withstand the demands of the role. As Jinx in the Bond film *Die Another Day* (2002), Halle Berry pays homage to the Ursula Andress role by wearing an orange modern version of the Andress swimsuit.

Once the initial hoo-hah had died down, bikinis retired to the 'gorgeous girls only' costume shelves of the film world. Other notable appearances include the bikini-type costumes of Raquel Welch in *One Million Years BC* (1966) and Carrie Fisher as Princess Leia in *Return of the Jedi* (1983). Welch's fur bikini was created by stage and costume designer Carl Toms, while the brass-and-cloth Leia bikini was invented by costume designer Aggie Guerard Rodgers. The hard truth was, and still is, that you must be toned and fit to look good in a bikini. There is nothing to hold you in or push you up, as any heavy constructive wiring would leave ugly

LEFT: Halle Berry in the Bond film *Die Another Day* models an orange La Perla bikini and hip knife in a direct tribute to the role played by Ursula Andress in *Dr No*. Andress's bikini top was constructed from one of her own bras, covered with ivory cotton, and fetched $60,000 (£41,000) at auction in 2001 – bought by Robert Earl, founder of the Planet Hollywood restaurant chain.

LEFT: Raquel Welch in the 1966 film *One Million Years BC* exhibited raw cavegirl sexuality in a fur bikini by costume designer Carl Toms. Fur bikinis had already made an impact: mink versions had a short-lived outing in the mid 1950s, worn by such starlets as Diana Dors and Carol Allen.

BELOW: In 1983, Carrie Fisher donned a gold 'slavegirl' bikini in the third instalment of the Star Wars saga *Return of the Jedi*. The bikini gained legendary status and made her an object of desire for many schoolboys at the time.

bulges above, below and out to the side. Marilyn Monroe was photographed in classic two-pieces early in her career but she shied away from the tiny bikini in the late 1950s and early '60s because she simply did not have the figure for it. The same was true for Elizabeth Taylor and most of the Hollywood old guard. New faces stole the big screen in the 1960s, more for their ability to look good in a bikini than for their acting talents. On television, however, the navel was still banned, and remained so until the 1970s with the *Sonny & Cher Show* and *Rowan & Martin's Laugh-In*.

LEFT: An early tankini from 1968 pairs a cropped vest top with generously cut bottoms. Like the shelf bra of years before, the tankini – or cami– top provided some midriff coverage and breast support.

RIGHT: A yellow crochet bikini from the 1970s features hip-slung bottoms – a low-waisted look that was so popular with jean and trouser fashions. The swimsuit offers no support, relying instead on the physical fitness and slenderness of the wearer to look good.

Bikinis Go Global

By the late 1950s, every boutique from St Tropez to Monte Carlo and along the Italian Riviera was selling its own version of the bikini. Though bikinis featured in the collections of most designers who dabbled in beachwear, they were rarely sold individually. It was almost impossible to buy a bikini on its own; you had to have the matching hat, shoes and dress, too. As an example, a bikini in white nylon piqué with black embossed flowers, complete with matching tunic and stack-heeled sandals, was available from Harrods department store in London in 1964.

However, department stores across the western world began selling their own-brand bikinis. More influenced by the traditional two-piece than by the Réard or Heim bikinis – or couturiers such as Jacques Fath who created ensemble pieces – the own-brands featured deep-sided 'classic' bottoms that finished on the hip line with tops in a variety of styles. Most popular in the early 1960s was the 'cami-top', an early forerunner of the tankini. This simply resembled the top of a chopped-off vest or tank top, and the British department store Debenhams boasted some magnificent Bri-Nylon versions in 1965. A combination of the words 'tank' and 'bikini', the modern tankini is considered a modest version of the bikini, and consists of a bikini bottom with a longer top, the edge of which lies somewhere between above the navel and the hip.

Cole of California launched its first mainstream bikini at the end of the 1950s; lined with a lightly structured bandeau top, it revealed the navel but was still relatively modest. In mainstream fashions the bottom crept lower only slowly over the years; until the mid to late 1960s, the bikini remained lined and with elastic at the waist and legs.

It was to take the arrival of Jean Shrimpton and Twiggy on the modelling scene to change the face of fashion and the bikini for ever. Skinny girls could get away with even less coverage than their bustier sisters, and they needed little support to hold up breasts or tuck in tummies. Along the French Riviera girls dispensed with bikini tops altogether and the resort became famous for its topless sunbathers. Ever since, the bikini has undergone many incarnations, the most notorious being the monokini, Rudi Gernreich's highly unflattering 1968 garment that featured two straps rising between the wearer's breasts and looping over the neck (see also page 203). It looked awful, generated unsurpassed publicity for Gernreich, and then sank without trace. However, the monokini performed an important task in swimwear terms, for it got the bikini noticed again by the fashion world. It ultimately led to the string, the tanga and such revealing strappy designs as the 'pretzel' or 'slingshot', in which the fabric strap crisscrosses the breasts and twists over the hips. The monokini is also a term used to denote just the bikini bottom, worn topless.

Liberated Bikinis

A shift towards liberation in the mid 1960s led to inventive use of materials and daring transparent trends. The bikini bottom slipped even lower, revealing the dimples at the derrière and the top of the pubic bone. As a result, the sides shrank to a tie, knot, ring or thin strap. The constructed cleavage-inducing bra top gave way to softer shapes with less fabric, such as halternecks, and straps became much narrower and less supportive. Rings and ties between the cups appeared. Self-adhering bikinis, which had an outing in the 1940s, emerged as a short-lived trend in the mid '60s as a bikini bottom with two bra cup pieces – named a trikini by the advertisers. The 1948 versions came with free glue, which was sadly (depending on how you looked at it) not water-resistant. Blow-up bikinis with flower designs featuring air valves on the nipples failed to catch on in the 1970s.

The creative use of grass, leather, denim and plastic followed trends in 1960s and 1970s fashions. Fishnet, crochet, macramé, chainmail and transparent fabrics were utilized to create 'peekaboo' swimwear designed to be seen through. The fashion designer Giorgio di Sant'Angelo declared the bikini to be the 'evening dress of the future' and in opposition to the work of such 'futuristic' designers as Paco Rabanne and André Courréges, he emphasized freedom, movement and comfort in his designs. He introduced ethnic influences such as fringing and hippy looks in his 1960s designs and created such groundbreaking swimwear designs in the 1970s and 1980s as the tanga, draped and crystal-beaded bikini. Extreme versions of the bikini, founded on natural materials, were seen on the catwalk: in 1968 Yves St Laurent's famous tulle-and-flowers bridal bikini ensemble was launched, called the 'Eve au Paradis', reinforcing the trend for beach weddings that enjoyed a sensational – and anti-establishment – vogue.

RIGHT: Bride and bridegroom 'Neptune' beachwear, modelled in Paris in May 1966, reflected the obsession for bikinis. Her white organdy bikini is worn with a floor-length veil and pumps; he wears vinyl swimming shorts.

Continuing the outdoor theme more than 20 years later, Moschino sent models down the runway in a thatched version with real grass growing from the bikini pant's band top.

Skimpier and Skinnier

From the 1970s, designers have embraced the string and tanga bikinis, going ever skimpier and reflecting a changing body shape – roundness and sportiness gave way to skinniness. String bikinis were not meant to run, swim or surf in as they easily untied and slipped. By the end of the decade the string halterneck, looping two triangles of fabric, got even tinier, reducing to barely nipple-covering. The string bottom – with ties connecting the front and back at low hip level – went higher on the leg to, by 1980, become the V-kini, featuring a very high leg line with a plunging minimal covering front and back. The focus shifted from the breasts and navel to the legs, hips and bottom, helped by influences from South American swimwear styles.

Today, jet-setters love Dolce & Gabbana, Roberto Cavalli and Missoni at the highest end of the market. Modern resortwear often features kaftans, sarongs and ponchos to match bikinis and swimsuits. Despite predictions in the 1960s and '70s by Rudi Gernreich, and even at Jantzen's headquarters, that everyone would be swimming nude by the twenty-first century, for most women, the bikini is still about as far as they are ever likely to go when it comes to stripping off in public.

ABOVE: A tanga bikini modelled by Luiza Brunet in Rio de Janeiro in 1988. The bottoms create the classic V-shape of low-slung front fabric and high-side strings. This is also an example of the adjustable bikini, where the amount of fabric covering the breasts and bottom can be widened or narrowed by sliding the fabric along the string casing.

LEFT: The skimpiest of styles ever created: the Chanel 'eyepatch' bikini from the spring/summer 1996 collection reduces the string bikini top down to mere nipple coverings in a stripper-esque 'pastie' style, adorned of course with the brand's linked double C logo.

chapter five

THE FABULOUS FIFTIES

THE 1940S MAY HAVE BROUGHT THE HOURGLASS SILHOUETTE AND THE SWEATER GIRL, BUT THE 1950S TOOK THE SHAPE SEVERAL STEPS FURTHER. The hourglass enjoyed its finest hour and a new, ultra-feminine body became the ideal. To hell with comfortable underwear and natural outlines: women wanted it all and they wanted it now. Traffic-stopping, eye-popping outlines were crucial. Underpinning all this was the foundation garment, from which swimwear design naturally benefited – internal scaffolding was constructed via wires, padding and elastic panels. What began in the 1940s as clever manufacturing tools for making swimsuits fit without the help of elastic, and aid in the actual sport of swimming, became the be-all and end-all of the garment: only styles that pulled in, pushed out and clung in all the right places could cut it. But that still wasn't enough: gold lamé, velvet, satin, spandex and sequins were all employed to add flashy luxury.

Postwar rationing had ended on both sides of the Atlantic and there was a new feeling of abundance. The Festival of Britain in 1951 was a huge celebration of everything new and modern, and cast a line into the

PAGE 144: Strapless swimsuits, like this gorgeous grey-and-white striped one from 1954, were à la mode in the 1950s, as were strapless dresses and tops. Support was achieved with stretch control panels on the tummy area and bra cups or boning for the bust, which gave a corset-like look. Thin shoulder straps were often optional.

LEFT: The front cover of the July 1957 issue of *Sketch* magazine. The hourglass shape of the 1940s continued in the 1950s and nowhere was the silhouette better displayed than beneath a swimsuit. It didn't matter how a girl achieved that shape, or how much undercover help she had, the glamour girl was here to stay.

future, building on a feeling of hope. The coronation of the young Queen Elizabeth in May 1952 undoubtedly had an effect and soon beauty queens, prom queens and teen queens were everywhere. In 1957 England's Prime Minister Harold Macmillan told a meeting in Bedfordshire that British people 'had never had it so good'.

The new female outline reflected the atmosphere of largesse. Out went soft curves and in came unabashed voluptuousness. The curvaceous silhouette was everywhere, not just in the case of Hollywood starlets but from architecture and furniture to designs for automobiles and even swimming pools.

Female stereotypes were carved into the social consciousness and it would take years, in many cases, to erase them again: *dolce vitas* types (young, sexy, dangerous), housewives (perfect, sexy, clean) and matriarchs (older, sexy, sensible) were just a few of the feminine icons to emerge. The Hollywood influence spread across the world, with Italian starlets Sophia Loren and Claudia Cardinale vying for press attention with Marilyn Monroe, Jane Russell and Lana Turner, all posing in their ruched, gathered, corseted one-pieces. But a young French starlet was to appear by the end of the decade and eclipse them all; everything about Brigitte Bardot said 'All change!' and as the 1960s dawned, Bardot's long hair, teeny bikini and lazy, smudged make-up said 'Loosen up', the key phrase of the next decade.

ABOVE: Here, a model wears a Catalina swimsuit for a Condé Nast magazine spread. Bright, sunny 'California' colours were dominant, and black swimsuits virtually unknown in the 1950s.

Va Va Va Voom

To keep up with the fashions, women needed super-curves. Swimsuits were formed with fully fashioned bone or metal-framed breast cups, with or without padding. Zips persisted – along a central back seam, sometimes in the side seam – to provide a corset-like appearance up until the 1960s. Corset manufacturers spotted the gap in the burgeoning swimwear market. The popularity of old-fashioned boned corsets waned with women's desire for freedom, shape and comfort, so lighter-structured underwear became popular and this carried through to bathing costumes. Thin metal boning made it possible to put 'invisible' corsetry inside swimsuits to really accentuate the body yet at the same time retain a structured shape that provided the necessary modesty. Fabrics mirrored corsetry and cut in presenting the curvy silhouette. New materials, like Lastex, a fabric woven from artificial chromspun acetate, were used to facilitate the form-fitting looks. Lined cotton fabric and elastic ruched waffle nylon were also popular.

Companies such as Flexees and Maidenform sprang up, their names reflecting the characteristics of their brand. A Flexees swimsuit from the mid 1950s clung to the wearer's body, a combination of Lastex and chromspun acetate giving that all-important tightly fitted appearance. Based on bra designs, the bodices had a pointed circular-stitched shape.

Breasts were big news and really came to prominence, so to speak, especially in the USA. Modest curves beneath fitted fabrics were not enough, and cleavage was on view. Times had moved on from the days when the American Association of Park Superintendents ruled that necklines should be no lower than the horizontal line from armpit to armpit. From the late 1940s onwards, the bra tops of many swimsuits took on an aggressive cone shape. Some even had nipple-like points where the seams deliberately met to create a sexy-looking extrusion.

ABOVE: Jantzen's Water Star sheath swimsuit features overall smocking with an inset of crystal jewels and 'shape insurance' for generous curves, created with Bates disciplined fabric. It was featured in the accompanying ad campaign of 1954, see opposite, but without its detachable halter straps.

RIGHT: A 1954 'Glimmer for Glamour' advertisement for Jantzen by artist Pete Hawley assures alluring curves all summer with its Water Star crystal-encrusted swimsuit and two other styles – the Summer Siren Lastex faille, top left, and the lamé Miss Photo Splash, bottom left. The'shape insurance' refers to a bra interlining that moulds the bustline. All the suits offer 'nice waistline deduction'.

glimmer
for glamour...
with
Jantzen
"shape-insurance"
if you ever had a yearning to be a glittering success, your hour has come and Jantzen will underwrite it...with the most beautiful make-believe diamonds permanently fixed on the world's most beautiful swim suits...and more important, with Jantzen "shape-insurance." "Shape-insurance" is a miracle bra interlining (technical name is ®Pellon and only Jantzen has it) that moulds and holds a lovely bustline forever..."shape-insurance" gives you a nice waistline deduction, assures a dividend of glamorous curves all summer. Left top, "summer siren," ®Lastex faille 16.95...left lower, "miss photo splash," gleaming lamé 18.95... right, "water-star," ®Bates Disciplined cotton 15.95 ...heavenly colors...at most stores.
Jantzen®
best of all swim suits
Jantzen Inc · Portland 14 · Oregon
nothing does as much for a body as a Jantzen

LEFT: The hourglass shape was the sought-after look of the decade, as this 1950s magazine advertisement for Slix swimwear shows. The British company was created in 1937 and launched in Australia in 2003.

ABOVE AND RIGHT: This pink strapless swimsuit features beautiful sequin workmanship, along with intricate embroidery and beadwork. Most swimsuits at the time were not heavily decorated, and this example seems to borrow elements from 1950s daywear.

FAR RIGHT: A 1950s fitted corset-style strapless sheath in light blue features a double-front bodice detail and side ruching. The style is designed to pull the body into shape and emphasize the hips and bust.

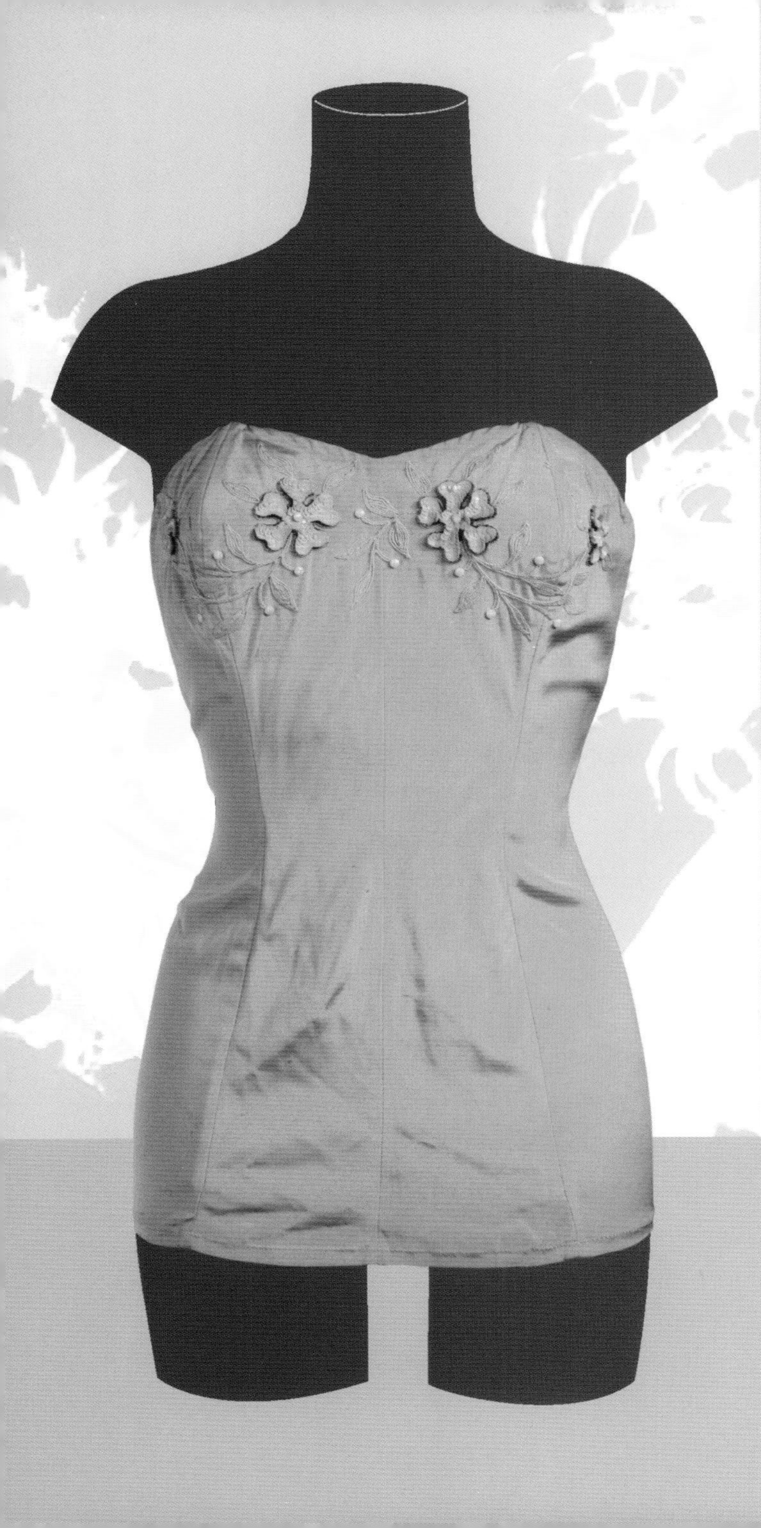
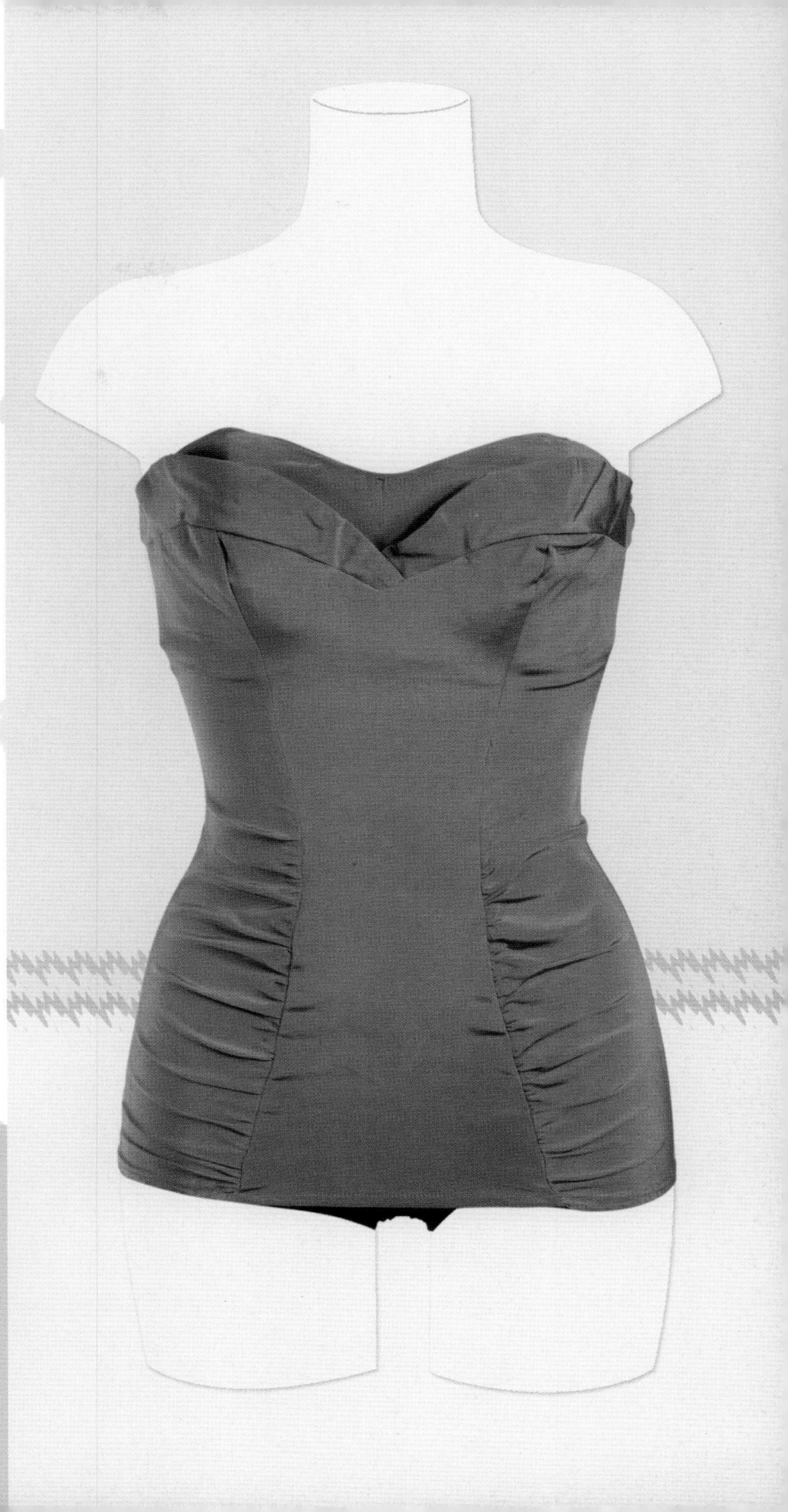

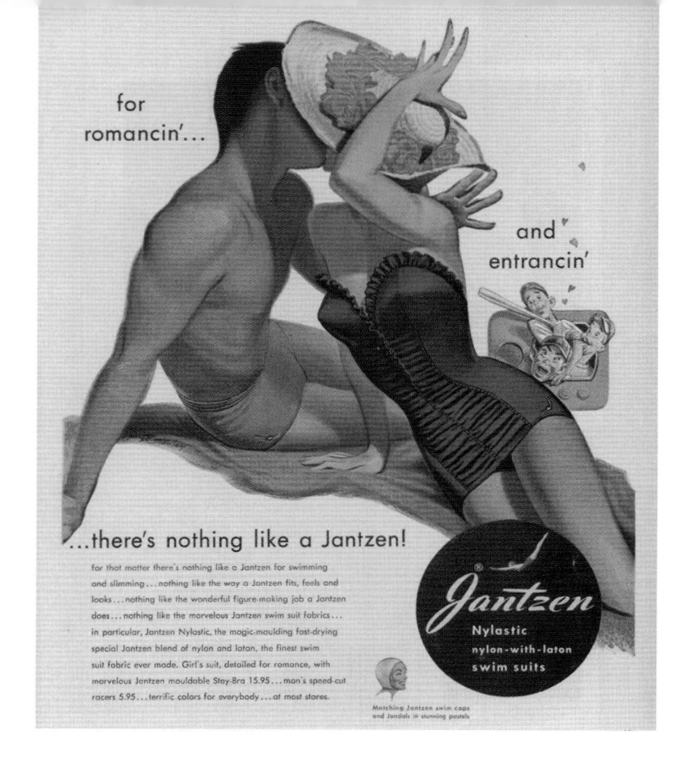

for romancin'...
and entrancin'
...there's nothing like a Jantzen!
for that matter there's nothing like a Jantzen for swimming and slimming...nothing like the way a Jantzen fits, feels and looks...nothing like the wonderful figure-making job a Jantzen does...nothing like the marvelous Jantzen swim suit fabrics... in particular, Jantzen Nylastic, the magic-moulding fast-drying special Jantzen blend of nylon and laton, the finest swim suit fabric ever made. Girl's suit, detailed for romance, with marvelous Jantzen mouldable Stay-Bra 15.95...man's speed-cut racers 5.95...terrific colors for everybody...at most stores.
Jantzen
Nylastic
nylon-with-laton
swim suits
Matching Jantzen swim caps and Jandals in stunning pastels

LEFT: A 1951 'For Romancin and Entrancin'' advertisement featuring the newest Jantzen Nylastic quick-dry swimming suits for men and women, illustrated by the artist Peter Hawley in 1951.

Nylon, liberated from wartime restrictions, was the miracle fabric of the age. Triumph, Warner's and Berlei created everyday girdles and brassieres in sturdy, stretch fabrics to keep the new body shape in place. Brassieres featured cantilever wiring to produce a balcony effect or conical stitching for that all-important torpedo shape. Special strapless corselettes featured deeply low-cut, cleavage-enhancing tops, which barely covered the breasts and centred around 'V' bodice shapes. The strapless styles were extremely popular as brassiere-style cups kept everything in place. Halternecks and shoulder straps were designed to create an overall shape around the décolletage, in a much more structured way than we see today, as formidable internal corsetry enabled straps to be more decorative than supportive. The shoulders, back and bustline were the focus. The 'falsie' trade took off with the first rubber breast enhancers, complete with built-on nipple shapes, doing a roaring trade and reportedly worn by such starlets as Jayne Mansfield, Marilyn Monroe and Jane Russell.

Even though the out-in-out shape ruled, other, more subtle laws still governed the wearing of swimsuits. The legline of the average swimsuit remained firmly sliced across the upper thigh, in a direct horizontal line across the crotch to form a modesty apron that hid the separate matching fabric gusset. Sometimes half-skirts or frills covered this frontal area, and even though leg lines crept up slightly towards the end of the decade, they still remained low-cut. The sexiness of the swimsuit was all in the cut from breasts to waist and hips, and the only big development from 1940s styles in terms of revealing flesh was the deepening of the cleavage. Strapless bustier tops were most popular, with double layers or single; otherwise, simple straps that plunged from the shoulder to down around the bust worked to lead the eye to the cleavage. Some suits featured frilled 'peasant-style' tops that could be pulled down and worn off the shoulder while others had decorative bodice details such as piping, eyelet trim, pleats or frills. The one-piece was still the preferred style, as the bikini was considered a little too risqué for anyone but film stars. Mainstream styles dictated that two-pieces were high-waisted so that the navel was barely seen, while the top retained the bandeau and halter-tie styles.

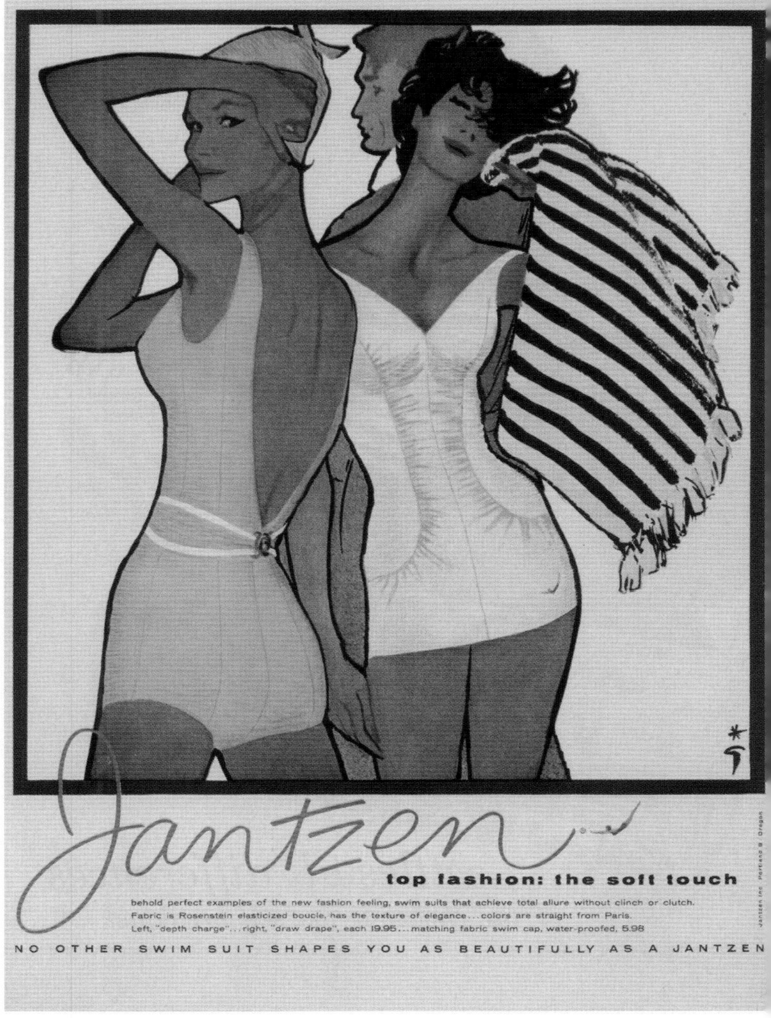

LEFT: In the 1950s, Jantzen updated their 'fun, sporty' family image with ads such as this 'Torso-oh!' one, showing more womanly shapes as well as their advances in fabrics and construction. Their unique 'shapemakery' – the inner support that lifted the bustline, shaped the garment and emphasized the waist – was designed to enhance the female figure.

ABOVE: A Jantzen 1958 'Top Fashion' advertisement promoting swimsuits soft to the touch and elegant in texture, reflecting fashion's softening shape toward the end of the decade. The longer shape was still in style but a less vampish look was coming into fashion for the beach. The artist was the renowned fashion illustrator René Gruau.

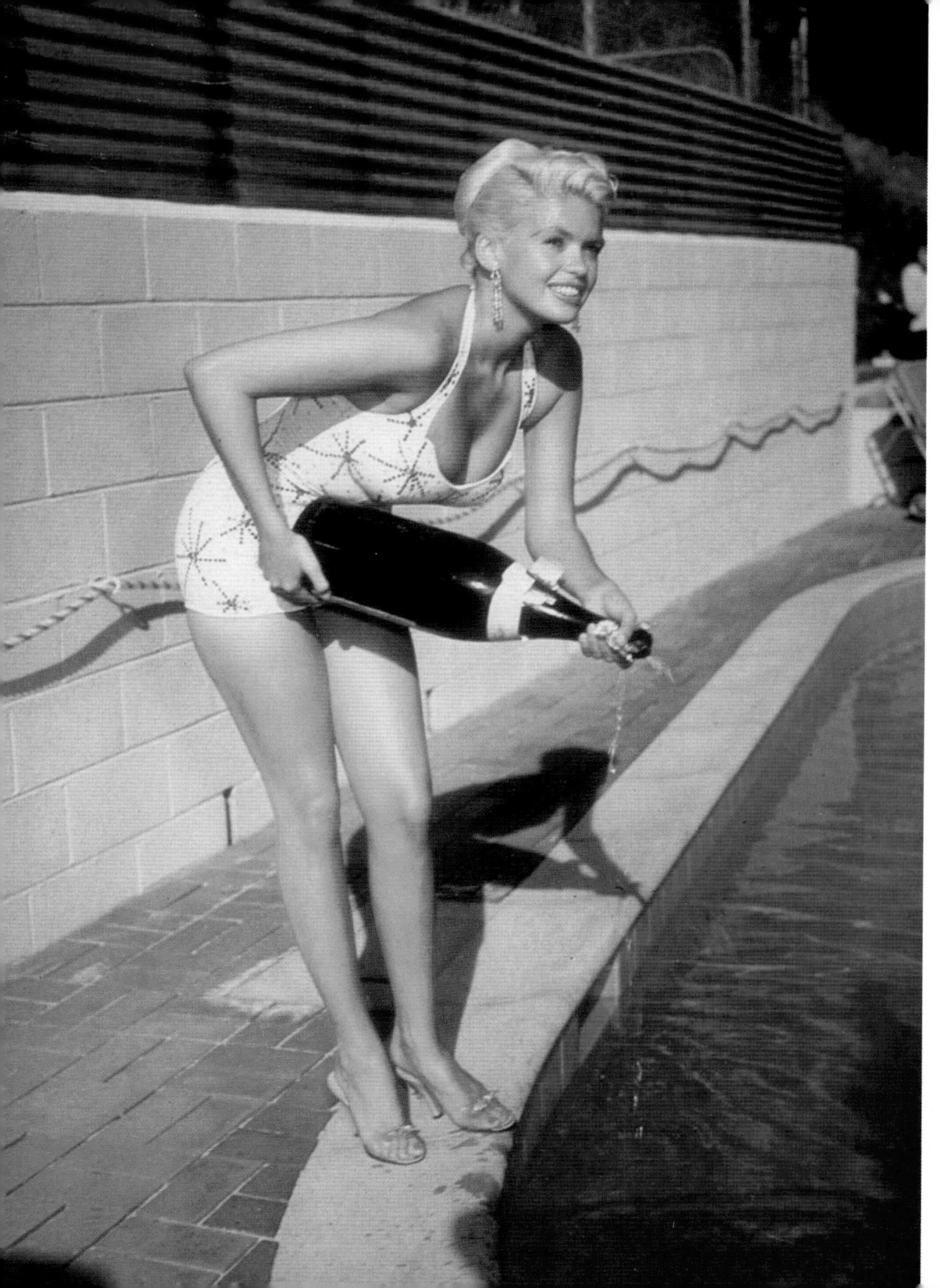

LEFT: One of the most recognizable icons of 1950s celebrity culture, Jayne Mansfield purposefully wore her swimsuit a size or two too small in order to enhance her sizeable assets.

RIGHT: Marilyn Monroe in 1953, photographed in the swimsuit she wore in *Gentlemen Prefer Blondes* while under contract to Twentieth Century Fox. The suit is a classic of its time, strapless with the demure, straight bottom edge.

FAR RIGHT: The one-piece was still the preferred style, as in the USA the bikini was still considered too risqué for the 1950s. Here, the dancer and actress Cyd Charisse models a Cole of California animal-print suit in 1956.

Glamour Girls

The Second World War brought great emancipation for women, and they wanted clothes to match their new mood. This new kind of woman was mirrored in the movie business, where feisty female heroines took on the likes of Frank Sinatra and won.

The flattering but simple one- and two-pieces of the early 1940s had been relatively unstructured, simple and long-bodied, but when the heady feeling of indulgence invoked by Christian Dior's New Look in 1947 broke loose, the swimsuit was swept along with it. The New Look was all about waists, hips and breasts, accentuated with full skirts, nipped-in tops and scoop necks. The female form was celebrated by fashion and this coincided with the rise of the Hollywood starlet as the major female icon of the time. It was the film industry that dictated the fashionable looks of the time. Stars such as Jean Harlow began posing for publicity shots in their undies in the 1930s – starting what became known as the glamour photography industry – but by 1950 every self-respecting Hollywood starlet was photographed in a swimsuit as part of their basic portfolio, with many going on to develop relationships with specific swimwear manufacturers.

Marilyn Monroe took swimsuit modelling to the next level. Although she began her career posing perfectly in neat, sweet swimsuits, she slowly unravelled that wholesome image. Pictured rolling in the surf, wet hair flying round her face, waves crashing over her wet bikini, she exuded earthy sexuality. With Monroe, the outfit was always secondary. She loved flirting with the camera and her mesmerizing sexuality tempted a thousand starlets to copy her looks.

The *Picturegoer Film Annual 1953–4* chose Marilyn Monroe as its Girl of the Year, stating: 'Around Hollywood she is thought the surest bet… she is the screen seductress par excellence.' Monroe's 1953 release, *Gentlemen Prefer Blondes*, cemented the style of the new vamp. A sweet temperament with a body almost too curvy to be real was every man's ideal. What's more, Monroe was overtly sexy – the girl literally couldn't help it.

The blonde sex symbol look caught on in the 1950s, and Jayne Mansfield, Mamie Van Doren and Diana Dors were a few of the better-known copycat 'blonde bombshells' who attempted to emulate Monroe's looks and professional success. Famously photographed at the Venice Film Festival in a mink bikini in 1955, British starlet Dors had the vital ability to look great in a swimsuit, eclipsing any other talents she may have had. A photo-call at such an event was probably, she later remarked, one of the few occasions when such an outfit was even mildly appropriate. The Italian supervixens Sophia Loren, Gina Lollobrigida and Claudia Cardinale may ultimately have had longer careers, better bone structure and more international recognition than the actress who – inevitably – was dubbed 'Double D', but she nonetheless retained a devoted fan base.

RIGHT: Brigitte Bardot single-handedly changed the face of the swimsuit and bikini when she posed in this mini denim two-piece in 1957. Up until then, the bikini had remained a modest, navel-covering ensemble. Bardot's wild beauty heralded the end of the beach vamp and the arrival of natural body shapes and simpler swimsuits.

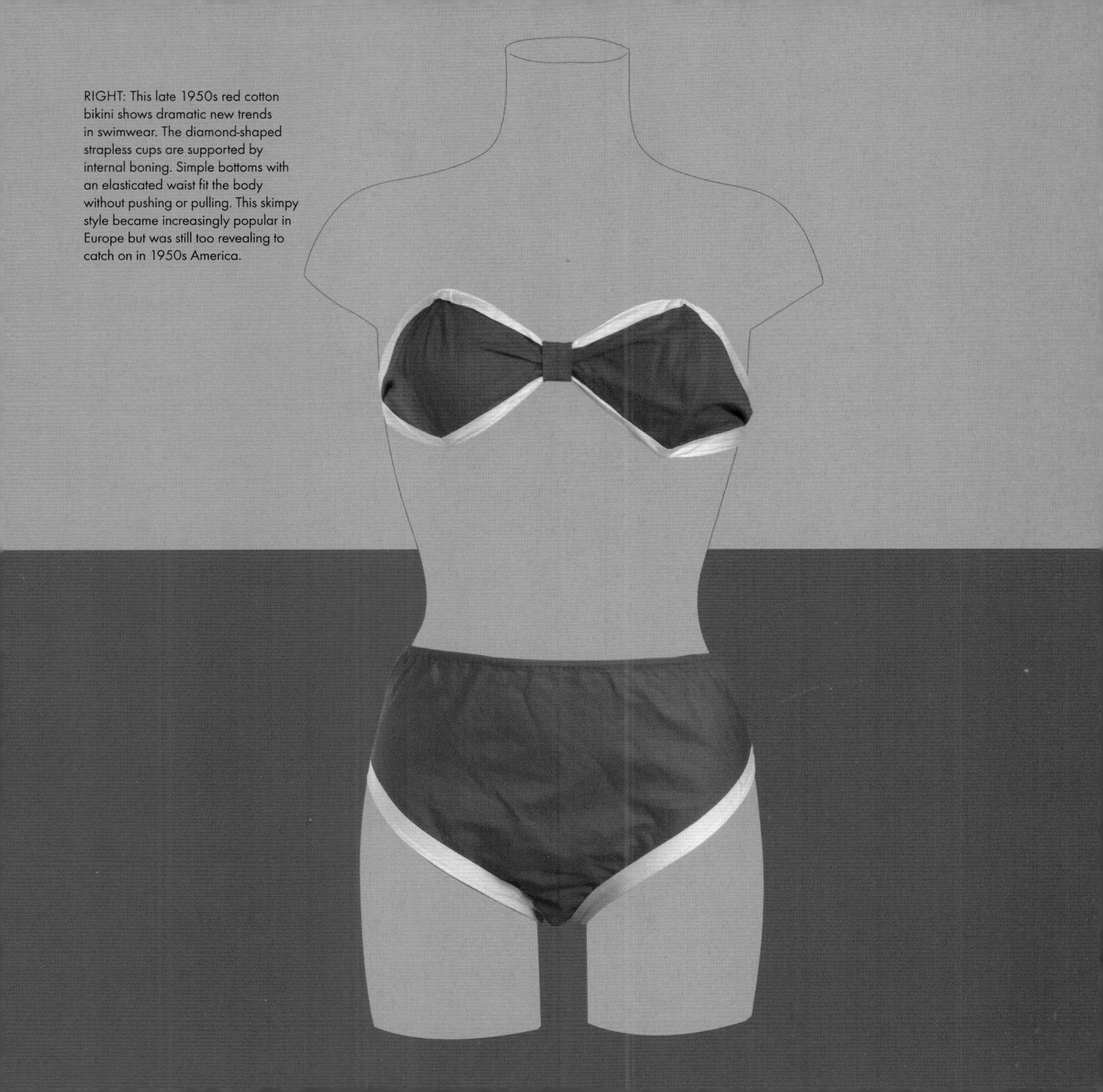

RIGHT: This late 1950s red cotton bikini shows dramatic new trends in swimwear. The diamond-shaped strapless cups are supported by internal boning. Simple bottoms with an elasticated waist fit the body without pushing or pulling. This skimpy style became increasingly popular in Europe but was still too revealing to catch on in 1950s America.

Annette Kellerman (Esther Williams) captures the fancy of New York when she stars in a sensational water extravaganza in the famous Hippodrome.
M-G-M's "MILLION DOLLAR MERMAID" Color by TECHNICOLOR

LEFT: Esther Williams collaborated with Fred Cole in the design of many of her swimsuits, notably the ones worn in *Skirts Ahoy!* and *Million Dollar Mermaid* (both 1952). In newspaper sports reportage swimmers were frequently lined up for photos, flashing big smiles and lots of leg. With her stunning good looks and tall, well-muscled frame, Williams stood out, and she went on to perform the same role for the film industry and Fred Cole.

Swimsuits provided the perfect opportunity for dressing like a starlet and women clamoured for copies of those worn on the silver screen. Esther Williams, star of 1952's *Million Dollar Mermaid*, cornered the market in sparkly sequinned numbers. During one particularly dramatic scene choreographed by the great Busby Berkeley, Williams plunged 15 metres (50 feet) into a mass of swimmers. Clad in a Latex net swimsuit of shimmering chainmail composed of 50,000 gold flakes, she was the ultimate diving goddess. It was great news for Cole of California, and thousands of copies of the suit were made from gold-coloured latex in the same shape but without the full chainmail effect. The swimsuit queen, Williams refused to wear bikinis full stop and redesigned the women's swimsuits for the American Navy after starring in *Skirts Ahoy!* (1952). Up until then, she claimed, female naval officers had to wear awful 'T-shirts' to swim in, so she devised a new streamlined navy swimsuit more appropriate for nautical duties.

Fred Cole secured Williams's services to promote his bathing costumes in the early 1950s and worked closely with her on many of the designs, launching an annual 'Esther Williams' suit. He had entered the swimwear industry via West Coast Knitting Mills, which was owned by his parents; Cole himself was a product of Hollywood, having been a silent movie star in the 1920s. Designer Margit Felligi joined Cole in 1936 and maintained her design leadership for the company over the next 36 years. During this time she created such noteworthy swimsuits as the Swoon and the Scandal. The first was a product of the war years; made from parachute silk (Cole of California produced parachutes for soldiers), it was available 'in parachute colours' that laced up at the sides, thereby conforming to wartime regulations on the use of rubber. The second was a one-piece launched in the mid 1960s that had net panels on its front and sides. At first look fairly modest,

LEFT: A Cole of California swimsuit from 1950, made of pink nylon satin. Fred Cole took the 1940s structured swimsuit and pared it down to make a one-piece that was more streamlined and glamorous than ever before. A publicity-aware entrepreneur, he recognized that swimsuits were not just for swimming but also for posing.

ABOVE: Esther Williams inspects the new 1951 range of swimsuits by Cole of California, with Fred Cole overseeing. Williams took a personal interest in the design of her swimsuit line. Essentially a sportswoman, she needed suits that could stay the course and maintain her allure during deep-water routines.

the Scandal suit actually afforded the viewer a peek at the body underneath. Cole even persuaded Christian Dior to design a swimwear collection for the company in 1955. At first Dior was reluctant, pleading that he knew nothing of swimwear, to which Cole responded, 'You're a designer aren't you? So design.' Unable to argue with this, Dior complied and produced his one and only swimwear collection.

LEFT AND BELOW: Catalina swimsuits occupied the middle ground between Fred Cole's high-fashion range and Jantzen's wide availability and family values. Sponsors of the Miss Universe pageant, Catalina's pretty, feminine suits were a firm favourite of ordinary American girls looking for a touch of glamour.

Showbiz continued to be the best swimwear parade ground, but Catalina also began sponsoring the Miss America contests, producing highly glamorous looks for the contestants. Unlike Cole, which was all about Hollywood glamour, and Jantzen, which had a sporty profile and promoted itself by sponsoring swimming education programmes, Catalina opted to build its swimwear reputation using promotional tactics, founding the Miss USA and Miss Universe pageants in 1952, after a falling out with Miss America when 1951 queen Yolande Betbeze refused to pose in a swimsuit. Catalina's styles largely appealed to the girl next door and her mother, though it did enlist the considerable services of head designer Mary Ann DeWeese, along with costume designer Edith Head.

Mabs of Hollywood dressed dancing star Virginia Mayo in the 1940s and 1950s. She starred in poster advertisement campaigns filled with swimsuit promise, including one for RC Cola and another that read 'Mabs figure-sculpturing swimsuit of elasticized nylon with a soft

LEFT: A lifeguard smiles at the prospect of lessened demands on him and his life preserver as he views the new 'ever-float' safety swimsuit worn by a model in 1953. Buoyant panels of fabric filled with a sponge-like substance were built into the suit. There is nothing to inflate or adjust in the suit, which could keep the wearer afloat indefinitely.

shimmer that highlights every undulating curve like artful screen lighting'. Wouldn't you buy it?

There were all sorts of tricks and gimmicks for selling swimsuits. Jantzen sold swimsuits based on bodyweight for many years, requiring the prospective purchaser to hop on in-store scales before making a purchase. By the 1950s this had been changed to a far more customer-friendly sizing system. In the big department stores, swimsuit salesgirls were advised on how to help women choose suits that would flatter them. Instead of saying, 'That would not fit you', it was suggested they say instead, 'This would look great on you'. Rudimentary sales training, but presumably necessary – and which some of us might wish was still used today!

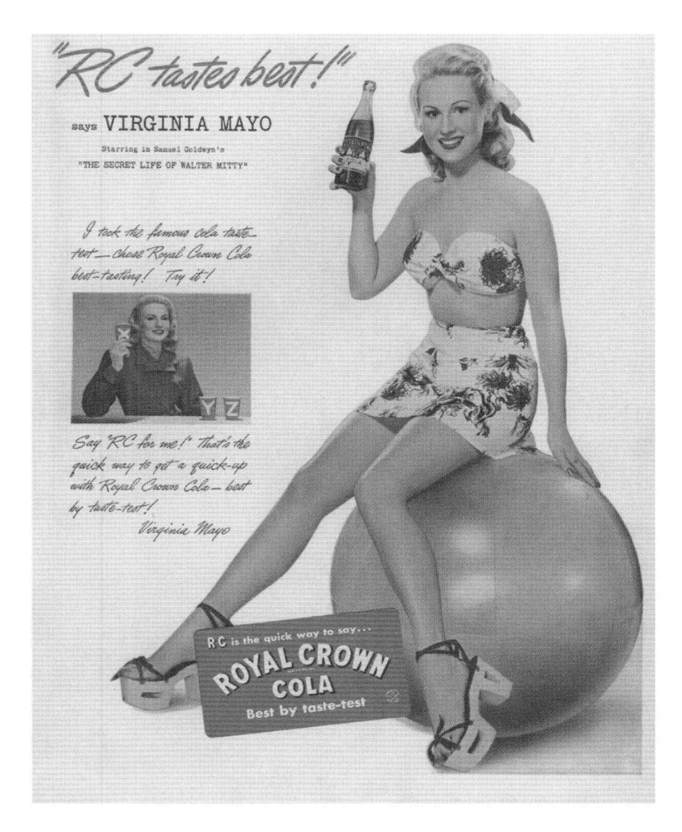

BELOW: Virginia Mayo, a chorus-line dancer who moved into mainstream films in the 1940s, became one of the great glamour girls of the 1950s after starring with James Cagney in the 1949 thriller *White Heat*. Here, wearing a Hawaiian-print sarong two-piece, she models for Royal Crown Cola.

ABOVE AND RIGHT: A blue polka-dot two-piece with white trim featuring hipster bottoms with decorative cut-outs. The top is an early example of an underwired bra style that started to become more widespread towards the end of the decade. The suit was worn with a white blouse with a blue-spot trim.

ABOVE: A 1950s halter-tie two-piece that has high-waisted bottoms with ruched side panels and a front zip. The legs are shaped high at the front of the leg, unlike the straight-across styles of previous decades.

RIGHT: A strapless one-piece made from fresh-looking blue gingham. with a skirt and internal bottoms. Fun playsuit-style touches include a frilled trim and bows decorating the top of the bodice and the waist. Brigitte Bardot popularized the fabric after her appearance in a gingham bikini in the 1956 film *And God Created Woman.*

Sexy Innocence

The return of the almost Victorian corseted hourglass figure was accompanied by a similar set of general standards, particularly in the USA. Young girls were unable to carry off the new, strong feminine looks and a broader age divide emerged, with mature women, rather than girls, becoming the sexual hub of modern culture. It was fashionable to look 'sexy', which in turn, created a dangerous tightrope for the modern young woman. Being sexy was at the core of one of 1950s society's biggest dilemmas: women wanted to look the part by resembling Marilyn Monroe, but they also wanted to attract the right kind of man in order to

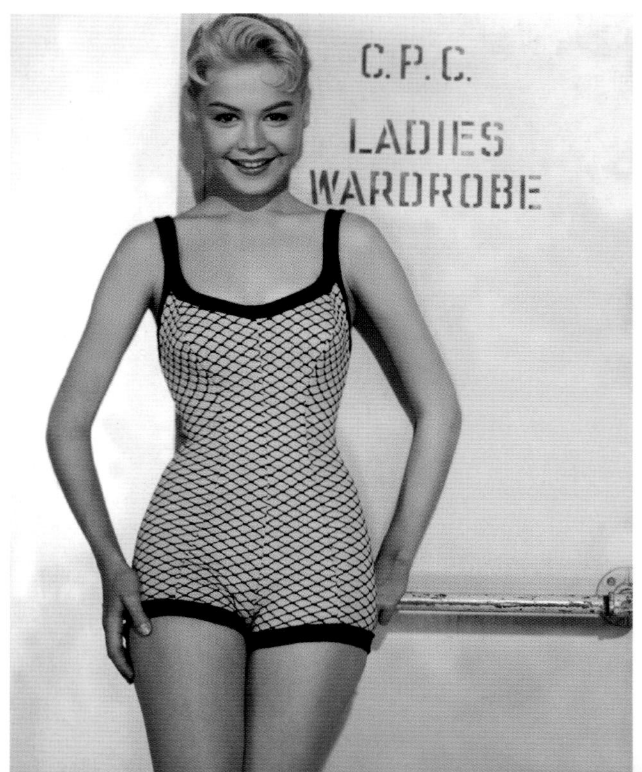

ABOVE: Model Pat Hall wears a two piece 'apron' style bikini from the mid 1950s. The gingham edging and noughts-and-crosses detail add a feeling of fun and 'innocence' to this beach playsuit, which probably wasn't worn for swimming. The lace-up sides add a slightly raunchy touch for contrast.

RIGHT: Sandra Dee's film role as beach babe Gidget in the 1959 film of the same name made her famous as the demure ingenue of feel-good films. The swimsuit, in a still from the movie, shows the modest, boy-legged look that encapsulated her sporty on-screen style as a surfer girl.

marry well and live happily ever after. To help her, the film industry obligingly turned out plenty of romantic comedies in which the modest 'good girl' got her man after an elaborate reeling-in process worthy of the Borgias. Such sagas set the scene for the Doris Day and Sandra Dee films of the early 1960s (see also page 185). It is worth noting that in Dee and Troy Donahue's films, the good girls always wore one-piece swimsuits, while the bad girls who get into sticky ends cavorted in bikinis. In fact, Dee herself was a 'victim' of this trend for sexy-innocent girls. In stark contrast to many of Hollywood's biggest stars, Dee was actually younger than her publicity age, starring in her first film aged just 14. Pushed on by her ambitious mother, Dee fought all her life to maintain the image drummed into her as a teen. She was dogged by anorexia while battling alcoholism and depression, reputedly caused by the nose-dive her career took after the age of just 26. However, as Gidget, the fun-loving surf girl, Dee captured the hearts and imagination of a whole generation of young Americans.

LEFT: Sandra Dee posing in a pink swimsuit that exhibits an alluring innocence. The frilled pink two-piece is similar to the swimsuit styles made for youngsters, yet Dee is clearly not a child. Taken in a suburban-looking backyard, Dee typifies the girl-next-door, with sex appeal.

Worn in the USA

'What you really need is a new suit for sunning, last year's for swimming and an extra one just for fun. A wardrobe of three or four suits isn't at all unusual any more ... and some women buy 12 or 13 at a time.'

Rose Marie Reid

In Europe designers such as Norman Hartnell and Elsa Schiaparelli were creating couture swimwear, and in the USA the swimwear market was booming – by the mid 1950s, Jantzen, Cole of California, Tina Leser and Rose Marie Reid, as well as the great names of previous decades, such as Clare Potter and Claire McCardell, created fashion swimsuit ensembles. One-pieces, two-pieces, overgarments, and hats and scarves to match soon joined together to form collections for the beach. The USA had a huge influence on international swimwear design. Paris may have supplied haute couture, but the looks women wanted to wear came from the USA. In London girls bought 'California bras' to get the right lift and separation. The 'American' swimsuit top was incredibly popular, featuring a high turtleneck and deep cut-away shoulders, giving a look

FAR LEFT: A 1950s halterneck playsuit with a smocked back and full skirt, which would have been worn with short bloomers underneath. The print is typical of the 1950s, when much of decorative art culture drew on iconic images such as playing cards and commercial postcards.

LEFT TOP AND BOTTOM: Examples of two beach towelling wraps from the 1950s displaying typical novelty designs of the time. Nautical and boating themes were particularly popular, as were travel, the Wild West, sports and tropical scenes.

RIGHT: Cyd Charisse photographed in 1955 wearing a Rose Marie Reid strapless bathing suit in nylon and rayon. Famous for her amazing legs and dance routines, Cyd preferred dance ensembles and a fresh un-vampish image to glamour-girl modelling.

that was flattering and made the arms and neck appear slender. It showed off suntanned shoulders and worked well with the highly fashionable halter-neck dresses as it left no awkward strap marks.

The undoubted sexiness of the tan led another swimsuit designer, Rose Marie Reid, to be the first to use photopermeable fabric in a swimsuit design in 1950. It did not quite catch on. Users reported patchy effects and the fabric was not available in the most fashionable colours of the time, nor was it suitable for the tight, fitted styles. Instead, Reid focused on fabrics such as chromspun acetate, a tight, shiny fabric popular across the swimwear scene. A 1956 advert features the Enchantress and the Rave Notice, two tight-waisted, cleavage-enhancing styles in glossy black chromspun. Reid's contribution to the glamour swimwear market of the 1950s cannot be underestimated. Her suits outsold those of many rivals, other manufacturers copied her designs, and Marilyn Monroe publicly thanked Reid for the contribution her swimsuits had made to Monroe's career.

RIGHT: A classic fashion shot from 1957 of two models posing on a Caribbean beach. Both wear Rose Marie Reid swimsuits. Reid, a Mormon and a strict matriarch, was a stickler for the underwired, super-glamorous suits so beloved of Hollywood stars.

First sold under the Reid Holiday Togs brand, her designs were later issued under her own name. As well as patenting several innovative under-swimsuit ideas including one particularly strong elastic tummy panel, Reid created ranges of swimsuits for different occasions. She called this matching of swimsuit to event 'imagineering', a technique often used in psychotherapy, which was also gaining ground at the time. Imagineering involves imagining oneself in a situation and thereby being better able to plan for it. Reid was also the first designer to show several lines a year, including a resortwear and cruisewear line, and during one of her many trips to Europe for inspiration she struck up a collaborative relationship with Emilio Pucci, who provided some fabric designs for her swimwear in the late 1950s and 1960s. In 1951 she launched the hourglass maillot, and as she told *California Stylist* magazine, 'The hourglass maillot, with firmly boned midriff with soft folds of a bra, soft shirred bloomers ... is the keynote of the couturier group.' She also suggested six female body types for suits to be fitted against – very tall, petite, superthin, perfect, big-hipped and big-breasted – and sales assistants were briefed to help customers choose their closest shape and then select the 'right' suit for their body. Reid genuinely cared about women feeling good in her suits and they were highly successful as a result. In a testament to her enduring legacy, the company is still manufacturing swimwear.

Artistic Influences

There were a few daring departures from the American swimsuit look, but Claire McCardell, one of the early pioneers, hated the corseted, vampish styles of the 1950s. She publicly stated that she simply could not understand why women wanted to wear swimsuits that looked like underwear. Even though McCardell's later swimsuits and playsuits were effortless combinations of glamour and practicality, they were risky market-wise. She designed soft woollen beach playsuits with the highest cut-away legs yet. And even Carolyn Schnurer's adventurous two-pieces did not reveal as much of the upper thigh and loin area as McCardell's. The less-than-sexy 'diaper' look was very much McCardell's leitmotif, and while it could look elegant, it was too revealing for the average woman. Combined with dark suiting fabrics and sophisticated but not very sexy draping, McCardell's playsuits did not lead to big sales.

Undeterred, McCardell headed to Paris, where in 1955 she tried to bring a touch of class to the swimwear business. A lover of fine art, she designed a range of resortwear in fabrics based on works by Marc Chagall, Pablo Picasso and Fernand Léger. She then had the designs photographed with the artists and their work for *Life* magazine. As was the case with Coco Chanel's work on *Le Train Bleu* in 1925, it was another instance of the successful and occasional marrying of swimwear with art.

McCardell's designs may have been a little outré for 1950s America, but the fabrics she developed for her 'Art' collection were very much in keeping with two important trends: first, exotic prints of all kinds and bright colours were everywhere as a reaction against the austerity of war; second, the popularity of Modern art was rising. The decade saw the opening of important new art schools in both Great Britain and the USA. After years of being the preserve of society outsiders, the art world became fashionable. People talked about the influence of art on design and architecture, because it was happening, quite literally, in front of them. The concepts and ideas from high art and fashion trickled down to the mass-market level, and manufacturers of swimsuits, with access to cheaper synthetic fibres and a burgeoning ready-to-wear industry, could copy haute couture designs for their own brands or for special department-store collections.

LEFT: A model wears a Schnurer-Cabana cotton-print two-piece with a lined towelling (terrycloth) cardigan on the beach in front of the Diplomat Hotel, Florida. Matching outerwear became highly fashionable in the late 1950s and was a Schnurer-Cabana speciality.

RIGHT: A 1957 fashion photograph of a model wearing a swimsuit by Imports International. This suit relies on its stretch fabric for shape and the clever diamond pattern for enhanced form. Designed to give a softer form, inner breast cups are all that remain of the traditional, aggressive hourglass styling.

FAR LEFT AND LEFT: Cotton poplin in pretty prints was a favourite swimsuit fabric. It could be stitched into ruching or gathered onto elastic and stayed strong enough not to rip. This cotton one-piece in a sheath style has a smocked back, with a simple lace-up fastening and pleated front centre panel. The side panels and elasticated back create contour and attention is drawn to the cleavage via the button detail. Lime green was one of the exotic colours first seen on swimsuits before going mainstream.

RIGHT: A Slix advertisement showing a swimsuit style from 1958, with a tie detail that draws attention to the bustline. The British company was known for using cutting-edge fibres and for their modest designs.

Swim in
Smart Circles...
...with
'SLIX'
SWIMWEAR
A glamorous 'Slix' model from the exciting, budget-conscious 1958 Collection. Price 65/-

British Bathers

Christian Dior's New Look prevailed; every woman wanted a full-skirted, tight-waisted dress after the lean war years. New quality British labels such as Dereta, Jaeger and St Michael from Marks and Spencer began producing copies of designer looks, making them readily available across the nation. These garments were unsuitable for young girls and teenagers, who were developing their own fashion looks and music.

However, the UK plodded along in the swimsuit market, as so few manufacturers were devoted solely to swimmies. With the changeable weather, investing in small, skimpy garments did not seem like a good bet for clothing manufacturers, so swimwear remained a division of larger fashion companies and department stores. The market was fabric driven, with Bri-Nylon, Drilon and rayon jersey more important than the designer, as is evident from leading advertisements of the time, when the fabric is mentioned before the designer or store name, as in 'Drilon for Jaeger'. The really big news came in 1958 with the availability of DuPont's Lycra, an artificial stretch thread made to replace rubber and compete with nylon elastics. At first, Lycra was used in control underwear, but by the end of the decade clothing manufacturers were employing the new thread in swimwear. Marvellously stretchy, Lycra maintained its texture for longer than elasticized fabrics. It was also less perishable and permeable.

Ladylike Swimwear

Elsewhere in the world, hotter climates were more conducive to creating swimwear. In 1949 a young couple named Lea and Armin Gottlieb left Hungary after surviving the Second World War and joined other Holocaust survivors at a transit camp in Israel. From there they moved to the up-and-coming town of Tel Aviv but they decided that their business, a raincoat factory, would not work there. Instead, they decided to manufacture swimsuits, buying their first fabric with the proceeds of the sale of Lea's wedding ring. The luxurious Gottex brand was born, inspired, according to Lea, by the desire to produce a new range of clothing and accessories based solely around the swimsuit. Colours were directly lifted from the blues, greens and golds of the Mediterranean climate of their newly created homeland.

Instead of the vampish shapes of Hollywood, Lea focused on colour and fabric. From the very inception of brand, she was aiming at an upmarket woman already emerging who would present a new, more refined public image to the world. Icons such as Grace Kelly and Jackie Kennedy epitomized this new glamour. They were rarely photographed in public clad in only a swimsuit. Instead, they wore matching outfits, perhaps with a two-piece, skirt and top all in matching fabric, or a one-piece with a matching shirt and slacks. These early combinations signalled the arrival of resortwear – though it was a concept still too sophisticated for the average woman, who did not spend enough of her time anywhere near stylish beach resorts.

Among the French couturiers, Jacques Fath designed suitable ensembles for these new ladies. His creations favoured more conservatively cut swimsuits with matching towelling-lined tunics to go over the top. Fath agreed with the view that bikinis were for sunbathing only and he continued designing modest swimsuits with skirted fronts well into the 1950s. During this decade Chanel disappeared from the swimwear market, focusing on outerwear. Dior was the only great Parisian designer persuaded by Fred

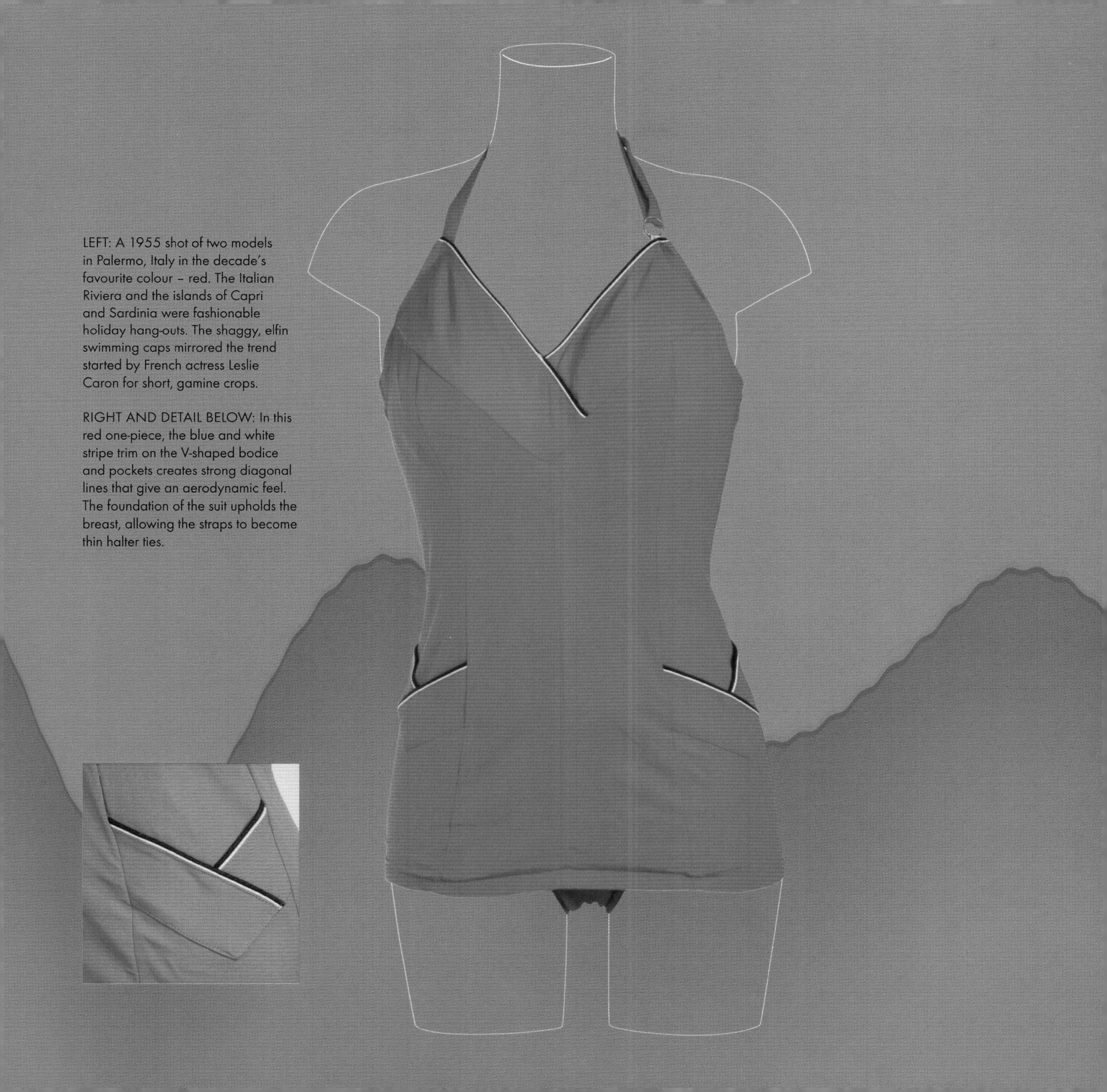

LEFT: A 1955 shot of two models in Palermo, Italy in the decade's favourite colour – red. The Italian Riviera and the islands of Capri and Sardinia were fashionable holiday hang-outs. The shaggy, elfin swimming caps mirrored the trend started by French actress Leslie Caron for short, gamine crops.

RIGHT AND DETAIL BELOW: In this red one-piece, the blue and white stripe trim on the V-shaped bodice and pockets creates strong diagonal lines that give an aerodynamic feel. The foundation of the suit upholds the breast, allowing the straps to become thin halter ties.

Cole of California to design a range of swimsuits in 1955. His ensembles of floral-printed swimsuits with halternecks and ties round the waist, with matching billowing beach coats for wearing over the top, followed his New Look silhouette. Such outfits were designed to take women off the beach and into the chicest of cocktail bars, hotels or shops without necessitating a change of clothing. These ensemble collections were a taster of the more ladylike elements coming on to the market.

RIGHT: Two models pose in Christian Dior beachwear in 1955. The sitting model wears a ribbed bathing suit with a halter neckline and flared skirt, which would have been worn for swimming. The standing girl is in a white poplin blouse designed to be worn over the top.

FAR RIGHT: A stylized, posed shot from 1954 showing a stripey swimsuit enhanced by matching sleeves and a burgundy-coloured bustle, neither of which were of much use in the water and probably wouldn't have been worn on the average beach. Several swimwear designers experimented with sleeve bands – either narrow or full-length as here.

chapter six

FAR-OUT GROOVES

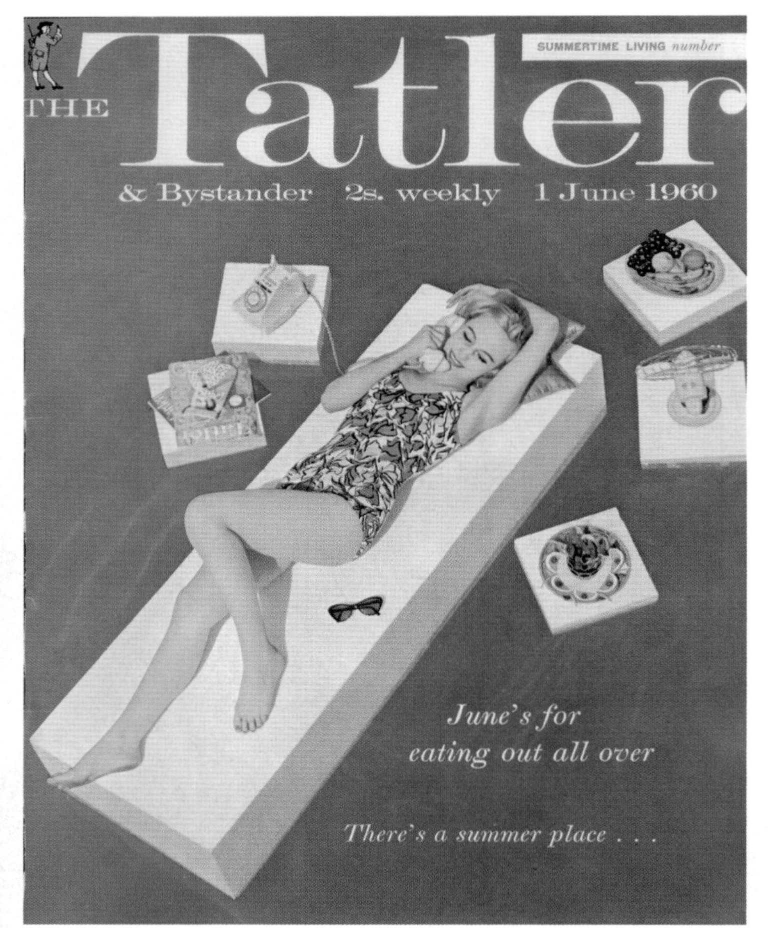

THE MOST NOTORIOUS DECADE OF THE TWENTIETH CENTURY DID NOT REALLY START 'SWINGING' UNTIL ABOUT HALFWAY THROUGH. UNTIL THAT POINT, 1950S STYLES AND MORALS HUNG ON BY THEIR FINGERTIPS. If anything, swimwear designs calmed down as a more ladylike style came in. Necklines went up, straps became thicker, suits gained a sportier, less-structured shape and among the manufacturers and designers there was a focus on comfort.

But revolution was in the air and the swimsuit changed to adapt. Stiff, wired underwear, tight girdles and corsets and stockings were all ditched for stretchier, more comfortable options. Tired of the stereotypes so prevalent in the 1950s, a new wave of feminists rebelled. Bra burning was the tip of a symbolic iceberg and women were saying 'we are man-pleasers no more' in actions if not words. There were other, quieter revolutions, too. In the UK the

PAGE 178: A 1966 photograph that sums up the 'feel' of California in the 1960s, home of the Beach Boys and surfing. The six models are wearing Jantzen bikinis. Corsetry had given way to the youthful trends that would dominate the decade.

ABOVE: A front cover for *Tatler* magazine, June 1960. The black, white and coloured-in graphic print was typical of the 1950s and '60s.

RIGHT: A magazine advertisement showing six different styles of sheath swimsuit from Catalina. The tagline read 'Part of the art of Eve...' with models pictured in a tropical Garden of Eden. Unlike European styles, American fashions were slow to move away from the demure one-piece with its low horizontal skirt panel or shorts, though vibrant prints and patterns were popular.

traditional seaside resorts began to see a downturn in visitors, as air travel became less expensive and more accessible. Holiday companies started taking people from the shores of Britain to Spain in search of the sunshine. By the start of the 1970s, international travel – to world-famous beaches along the Mediterranean, American resorts of Miami and Malibu and to northern Africa and India – was an unstoppable phenomenon, and swimwear manufacturers reaped the benefits.

Meanwhile, the bikini was embraced by teenagers. Suddenly, the awkward transition between childhood and adulthood had a new name, the teens, and parents all over the USA and Europe were battling with their offspring like never before. Combined with a growing wave of popular culture – when art, music and theatre truly began to reach the masses – a new freedom was turning society upside down by the end of the 1960s. What began in the 1940s as a slight restlessness among the 17- to 20-year-old demographic (who, after all, had friends and relations who had been to war at the same age) became a lifestyle trend. Even more alarming for parents, teenagers got together and started making decisions for themselves. At the start of the decade, they were organizing beach barbecues but by the end they were staging sit-ins at their universities and attempting to overthrow the 'establishment'. As a barometer of the decade, no item of clothing conveys it better than the bikini: what started out as a sturdy, elasticated garment for holding everything in, pushing bits up and flattening out the rest, ended up as a few flimsy strips of fabric. By 1969, all that was required for a woman to pass muster on the beach at St Tropez was a tiny pair of bikini bottoms – the top having been dispensed with altogether.

The California Scene

Conical-breasted one-pieces in ruched and rucked styles were now passé. A few leftover, big-bosomed babes hung around and starred in wan pastiches of their former glory. Mamie Van Doren's *Voyage to the Planet of the Pre-Historic Women* (1968) hit a hilarious low. Grace Kelly, now Princess Grace of Monaco, set a new trend for sophisticated, modest hair and make-up. She was slender like Audrey Hepburn, and lit up cinema screens without the use of torpedo bosoms and masses of hair. A vamp backlash kickstarted by Brigitte Bardot ensued and the big studios suddenly found their swimwear tie-ins were less lucrative. The newer screen stars did not want to pose in swimwear or sell themselves as 'pin-ups', so there was a parting of the ways between the sexy glamour girls and showbusiness. Many women continued in both worlds and still do, but ever since there has been a constant tug – to undress or not – for females searching for stardom on stage or screen.

BELOW: In this national advertising campaign a billboard from the mid 1960s shows the Jantzen Smile Girls, college beauties from around the country. They join the surfing revolution with the latest in fashion, and proudly 'Just Wear a Smile and a Jantzen'.

RIGHT: A two-piece in red, white and blue from 1966 shows the boardshorts styling borrowed from men's surfwear. The influence of surfing as a leisure pastime led to a more casual approach to beach fashions – swimsuits needed to be sporty and less rigid for a more active life, but not too revealing.

just wear a smile and a jantzen

Catalina and Jantzen looked elsewhere for promotion ideas and became heavily involved in beauty contest sponsorship. In 1960 Jantzen launched a new advertising campaign 'Just Wear a Smile and a Jantzen', and set up a chain of local 'smile' contests tied to this theme. Sponsored by Jantzen and six leading manufacturers, the winners were selected in Cypress Gardens, Florida, and in Hawaii. The winners were then featured in national advertising and promotional store campaigns throughout the year. Competitions by other manufacturers followed, including Miss Hawaiian Tropic, a competition to find the face of one of the USA's leading suntan formulas.

Meanwhile, surfing was growing in popularity as a sport along Pacific coastlines from California to Australia, via Hawaii. What began as a simple Hawaiian fishing method became an international phenomenon.

Surfing swimwear needed to be stronger than the average swimsuit, with more body cover to help prevent bruising and protect modesty. Early surfers wore shorts and tops especially designed for comfort. Fun, casual and young, the surf look quickly became popular, and by the late 1960s, the Hang Ten brand in the USA was born. Founded by surfer Duke Boyd and seamstress Doris Boeck in Long Beach, California, in 1960, Hang Ten, named after the special ten-toe-grip needed to stay on a board, launched a whole new look.

Not to be outdone, the highly competitive Australian surfing market launched their own brands –

Annette

Shy violets not shy enough to seek cover
pop up in a Jantzen Bashful Bikini.
Who wouldn't smile upon nature at its best?
Even more glamorous when wet 15.95.
just wear a smile and a jantzen

LEFT: The guitar-playing, singing actress Annette Funicello starred opposite Frankie Avalon in many 1960s beach movies. Here she is photographed in a still for her 1964 movie-soundtrack album *Muscle Beach Party*. Apparently it was Walt Disney who suggested that Annette appear only in a one-piece, in order to uphold her public image as a family entertainer.

ABOVE: Jantzen's Shy Violets billboard from 1960 provided advertising impact and slowed traffic along the heavily travelled Sunset Strip in Hollywood, California. Early 1960s swimsuits closely resembled those of the 1950s with their conservative, prim styles, and the one shown in this campaign was a high-waisted, modest number named the Bashful bikini.

Hot Tuna in 1969 and Quiksilver in 1970 became hugely popular. Earlier, in December 1954, the first major surfing contest took place in Makaha, Hawaii, paving the way for future competitions, which became sponsored by major surfing brands, including Quiksilver.

Hollywood looked to the beach to rekindle some film successes while still featuring girls in swimwear. To tie in with the new generation of worried parents, it made films demonstrating how, using a swimsuit, a neat hairstyle and a pretty smile, any girl could snatch a man from the talons of an hourglass-shaped vamp. The beach movie became a genre; plots usually centred on a gang of teens (though everyone looked at least 30) living near the sea and enduring the usual growing pains. Sandra Dee and Troy Donahue's *A Summer Place* was a smash hit in 1963. Lots of towelling and cotton swimsuits featured, without a spandex or mink bikini in sight. The bikinis that did make an appearance were sweet, with hipster pants and modest tops.

The chaste message got through and for the first half of the decade, swimwear designs reflected the new trend. Young girls wore bikinis, while the over-30s went for swimsuits. Doris Day and Jacqueline Bouvier Kennedy epitomized the new elegance. Day had more than 50 costume changes in *Do Not Disturb* (1965) and her films stayed in the top ten for six years from 1960 to 1966. The kind of swimsuits Day might have chosen would have been made in some of the new sturdy, flexible fabrics emerging from the nylon industry.

Stretch and Simplicity

There were a few technological advances during the early 1960s that enabled designers to retain the shapely look of modest swimwear without having to depend on elaborate internal structuring and corsetry. Piqué, a textured nylon with a knobbly pattern in the weave, was thick enough to give shape on its own; Bri-Nylon was a new wonder fabric that kept its shape when wet, was cheap to produce and came in

Cole of California style the swimsuits
BRI-NYLON gives the flattering fit
It makes a real difference what your swimsuit's made of. Swimsuits in BRI-NYLON fit you in the most flattering way, always. They keep their lovely colours, dry quickly. They're beautiful and comfortable in and out of the water. Take these two from Cole of California. The button-fronted suit in the foreground has a sweeping low back. Sizes, 32-38, about 75/-. The zip-front one-piece with the sealskin look costs about 85/6. Sizes, 32-36, black or white only.
IT'S THE BRI-NYLON THAT MAKES THE DIFFERENCE
12

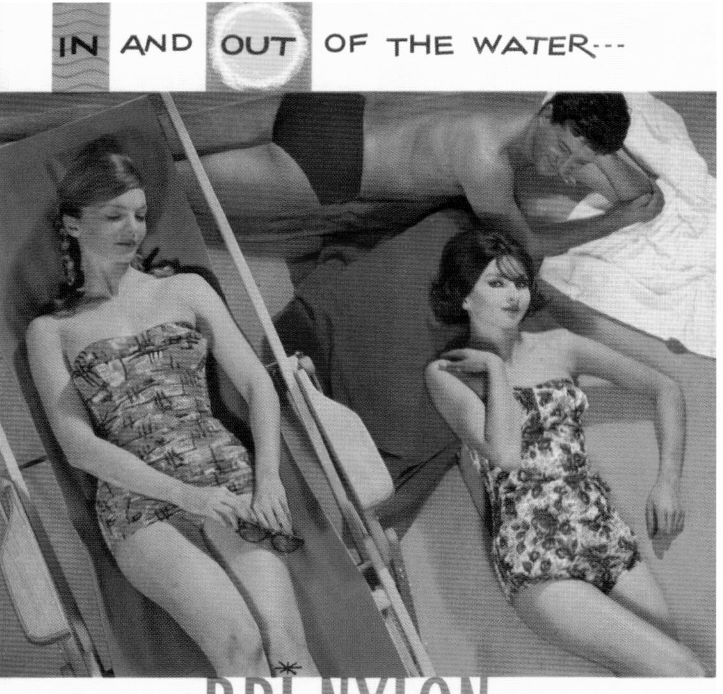

IN AND OUT OF THE WATER---
BRI-NYLON
makes fashion sense
This summer GOSSARD and BRI-NYLON get together to give you a mermaid-like poise and pride. In these new swimsuits, Gossard expertise in figure-fitting combined with the super-light, super-strong, non-shrink, non-rot qualities of BRI-NYLON, make for just one thing. Seaworthiness of a special kind. So swim with the stream this summer—you're destined for a BRI-NYLON swimsuit by
Gossard
(Left) SOUBRETTE, SW 57 in exciting new print. With original lintafoam lined bust and detachable shoulder straps. In four colour ways: Blue, Red, Green and Flame. Sizes 32-38". Approximate price 89/6.
N.B. The man's trunks are by Jantzen.
(Right) SIMONA, SW 54 in exquisite rose print. With preformed lintafoam lined brassiere section. In four colour ways: Purple, Royal, Turquoise and Gold. Sizes 32-40". Approximate price 89/6.
REGISTERED TRADE MARK OF BRITISH NYLON SPINNERS LIMITED
BRI-NYLON for the best in nylon

ABOVE: Ladylike fashions were given a new lease of life by the miracles of technology with the use of Bri-Nylon in fabric, which aided a flattering figure-hugging fit. The orange-and-white suit on the left has a button front, whereas the sealskin-look suit has a zip front. This Cole of California advertisement dates from 1964.

LEFT: Bri-Nylon teams up with Gossard in this 1961 ad proclaiming the quick-drying, non-shrinking, non-rotting qualities of the fabric, as well as its shape-fitting virtues. The strapless swimsuit, which was so popular in the 1950s, continued to hold appeal for women throughout the 1960s.

different textures. Many manufacturers advertised their swimsuits made of Bri-Nylon in expensive advertising campaigns. The fabric also allowed greater expression in the form of pattern designs. Animal prints were big fashion news for swimsuits and one 1964 black Bri-Nylon bikini came in suede effect with shorts-style pants and featuring zebra-edging. In the same year Slix produced Bri-Nylon tiger-print bikinis and swimsuits – the pants were cut on the large side so that the navel barely showed, and the tops were cami-style. Other key swimwear fabrics of this period were Drilon, rayon jersey and Helanca – all thick, practical and sturdy. Swimsuits became far less structured due to the flexibility of the fabrics, and no matter how drip-dry or stretchy, the styles mutated into very simple shapes. Catalina stopped putting zippers in their suits, a fastening detail that had lasted 30 years. Bikinis featured large-cut bottoms sometimes even fastened on to an elasticated waistband so that the navel remained covered. Scoop necks, square necks and long bodies returned and for a while, early 1960s swimsuit designs resembled those of the 1920s, with only slight alterations in body length and fabric. However, all this was to change when the European influence spread across the Atlantic to the USA.

LEFT: With their navels showing, models Pam Gail, left, and Rita Thiel pose at an outdoor café in swimwear by Rose Marie Reid in 1963. Gail's three-piece outfit includes a bikini bra top, tight shorts and a V-neck sweater slung over her arm. Thiel wears a paisley-print cotton Scheherazade suit consisting of a hip-rider bikini bra and bottoms set worn with a sleeveless cover-up jacket.

RIGHT: As the 1960s progressed, textile prints became more vibrant and outrageous. Paisley was a dominant pattern in swimwear, as seen in this detail from a 1960s nylon swimsuit. Colours became more exuberant, and floral designs bigger and bolder.

LEFT: The first-ever swimsuit cover from *Sports Illustrated*, dated January 1964, with model Babette March in a white bikini by Rose Marie Reid wading in the surf in Cozumel, Mexico. Deemed the height of sexiness, *Sports Illustrated* covers launched the careers of the first supermodels.

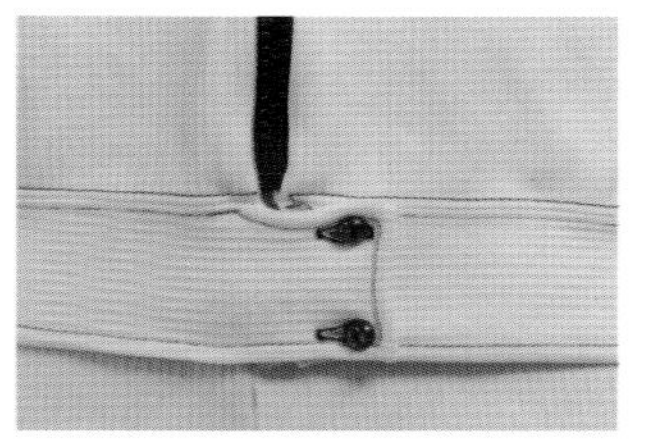

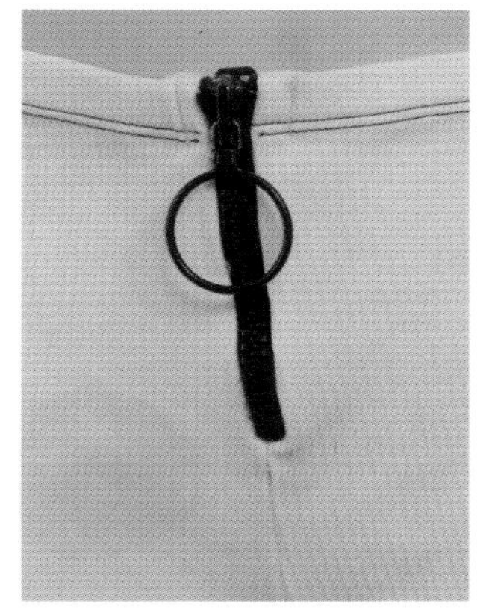

ABOVE: Unmistakable 1960s details such as circular ring-pulls, zips and topstitching in contrasting colours adorned beachwear as they did daywear. Coloured zips were meant to be seen rather than concealed and became features in their own right. Synthetic elastics such as nylon and spandex allow clothing to be closer-fitting and follow the natural outline of the body.

RIGHT TOP AND BOTTOM: A three-piece swimwear set in a sporty style reflects the obsession with surfing. Cleavage is de-emphasized with bra tops that are soft, comfortable and unstructured. Straps become narrow but the string has yet to develop. Necklines are wider and more open, and fashion completely abandoned the cleavage-inducing corset styles of the 1950s.

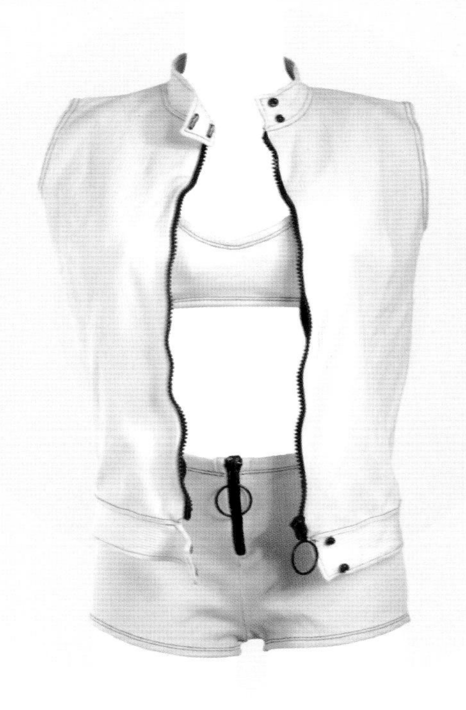

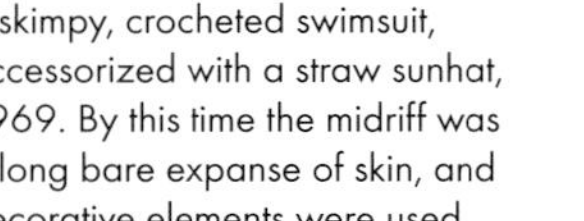

FAR RIGHT: A young model wears a skimpy, crocheted swimsuit, accessorized with a straw sunhat, 1969. By this time the midriff was a long bare expanse of skin, and decorative elements were used to draw attention to the area. Crochet was a popular material for swimsuits – daringly see-through yet also tapping into the trend for ethnic styling.

ABOVE: A black-and-white 1965 gingham two-piece by Jantzen is trimmed in ribbon-threaded eyelet. The fabric is a Dan River Fortel polyester and cotton.

RIGHT: This 1960 Bold Violets one-piece is a sheath version of the Jantzen Bashful bikini pictured on page 187. The style featured a print of violets on delustred satin.

Pretty Europeans

Europe's influence was increasing. French stars Brigitte Bardot and Jean Seberg looked great in casual checked gingham and simple white lace styles. Prettier fabrics made successful sellers and artificial fibres were created to mimic denim and cotton prints. Cotton bikini tops and bottoms were gathered on to elastic edging, giving them a slightly puffed-out, pretty look. This trend followed the fashion for puffed sleeves and full skirts that caught on between 1960 and 1964, and soon bikinis with smaller bottoms and skimpier, bra-like tops were being worn by younger women.

Swimwear followed the major trend for lace mid-decade, when, in particular, white lace was ubiquitous in various forms. It was possible to buy a swimsuit made from white Lycra elastomeric lace, a thick stretchy fabric resembling real lace, fashioned into a classic maillot-style suit. The maillot returned and reasserted its claim to classic status, though with new fabrics. Experiments with fabrics continued, and crochet was popular for the beach. With the appearance of wool, crocheted nylon could survive sand and sea, and was fashioned into waistcoats, tunics and lightweight cardi-jackets to match bikinis. Such outfits were called 'tease sets'. Lycra was also used more often, because the threads were much lighter than other stretch nylons and so could be woven into finer, less bulky fabrics.

RIGHT: A 1969 multicoloured crochet bikini with tassels on the bottoms by Allen & Cole. Crochet was part of a wider trend for crafts-inspired fabrics and natural materials. at this time. There was also a greater interest in fastenings of all kinds, and along with tassels and ties, there were straps, rings and knots. The influence of the next decade can be seen in the hippy styling and gold coin belly chain. While this bikini looked sexy on the beach, it may not have stood up well to a soaking.

Later, stretch towelling would be a frequent fabric choice for companies such as JerSea and Baltrik. In 1969 each company produced a range of bikinis and swimsuits with matching tops in towelling. Baltrik's featured a lace-up detail, with bootlace cords fastening the top, slotted through silver eyelets. It was a sexy look, and picked up on the 'lace-up' trend.

Colours were brown, black and cream, and the palette that started off bright darkened as the 1970s approached. The vivid, psychedelic colours of the decade were gradually replaced by more sombre shades as fashion discovered a passion for the Victorian and Edwardian eras.

The word 'psychedelic' literally means to expand the awareness of the mind. Drug users of the 1960s claimed that substances including LSD had this effect, and the word was hijacked to represent a movement that encompassed fashion, music and art. Vivid coloured patterns that almost swirled before the eyes were key to the fashion look of psychedelic print-master Emilio Pucci, but also featured in the styles of other swimwear designers and manufacturers.

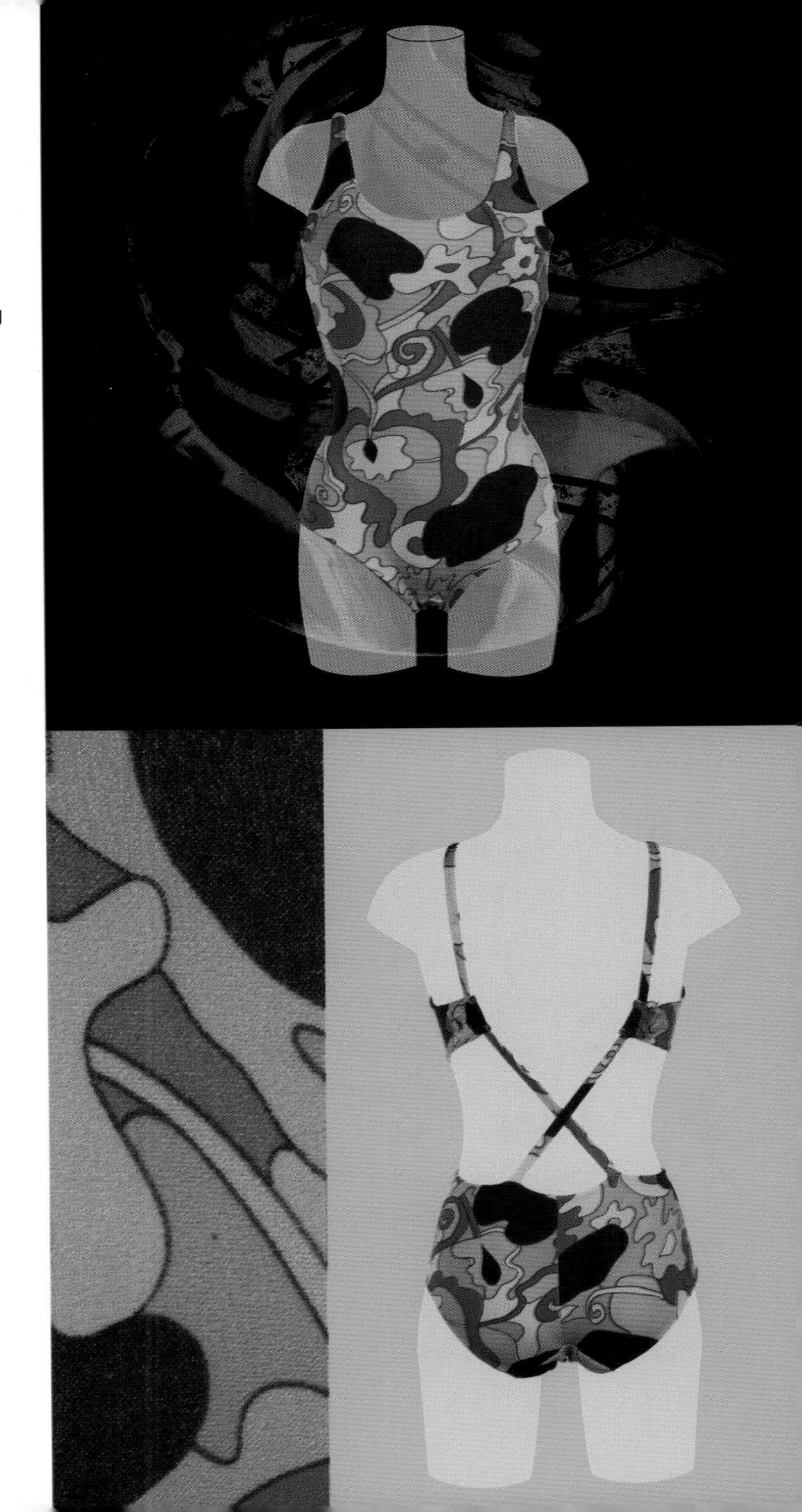

RIGHT TOP AND BOTTOM: A psychedelic-print 1960s swimsuit in pink, orange and brown with a crossover back through button loops. During this decade, the legs gradually became more high-cut at the hips and the back plunged lower.

LEFT: Model Marisa Berenson wears a Pucci slip on a beach in Sardinia in 1967. Emilio Pucci developed the first resortwear line of clothes with his beach pyjamas, bikinis and wraps in bright swirling colours.

RIGHT: The model Veruschka wearing a gold-and-black Ken Scott swimwear ensemble in 1965. Scott was known for his bold, intense graphic designs, particularly of exotic flowers.

The Jet Set

After years of war in Europe and then the threat of the H-bomb in the 1950s, northern Europeans started travelling again, and as always they followed the lead of those in the spotlight. Celebrities and their aristocratic friends carried on partying abroad in the postwar years. The speed and efficiency of air travel earned them a new name, the 'jet set', and their destinations included the French and Italian Rivieras, Tunisia, Morocco, the Greek Islands, the Balearic Islands, Hong Kong, Miami, Acapulco in Mexico and Rio de Janeiro in Brazil, while Spain became a popular destination for British, Swedish and German tourists. Everyone loved the sunshine and there were now more opportunities to soak it up.

Jet-setters chose designer labels for their swimming costumes and resortwear. An exoticism returned after a quiet patch and new names gained a glamorous following. One of the more well known was Emilio Pucci, still immensely popular today. In 1963 Pucci launched the most exciting, gorgeous range of printed silk fabrics anyone had seen in fashion until that point. Daring candy-coloured combinations on white backgrounds, they were crisp and vibrant enough to make any woman look stunning, regardless of her age or colouring. Pale beauties and tanned goddesses all looked amazing and wealthy in Pucci. The designer specialized in shirts, shift dresses, capri pants, bikinis, swimsuits and scarves for summer dressing, but he also created long evening gowns with slashed-to-the-thigh sides, short tops, miniskirts, beach pyjamas and kaftans. Now hugely collectable, Pucci was the choice of icons including Jackie Kennedy Onassis, Elizabeth Taylor and Claudia Cardinale.

LEFT: The model and actress Sharon Tate, pictured here in the late 1960s. The silver metallic swimsuit she wears is an example of the decade's obsession with 'space age' fabrics.

RIGHT: Veruschka models a white nylon bikini in Brazil in 1968. The top and bottom are held together with huge chain hoops, a trademark of Pierre Cardin but in this case employed by Bill Blass.

The expanding European market opened doors for other high-end designers. A Christian Dior design from spring 1966 features a white lace see-through dress worn over a bikini. Elaborate, almost fantasy designs were tried out in resortwear as the decade progressed. Paco Rabanne, André Courrèges and Pierre Cardin were Paris-based designers who experimented with swimwear styles to dramatic effect. Rabanne loved metal-work, hoops, studs and leather, and created swimsuits covered in huge gold discs sewn on to mesh. His designs also featured chains and hoops connecting bikini tops to bottoms, and plastic discs as decoration Even more futuristic in his approach, Cardin made his name with 'space age' designs inspired by the Apollo rocket programme of the late 1960s.

As the 1960s progressed and swimwear merged into resortwear, particularly at the higher end of the market, other designers entered the field. Many crossed over from the world of entertainment into fashion, including Oleg Cassini, an Italian-born

ABOVE: A 1966 silver maillot by Sylvia de Gay for Robert Sloan. Obvious synthetics were fashionable, particularly with the young in-crowd, with futuristic-looking metallic and wet-look vinyl worked into swimwear, daywear, footwear and accessories.

RIGHT: A revealing swimsuit designed by actress Elizabeth Taylor and her American partners Mia Fonssagrives and Vicki Tiel on show at Maxim's in Paris in January 1968. Fonssagrives and Tiel were known for sexy 1960s 'youthquake' fashions and also collaborated with Taylor on wedding dresses.

American who began his career designing costumes for Hollywood productions. From 1960 onwards he dressed Jackie Kennedy at the White House, creating her signature looks including A-line and sheath dresses. For the beach Cassini created matching ensembles of bikinis and swimsuits with over-shirts, dresses and accessories, and developed his own ready-to-wear line. He designed tennis clothes for Munsingwear and swimwear for Waterclothes under his own label. Waterclothes also employed the skills of American swimwear designer Tom Brigance, as did Sinclair and Gabar, in the late 1950s and 1960s. Anne Fogarty, who was one of the first Americans to produce bikinis, worked initially for Saks Fifth Avenue.

Jet-setter swimsuits, featured on models in magazines and posed beach pictures of film stars, were far more glamorous than those of ordinary women, and constituted great free advertising for designers. They also captured the eye of those in the ready-to-wear market and eventually designer details filtered down the market to high-street chainstores. Details copied by ready-to-wear manufacturers included lace-up front bodices, cut-away details at the sides and tie-sides on bikinis. The beaches of St Tropez were particularly influential in terms of European trends. Big-label designers despatched scouts to discover what the local boutiques were creating; then sent sketches back to their head offices to be made up into similar styles.

Skinny-Dipping With Rudi

The idea of feminine beauty changed again in the mid 1960s with the discovery by photographer Justin de Villeneuve of a young London girl called Lesley Hornby, known by her nickname Twiggy. As thin as her name suggested, she had a skinny but feminine look and short hair that was in direct contrast to the big, long looks around at the time. Skinny body fashions created a market for even smaller bikinis. The way to look good in swimwear unfortunately involved a starvation diet rather than a bit of decent corseting.

BELOW: Sex symbol Elke Sommer, photographed in Hollywood 1967, wearing a fashionable hipster bikini with a front-tying top.

BELOW RIGHT: A late 1960s bikini in striped cotton features a front-tying halterneck top with low-waisted elasticated bottoms.

BELOW FAR RIGHT: A fringed navy swimsuit with red-and-white trim. Fringing and Native American themes were key inspirations for fashion design during the 1960s, finding their way into daywear, coats, boots and handbag designs, as well as swimwear.

It was tough on older women, and continued the age divide in fashions between young and old.

Innovations flourished. Skirts were getting shorter and the mini-skirt was headlining news in the mid 1960s. The futuristic fashion designer Rudi Gernreich was already producing skimpy daywear in easy-clinging fabrics when he was commissioned by Warner's to design the first 'invisible' underwear in 1965, the bra of version became renown as the 'no-bra bra'. This silky, stretchy collection was seam-free and the centrepiece, the Warner's bodystocking, could be worn beneath any outfit for a smooth, line-free look.

Production of underwear that was seamless and comfortable coincided with the feminist movement sweeping the world. Going bra-less became a political statement for many women, who saw restrictive 'body-shaping' underwear as a symbol of female repression. However, the truth about whether or not any actual bra burning took place remains shrouded in myth. It is certainly true that the 1968 Miss America pageant was stormed by feminists, protesting about the beauty queens feeding into the traditional, man-pleasing female stereotype. To demonstrate their disgust the feminists tossed bras, girdles, corsets, girdles and even hairspray into a litter bin outside the competition venue. Some reports say that the receptacle was subsequently set alight, but there is no official confirmation of this. Nevertheless, the legend spread.

Gernreich had been designing modern-looking swimwear in simple colours and fine, clingy fabrics, but he wanted to investigate how far women were prepared to go for fashion, comfort and innovation on the beach. St Tropez and a few other spots along the French Riviera were famous for their topless sunbathers, but although the French were once again admired for their daring, bikini tops stayed firmly fastened elsewhere in Europe and the USA. Gernreich

ABOVE DETAIL AND RIGHT: A midriff-baring 1960s swimsuit with white flowers on a navy field. As the navel became more exposed, so did inventive ways of revealing the abdomen area. Whereas the 1950s were all about bosoms and hips, the 1960s focused on the midriff. The swimsuit looks like a bikini from behind, but note that the bottoms' sides are hipster-like in their generous width. There is an extra cut-away area where the bra top meets the centre panel.

believed that it was only a matter of time before all the beaches of the world became topless, and was genuinely abashed at the worldwide reaction to his 'monokini'. After working on the design for four years, he showed his first full monokini collection in July 1968. It met with outrage: the Vatican ruled it to be immoral and, to be honest, the monokini did very little for its wearer. Crafted as a single garment, the swimsuit featured bikini-style bottoms with a set of two straps crisscrossing between the breasts then passing over the shoulders and fastening behind, bib-and-braces style. Fashion pundits then and now still firmly believe that it was the out-and-out unattractiveness of the monokini rather than international prudishness that killed it off. It apparently sold well in San Francisco, home of Flower Power culture, for one summer.

Topless sunbathing continued on the beaches of southern France and over the years spread to other destinations along the Mediterranean. The fact that it began in the 1960s is coincidental, and it was not an outcome of the women's movement. Topless sunbathing is mainly about getting an all-over tan, though it has been 'blamed' for everything from the arrival of the Pill to bra burning; the monokini was a response to the decreasing size of bikinis and a product of Gernreich's exploratory motivation – the same sort of motivation that drove Carl Jantzen to develop a

LEFT: This blue 1960s swimsuit with white trim has straps that attach at a back button, revealing a long stretch of back but still keeping a modest high waist. From the front the suit looks like a shorts-style two-piece.

tighter-woven knit or Fred Cole to pioneer Lastex. Gernreich wanted to take the swimsuit even further forward, to give women something different, new and adventurous to wear. True, it matched the female spirit of the times but might not Gernreich have designed it anyway? Ultimately the commercial success of a piece, rather than its route into existence, is reliant more on the needs of real women than on the aims of fashion.

RIGHT: The model Rose McWilliams, wearing the original monokini – a topless bathing suit – by Rudi Gernreich, relaxes pool-side after a rooftop fashion show at the Continental Hotel in Hollywood in 1964.

chapter seven

THE BEACH BABE REVOLUTION

EVERYTHING SHRANK SWIMSUIT-WISE IN THE 1970S. BIKINIS WERE REDUCED TO FOUR TRIANGLES AND TWO PIECES OF STRING, OR IN THE CASE OF THE THONG, THREE TRIANGLES AND TWO PIECES OF STRING. Swimsuits were cut away at the front, back and sides until they resembled bikinis with just a few extra attachments. Beauty contests were enjoying their final fling before collapsing in the face of feminism but still managed to influence swimsuit styles until the middle of the decade. European companies including Slix, Silhouette and Gottex took hold of their home markets while the power of the larger American swimwear groups was confined to their home country and Latin America. Sporting swimwear brands including Speedo and newcomer Arena created 'second skin' stretchy fabrics, specially formulated for performance swimming.

The glamour business provided a new background for swimsuit modelling and in the USA a sporty new style of model appeared on the scene who was a world away from Europe's skinny waifs. Christie Brinkley, Cheryl Tiegs and other *Sports Illustrated* models brought back the body beautiful, only this time the curves were real and the corsets were gone.

High-street retailing took off and shopping malls with chainstores full of affordable clothes spread throughout towns and suburbs. Denim was everywhere, and on the beach cut-off jeans and a bikini top worked as well as a matching bikini. Unisex style was cool: men and women dressed in the same denim blazers and jeans or knee-high boots. On the beach women went topless in southern Europe and men wore tight-fitting Speedo trunks. Blame the decade: small tight trunks were genuinely fashionable then and even today there are those who think the look is still in style.

PAGE 204: A classic Norman Parkinson fashion photograph for *Vogue* from the early 1970s of the iconic Apollonia Von Ravenstein wearing a white jersey swimsuit.

LEFT: Seen here in the February 1975 edition of *Sports Illustrated*, Christie Brinkley wears a red-and-orange ringback tanga by Giorgio di Sant'Angelo, in one of the first showings for the Brazilian-inspired swimsuit design.

RIGHT: Vivien Neves models a buckle-fronted Lycra bikini in 1975. Cerise with gold buckles, this swimsuit became a bikini classic. It is possible to buy virtually exactly the same design from most major manufacturers today. A popular glamour model, Neves was also the face – and body – for Nelbarden swimsuits.

Swimsuits Cut Loose

In terms of fashion, swimsuit trends headed in several directions. The swimsuit fabrics that exist today evolved in leaps and bounds, with stretch fabrics and nylons taking on glossy, satin sheens and colours becoming more vibrant. Hawaiian and tropical prints remained big news in the mass market, along with animal prints such as zebra, leopard and tiger skins. Large companies specializing only in swimwear entered the European markets and soon dominated: almost everyone owned a decent beach or swimming outfit and there were few reasons not to – every town had a heated indoor pool and swimming became a prime way to keep fit.

While there was a huge market in swimsuits for the average woman, high fashion gave up on resortwear for a time. Hippy and ethnic trends did not sit well with the full-on resort attire of the past. It was the end of the line for designer beach-side outfits, complete with matching shoes, bags, dresses and headscarves. These were changing times. The hip jet-setters heading out to Marrakesh or the Med simply threw kaftans over their swimwear, if they wore any swimwear at all. Bikinis were tiny and sometimes only bottoms were required.

The skinny body silhouette of the previous decade established itself as the norm for fashion models and magazine photographers. Big, curvaceous bodies were 'out', and fashionable styles accentuated the long, skinny look. Girls wore their string bikinis with cut-off denims over the top and a pair of high cork-heeled wedges. This was the time when the USA started making real inroads into the fashion business, first with home-grown fashion models who went to Europe and took the place by storm, and second with fashion designers such as Calvin Klein and Donna Karan who were busy serving their apprenticeships in preparation for world domination. Jerry Hall, Rene Russo, Rosy Vela and Margaux Hemingway were just a few of the American names arriving on the fashion scene in the 1970s. British and European models were looking

LEFT: After the hippy, floaty, arts-and-crafts vibe of the early 1970s, the end of the decade was characterized by a strong new look. Futuristic, lean and dangerous, all the padding fell away from the swimsuit and left behind a few strips of tight, gleaming Lycra fabric, as shown in this 1977 shot by French photographer, Jacques Malignon.

BELOW: Two simple swimsuit styles designed by the masters. Uber-babe Jerry Hall (left) wears a red maillot by Cole of California in this 1977 photograph, while her modelling partner sports an adjustable Gottex number with side-ruching and ties. Both brands are still successful.

jaded and faded, as drugs and partying took their toll. The new, fresh American girls with their sleek bodies, tanned skin, long legs and ability to look incredible in a swimsuit put the pale Euro babes with their pasty legs and black eyeliner firmly in the shade. By the end of the decade, an even stronger silhouette would emerge from the USA and lay the foundations for the supermodel trends of the 1980s.

Battle of the Beaches

Spending time in the sun was the ultimate holiday goal. In the decade before the risks of skin cancer were known, the suntan was the essential sign of health and beauty. Models were photographed with tans in summer issues of the top fashion magazines, the darker the better. A famous advertisement for suntan lotion from the European brand Bergasol featured two topless girls sitting with their backs to us on a pool edge, one a sexy nut brown, the other a pale shade of pink. Of course the girl with the best tan was the one using the product. By the

BELOW: Jantzen's 1975 'Heat Lightning' advertisement promoted their geometric-print bikini and matching patio dress, which made an elegant ensemble for 1970s beach attire.

RIGHT: A Coppertone suncream advertisement from 1979 showing a tanned model in a yellow string bikini. Deep suntans were highly fashionable in the late 1970s, before the bad news about skin cancer and premature ageing hit the headlines.

Heat lightning.
Swimwear that's sophisticated and soft
in Du Pont ANTRON® nylon and LYCRA® spandex.
Patio dress and bikini about $44 and $18.
To stir up a storm this summer,
just wear a smile and a Jantzen.
Jantzen
A source of pride
LYCRA for the easy life.

FLASH 'EM A COPPERTONE TAN
Flash thru summer in a Coppertone tan.
Coppertone Dark Tanning Oil or Butter for the fastest, darkest tan.
Or Coppertone Suntan Lotion for a fast, rich tan of honey gold, while it helps
protect against burning. And there's Coppertone Shade, with extra
sunscreen protection, for a gradual tan.
The moisturizers in Coppertone help keep your skin looking
young. So get quick-as-a-flash looks wherever you go this summer.
Flash 'em your Coppertone® tan.
Coppertone
2
Minimum Protection
Coppertone
2
Dark Tanning Oil
The Fastest,
Darkest Tan
Coppertone
4
Suntan Lotion
A Fast, Dark Tan
Extra Protection
Coppertone
6
SHADE
A Gradual Tan
©PLOUGH INC. 1978

1970s, a suntan was virtually compulsory for any stylish woman. Tanning lotions were all about getting darker, with the idea of sun-protection low down on the list of prerequisites. Suntan oil was hugely popular, despite the fact that it left a greasy film on swimming pools and stained light-coloured swimwear. Fake tans were unsuccessful, foul-smelling creams that left the wearer streaky or orange coloured and the tanning tablets which many women took, simply dyed the skin a pallid orange colour. The only real option was a natural tan, as the swimwear ads of the time show.

During the 1960s and '70s, the suntan became a great leveller, just as it had been in the 1920s. Spending leisure time in the sun did not just mean that you were wealthy but it also showed that you were willing to take your clothes off and enjoy a sense of freedom. No wonder so many young people decided to chill out on the beaches of farflung destinations.

The hippy trail included such hotspots as Turkey, Iran and Afghanistan, and all you needed was a kaftan and a duffle coat. People wanted to experiment culturally and travelling was essential for this. Students dropped out of university and took the famous 'magic bus' from outside the American Express building in Amsterdam all the way to India. Rich hippies returned from India, Tunisia and Morocco in kaftans, cheesecloth and crochet clothing, and ethnic and bohemian styles filtered through to high fashion and ready-to-wear. Cheesecloth and crochet were natural fabrics that either became see-through when wet (as in the case of cheesecloth) or offered the peek-a-boo allure of open-weaved fabrics. Handmade textiles and surface decoration like those seen on the hippies'

LEFT: With a bicycle print that references the 1920s, this 1970s scoop-back swimsuit has a full modesty skirt, making it a conservative option and probably marketed with the middle-aged woman in mind.

RIGHT: Simple JerSea of Sweden nylon designs from the mid 1970s. White edging was a popular fashion detail, as was the string tie at the neck. Bikini bottoms shrank, barely covering the hipline, before evolving into the even skimpier thong.

LEFT: A photograph from 1974 shows the boyish look that ran alongside mainstream fashion. Vamps such as Jerry Hall stalked the catwalks, but many healthy, natural looking models featured on the pages of the growing number of women's monthly magazines. This ad is for Silhouette swimsuits, featuring a brightly printed bikini and tankini set.

BELOW: A 1970 Jantzen swimsuit is an example of a miokini, with its cut-away sides and midriff-baring plunging neckline, combined with a bikini back. Called the Aquarius, the suit features a bright nylon print and front-lacing ties.

travels also became popular. Fringing, tassels, embroidery and beading appeared around on clothing and carried through to swimwear.

In the UK holidaymakers deserted the traditional seaside towns in droves and many of the once-popular lidos closed down because there were so few customers. You couldn't simply buy the glamorous, all-important tan in Blackpool or Torquay. The demise of the British seaside was one of the contributing factors to the dwindling popularity of the beauty contest. The major contests remained based around seaside resorts and sponsorship was never really taken up by manufacturers of suntan lotions of swimwear as had happened in the USA. Simultaneously, the feminists were finally winning their argument about the principal factor governing the concept of the beauty contest – namely that central to it all was the swimsuit parade. How could a woman be judged personally on her body shape, they argued. But the swimsuit industry still benefited from contests that survived in that they continued to be a showcase for demonstrating trends that included the return of the halterneck, lace-up fronts, mesh cut-outs and hoop or buckle details attaching two-piece suits together. If Miss World wore a certain style of swimsuit, it was guaranteed to be copied for the stores.

ABOVE DETAILS AND RIGHT: A late 1960s or early 1970s swimsuit with cut-away latticing at the sides features a Pucci-inspired psychedelic print in a large-scale paisley design.

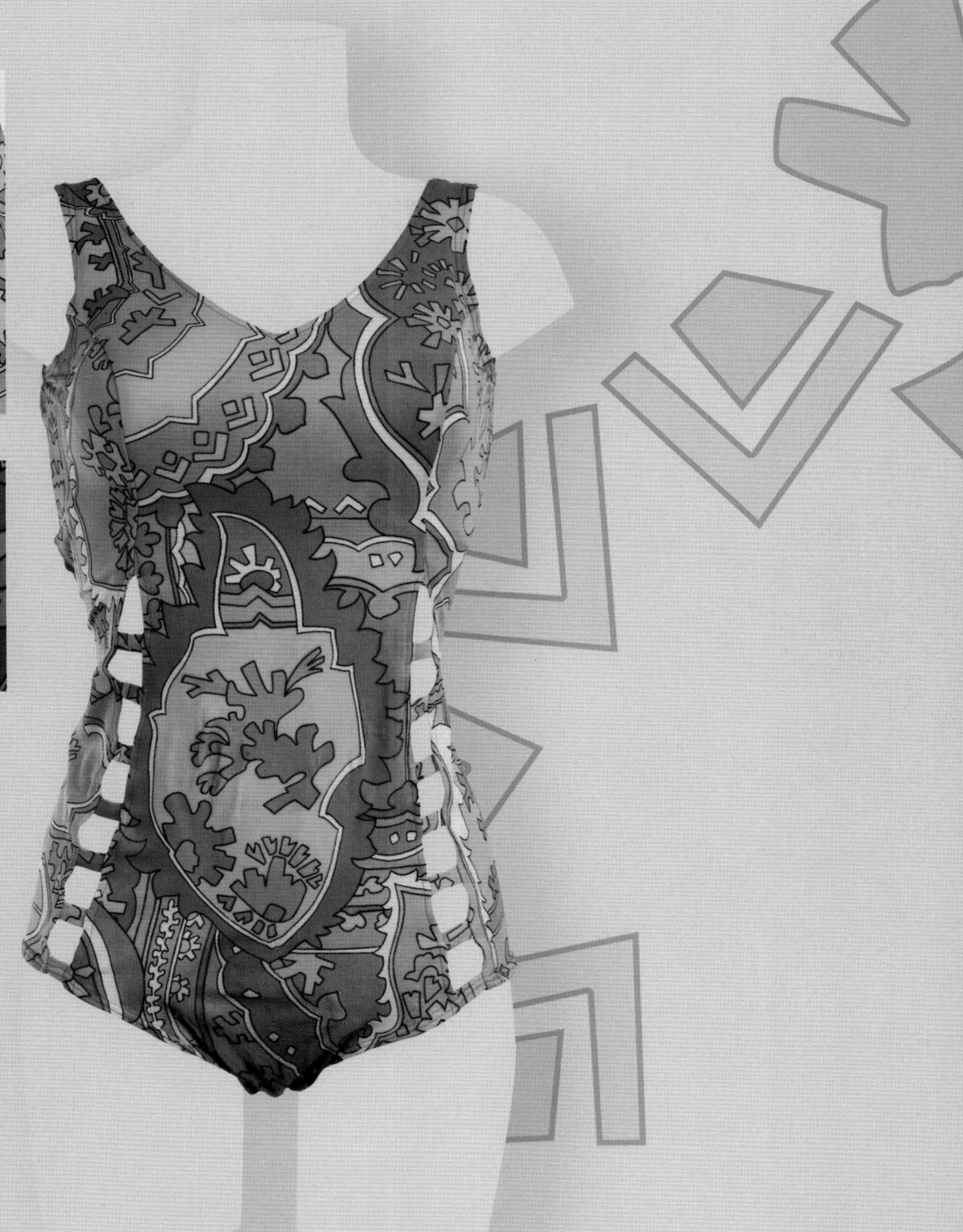

RIGHT AND FAR RIGHT DETAIL:
A lime floral one-piece from the early 1970s is notable for its exotic print and colour combinations, though the sheath-like shape with a straight-across hemline is more reminiscent of the early 1960s.

Some great swimming brands came to the fore in the 1970s. Companies including Gottex, Nelbarden International, JerSea and many more offered women huge choices in the styles they chose for a mid-market price. Generally, the rule was that the skimpier the suit, the higher the price. Basic department-store styles were chunky, thick Bri-Nylon one- or two-pieces and not too revealing, but more stylish versions featured cut-away sides and elaborate detailing. Various mutations of one- and two-pieces emerged, one of which was the miokini – an abbreviation for the maillot-bikini and easily confused with the cut-out maillot. This featured a plunging neckline to below the navel, high-cut legs and narrow side ties to a tanga or brief bottom at the back.

Be noticed in all the right places.
Miss LadyBird
Sleek, bright swimwear at under £3 a piece (or 2-piece).
For a leaflet, send this coupon now.
Name
Address
Dept.A
Ladybird Ltd., Langley, Bucks.

Nelbarden International
Send for your free copy of our new, exciting 1976 brochure.
Dept OV1
Nelbarden House
Mortimer Street,
London, W1N 7RD
Telephone: 01-637 8301
Nelbarden International
1976
6105
Swimsuit
£9.75

ABOVE: This 1970s bikini advertisement shows a typical print and colourway from the decade. The bigger-style bottoms were still popular with the average woman and were sold by budget lines such as this one, Miss Ladybird.

LEFT: A magazine advertisement for Nelbarden swimsuits from 1976. Cut-out sides and lacing were strong details in the 1970s, and thong ties made use of the newer, stronger Lycra fabric that could be pulled tightly into place without ripping.

Dare to Bare

Perhaps one of the most controversial looks to be introduced to the swimwear market was the thong or tanga brief. As part of a bikini or even a skimpily cut one-piece swimsuit, it was the most revealing 'garment' available. First spotted on the beaches of Rio de Janeiro in the early 1970s, the thong soon spread as a beach fashion among the young and nubile. Rudi Gernreich, designer of the monokini, obliged the world with a 'tanga' – the lingerie world's word for 'thong' in 1974. Gernreich, like some of the large swimwear companies, genuinely believed people were heading towards total

ABOVE: A typical day out in Rio de Janeiro, Brazil, from 1973, showing the string bikini with a central tie neck. This was a hugely successful fashion detail in the 1970s, found on everything from dresses to tops, as well as on swimwear.

LEFT: A photo from 1974 that quite possibly shows the bikini at it's very best, as these four fit females take a stroll along Copacabana Beach. Tight and teeny was the bikini rule in Brazil, and shots such as these ricocheted around the world in the early 1970s. What started out as a local, Latin American fashion was soon a worldwide glamour look.

RIGHT: A *Sports Illustrated* cover from 1978 celebrates the beauties of Brazil, including the model Maria João on the cover, wearing a revealing red miokini with a plunging neckline.

nudity on the beach, and certainly the styles coming out of South America were the most revealing yet.

Brazil's economy grew rapidly throughout the 1960s and 1970s. With its Latin American flavour for dance music, nightclubs, fabulous beaches and fresh, exotic food it became an American beach destination and a jet-set mecca. The laidback mood on the beaches was enhanced by the glamorous girls who flocked there, and a swimwear industry grew up. Tiny, string bikinis were just the start. The thong swimsuit was born, worn by men and women alike on Brazil's beaches, though it did not reach the USA in any dominant way until the mid 1980s. Worn for decades by exotic dancers, the thong takes various forms, such as the G-string (which forms a string T-back), the V-string (which forms a string V-shape) and the rio (a narrow band of fabric that is also known as the Brazilian).

However, just like its predecessor, the monokini, the tanga never became mainstream in Europe or America, despite the fact that the decade was about revealing flesh more than anything else on the beach. The tanga was more often a useful way for professional models to show off their bodies on a fashion page than for real women to show off in on the beach. However there's no doubt fashions were more revealing. Models appeared in fashion magazines semi-clad, showing nipples, navels and bottoms. Nudity on such a scale had never been seen before in the mainstream media, nor has it since. Nude scenes became acceptable in films provided that they came with an over-18 certificate, as the Hays Code was finally laid to rest.

Disco Influences

Towards the end of the 1970s, nightlife dictated a whole new fashion look based around leotards and footless tights for the evening, accessorized with sparkly accessories, big belts, miniskirts or wraps. Swimsuits came in the fashionable colours of shocking pink, turquoise, royal blue, purple and canary yellow. In silky, almost metallic-looking Lycra, these suits could be worn on or off the dance floor and for a brief period women actually went out in the evening dressed in their swimsuits. Designs were simple maillot styles, but straps over shoulders were ultra-thin, and 'high-cut' bottoms came in. The idea of a 'high-cut' leg is that more thigh or loin area is revealed, supposedly making the legs look longer. This can work if legs are lean enough, but if not the effect can be less than flattering. High-cut legs reveal far more than other swimsuit styles so bikini waxing was added to the menu at many beauty salons. Ever prepared to suffer for fashion, ordinary women gritted their teeth and went for it in order to be able to wear the latest styles on the beach or to the disco.

LEFT: This stylized photograph from 1975 demonstrates fashion's disco direction, putting the swimsuit at the forefront of glamour once again. In the late 1970s a swimsuit in spandex and Lycra might be worn with a gold belt, matching sandals and leggings or legwarmers.

RIGHT: More than anyone else, the house of Christian Dior dictated the glamorous, glossy-lipped look of the 1970s and created designs that were copied by others. Here, the ultra-sexiness of Dior swimsuits is exploited in a slick magazine advertisement from 1977.

LEFT: Cheryl Tiegs in a shiny pink string bikini. Although a fashion model, her main claim to fame was a long-running affiliation with the *Sports Illustrated* swimsuit issue, which featured her on the cover in 1970, 1975 and 1983. While posing for the 1978 issue, Tiegs took a quick dip in the ocean wearing a white cotton fishnet swimsuit. When she emerged from the water, photographers – both professional and amateur – flocked to her and asked her to pose; she later claimed she had no idea why.

RIGHT: The ex-Bond Girl who also became known as the 'Captain's Rum' girl, Caroline Munro, poses on the shoreline. Her Lycra bikini is a classic shape, showing how simple, stretchy and comfortable the 1970s version was compared to those early 1930s and 1940s two-pieces.

The Beach Girl

Nothing epitomizes the sexy modern woman more than a model on a beach, clad in a simple bikini, with 'out-there' hair, tanned, fit and free. It is an image first celebrated in the 1970 *Pirelli Calendar* by photographer Francis Giacobetti on location in Majorca, but the look soon became a standard of modern, sexy glamour that remains potent today.

Beach beauty separated out from mainstream fashion in the 1970s. Wild, beach-tousled hair with sun-bleached ends replaced more 'done' coiffures. Fashion-wise, sun-bronzed skin translated into a glossy-body look in fashion photographs, with slicked-back hair, glistening lips and sunglasses. Sporty glamour models emerged in the USA who steered clear of the catwalks but represented the arrival of the beach babe for good. Cheryl Tiegs, a favourite of *Sports Illustrated* magazine, and co-star Christie Brinkley were virtually unknown outside the USA, but in their home country they were superstars. Sporty, tanned and toned, these blondes were the prototypes for modern Hollywood female stardom and were rarely photographed in anything but a swimsuit or bikini. The US television show *Charlie's Angels* starred Farrah Fawcett, who personified this look. Married to TV's *Six Million Dollar Man,* Lee Majors, Fawcettt helped launch the California beach babe on to the international stage; the poster of her in a red swimsuit hung on thousands of boys' bedroom walls. European beauties evolved their own superstylish version of the beach babe look, thanks to photographers like Helmut Newton and Francis Giacobetti. Soon the swimsuit photographs that were being shot for the fashion pages of magazines were far sexier, more outrageous and gutsier than anything previously published in the name of fashion.

In the USA, sport was a national passion and home-grown swimsuit models represented the best of what the country had to offer – the great outdoors. Europeans increasingly holidayed abroad during this period, in Mediterranean resorts without space to swing a cat let alone start a game of beach volleyball. Culturally, the swimsuit modelling business diversified after the rise of *Sports Illustrated* and American beach babes.

The glamour industry gained new ground with the rise of the centrefold as an icon. The *Playboy* empire flourished and looking good in a swimsuit once again became a legitimate way to make a living. The film industry was exploring new genres in all sorts of different directions, so it was left to the growing soft-porn market to mop up the leftovers. Women who were willing to pose in the nude or semi-nude in return for a whiff of fame could do so for the glamour magazines. It was hardly surprising that the feminist movement grew alongside the rise in the 'glamour' game. As hard-core pornography developed, campaigners came out of the moral woodwork to challenge men such as *Playboy* chief Hugh Hefner. In Europe fashion took hold of the swimsuit in terms of photography, and masters including Helmut Newton and Norman Parkinson created new, outrageous images for fashion magazines. Newton in particular dabbled with pornographic imagery, yet managed to escape the wrath of the feminists by his artistry.

LEFT: Christie Brinkley in a simple maillot designed by Ariel for Have Designs, an exclusive American brand. This photograph is from 1977, when Christie's star was rising fast. Her groundbreaking horizon pose here was much copied in future suntan product advertising.

RIGHT: Tennis-pro sisters Yvette and Yvonne Sylvander pose for *Sports Illustrated* in 1976. Their grass green and turquoise bikinis by Monika for Elon are fashioned from metallic-sheen spandex, a brand-new but hugely popular finish.

Racing Ahead

While swimsuit fashions moved on through the decades, swimsuits worn for sports and competitive swimming also developed, but in different ways. The goal with a racer's swimsuit is for it to fit as closely to the body as possible, eliminating drag and maximizing speed. Speedo dominated the competition world until 1973, when Arena swimsuits were launched by Horst Dassler, the creator of the Adidas trainer brand. At the time, competitive swimmers were looking for as nearly nude an effect as possible in the pool. Such was the belief in the 'naked effect' that many professional organizations believed swimmers would be competing in the nude by the 1980s Olympics. Before the 1970s there had been several innovations in the racing market, including suits that came with an adhesive to stop slipping or air bubbles getting beneath the suit to cause drag. These were tried out by the Swiss national team before the 1972 Olympics. However, they reported the pulling-off process to be too painful and the team returned to experimenting with fabrics as the answer. Arena came up with a Lycra-based fabric that was almost skin-thin, which eventually developed into Powerskin.

Early competitors who tried Powerskin reported that the fabric did indeed feel like a second skin and it was

LEFT: A collection of close-fitting swimsuits by dancewear and fitness manufacturer Danskin. Their outfits crossed the dancewear–swimwear divide, as this 1977 photograph by Alberto Rizzo demonstrates.

RIGHT: A blonde beach babe poses on a jetty off Cap Ferrat in the South of France in 1976. As the popularity of beach holidays grew, so did water sports – looking good while surfing, snorkelling or waterskiing was as important as when sunbathing.

adopted for use by the British and American swimming teams. At the Montreal Olympics in 1976, 37 medal winners won wearing Arena suits. Along with Speedo, Arena has remained the first choice for swimmers in all major competitions. The suits made by these companies are designed for function: they are high-necked to prevent water getting into the cleavage on female swimmers and waterproof enough to prevent saturation, which would add weight. It took much effort on the part of amateur associations to get competitive garments changed for the better as it was still difficult for the public and media to separate the swimsuit from its image as a 'sexy' garment, even though women's competitive swimming had become a serious sport.

Another sports brand, Danskin, made a natural progression from dancewear to swimwear in 1976 when they extended their basic leotard line to bathing suits. Danskin invented a shiny, stretchy fabric that blended nylon and spandex and used this in a maillot, which, like the leotard, fit the wearer's body as closely as a second skin. Although the 1970s may be thought of as the era of barely-there bikinis, strides in technology led the way for the body-conscious boom of the next decade, when fabric would once again aid in sculpting the body.

Calendar Girls and Pin-Ups

At one time being a calendar girl was a respectable modelling route to follow for a girl who could carry a swimsuit. From the early days of the seaside postcards through to the 1960s, calendars were, by and large, cheerful, wholesome and fun. Times would change. By the 1970s, The Pirelli Calendar *had come along and altered the future for good. Originating in 1964 as a trade edition for Pirelli tyres, the exclusive girly calendar became an annual publication available only as a corporate gift to a restricted number of customers and celebrities. Pirelli considered only the most feted photographers, models and actresses of the day for inclusion in the calendar. The calendar had style but the hundreds of imitations lowered standards. Soon all self-respecting car mechanics had a copycat calendar on their garage wall and they became part of the soft-porn industry. Swimwear fell from favour and was replaced by a few pieces of lingerie and naked breasts.*

Admiring the Beauty.

The Bathing Beauty Boom

Calendar girls were born at the start of the twentieth century from something far more exciting, the arrival of the camera itself. By the 1910, every seaside resort had its photographer, who in turn printed up their pictures of the local bathing beauties for a thriving postcard trade. Photography led to the arrival of the pin-up. Beautiful girls dressed in swimsuits or lingerie shocked society but sold everything from soap to soft drinks. Coca-Cola famously hired one of the first pin-up

LEFT: A sketch from the early 1900s entitled 'Admiring the Beauty' shows the sheer novelty of the swimsuit's arrival. It was not long before the bathing beauty business was booming. Photography moved on in leaps and bounds as an industry as money poured in from eager purchasers of early glamour pictures.

girls to appear in its advertisements. Homely Hilda Clark became the face of Coca-Cola in 1901, retaining a demure, respectable image for the exciting new beverage. The company pretty soon realized the value of a pretty face to advertise its products and began publishing calendars, which were eventually sold as products in their own right.

Some of the earliest seaside bathing beauty postcards make truly hilarious viewing now. It is hard to imagine that such images – of girls posturing in horrible knitted all-in-ones with odd frizzy hair and strange facial expressions – were considered sexy. Of course, there was no such word then; instead, the idea was that such pictures were all about good, clean fun.

As idealized representations of women, an early example of the pin-up was the Gibson girl, drawn by the New York artist Charles Dana Gibson. His work led the way for later pin-up illustrators such as Alberto Vargas, Rolf Armstrong and George Petty. In Paris the fashion model or mannequin was another departure for the pin-up girl. Vera Ashby was one of the most famous, becoming a house model for the designer Edward Molyneux in the early 1920s. Yet, she later claimed, it paid her very little money. She became one of the most photographed faces of the age but could not afford a winter coat because, she said, she refused to take on a lover to keep her in style as other girls did.

ABOVE: This Rolf Armstrong glamour fantasy, 'Sunny Skies', is typical of his work in the 1940s. The girl resembles Dorothy Lamour, star of the Bing Crosby and Bob Hope *Road to...* films. Her Hawaiian sarong two-piece reflected fashion trends. An illustrator for *Pictorial Review* in the 1920s and the best-selling calendar artist at Brown and Bigelow, Armstrong also illustrated pin-up girls to sell RCA products in the 1930s.

Hollywood Calendars

As the swimsuit evolved, so did the business of posing in one. Soon young starlets were earning enough to buy their own small apartments in Hollywood or at least clothe themselves in Paris, through posing for photographers. The artist Rolf Armstrong created some of the most famous glamour girl calendar images through half-photograph, half-painted plates. Jean Harlow was his muse, and his imagery of the 1930s star with red lips, curled hair, wide hips and pert breasts summed up the calendar pictures of the age.

During the Second World War calendar girls played a huge part in keeping troops cheerful while posted in war zones. By then, it was seen as a sign of impending Hollywood success if you were given the chance to pose for your own calendar. Ava Gardner, Betty Grable, Rita Hayworth and Marilyn Monroe all began their careers as pin-up girls at the end of the 1940s.

Ava Gardner made her film debut in 1947's *The Hucksters* and demonstrated genuine acting skills. Monroe never needed any, and became a veteran of her own calendars. Famously, it was a calendar shot of Monroe that graced the launch issue of *Playboy* magazine in 1953. As the first Playmate of the Month, Monroe set the bar for a certain type of glamour that would remain in place until the late 1960s. Curvaceous, made-up and traditionally posed, the girls on the *Playboy* calendar were simply modern 'cheesecake' versions of the overstyled bathing belles of old.

ABOVE: 'All Clear', a 1940s print by Merlin Erabnit, was featured in *The Daily Sketch*, a British tabloid paper. This illustrated model has perfect curves and contours, designed to fuel the imagination of male readers.

After seeing the success of *Playboy* magazine lead to an empire of clubs and lucrative publications, imitators followed. Hugh Hefner put an image, label and price on a lifestyle that had previously eluded definition, that of the international millionaire with a lust for life, luxury and gorgeous-but-sophisticated-looking girls. *Playboy* helped produce a world that divided up the glamour industry once again, creating different tiers of modelling, from low-level porn right up to high-end, semi-nude glamour. It was the perfect backdrop for the arrival of the most famous pin-up calendar of them all, *The Pirelli Calendar*.

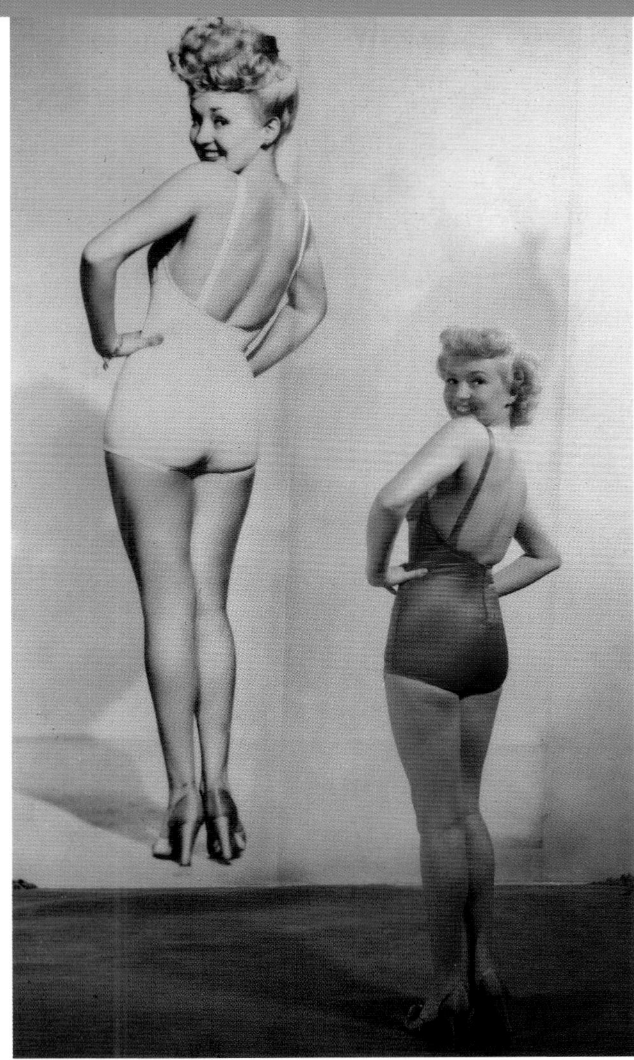

LEFT: Universal movie star Yvonne De Carlo gives a photogenic New Year's greeting clad in a bikini from her 1945 film *Salome, Where She Danced*. De Carlo became best known for her role as Lily Munster in the American television show *The Munsters* (1964–6).

ABOVE: A 1950s photograph of Betty Grable posing in front of one of the original glamour shots that helped her make it bigtime in 1940s Hollywood. Grable was one of the few stars to be a pin-up first and an actress second. She was by no means the last.

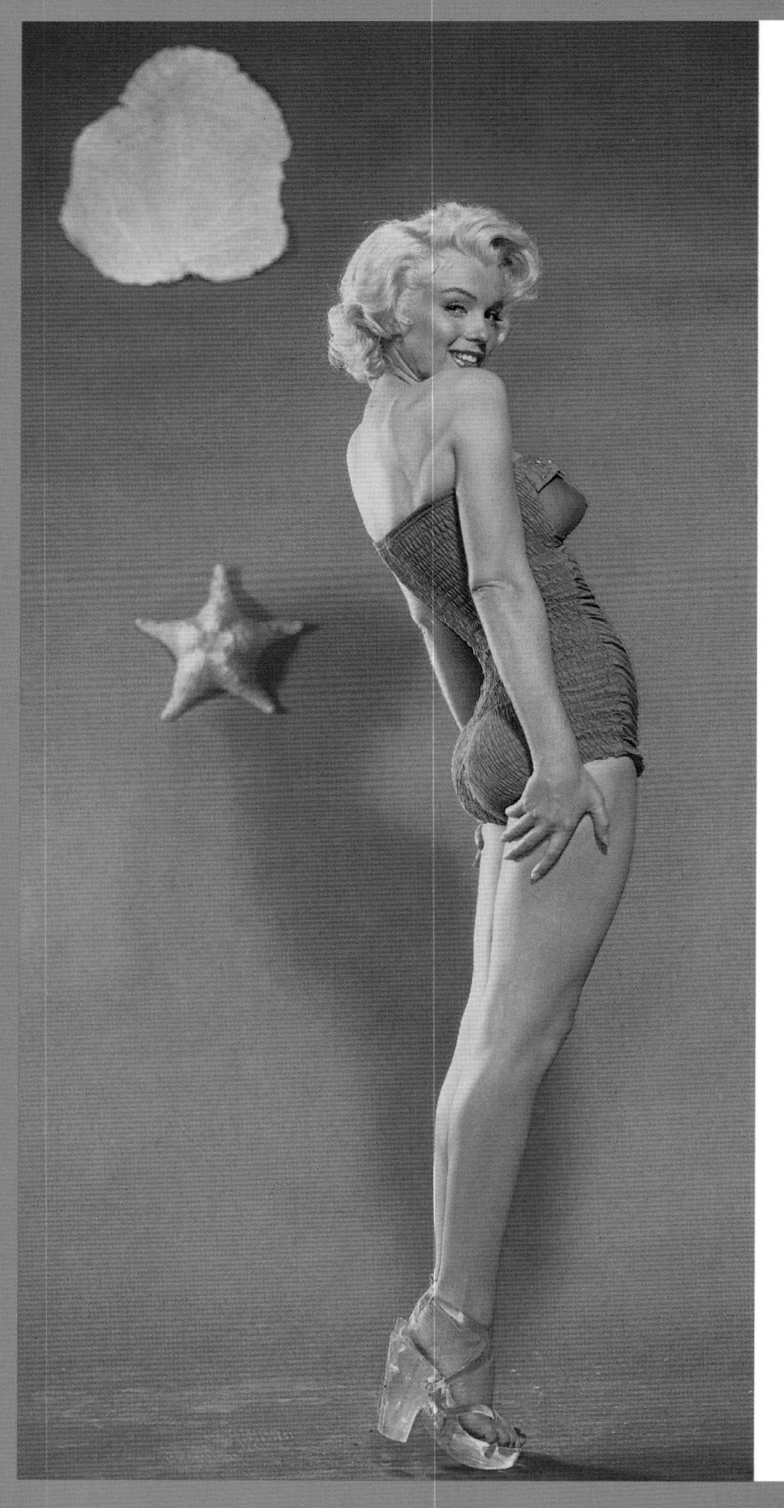

'Undone' Glamour

In 1964 the people at Pirelli decided to create a pin-up calendar for their upmarket customers featuring girls looking gorgeous in swimwear, along the lines of, but different from, the *Playboy Playmate Calendar.* The photographer Francis Giacobetti created some of the most iconic glamour images of all time for the 1968–9 editions. His girls were lean, strong and tanned – their curves were smooth and they wore sporty swimwear in neutral colours.

The Pirelli girls had a Bond-girl glamour and left the blousy, busty pin-ups of the past in the shade. Their swimwear was basic in styling, with lace-up, thong-style fastenings, and deep V-fronts or -backs. Corsetry and underwiring were not needed by Pirelli girls, whose natural, lean lines and fit bodies were already the ideal shape. Similarly, their hair was roughed up and blown about by the wind and make-up barely there. Although these looks took as much art to create as a fully made-up Monroe, the Pirelli girls had a wild, 'undone' look that was shocking to some at the time. But the fact that the girls were always photographed 'tastefully' – leaving more to the imagination than other glamour shots – made the calendar more sophisticated in the eyes of the establishment.

Both Pirelli and *Playboy* led the way for the pin-ups of the 1970s and 1980s. Bo Derek, Farrah Fawcett and Cheryl Tiegs dominated the 1970s, while Christie Brinkley and Kathy Ireland were two favourites in the

LEFT: A young Marilyn Monroe poses in an early shot from her career in 1952. Her slim, youthful body and hourglass curves were complemented by her dyed blonde hairstyle. Her swimsuit, a basic ruched Lastex version, features a cleavage-enhancing cuff on the bust. She was the *Playboy* Sweetheart of the Month for December 1953.

RIGHT: The beautiful and the damned, April 1980. *Playboy* model Dorothy Stratten, in a nearly transparent suit, poses four months before her murder by her jealous, estranged husband. Stratten's murder shocked the glamour world and revealed the dark side to the industry.

1980s. The 1978 poster of Tiegs in a pink bikini became an iconic pop culture image, as did posters of Bo Derek from the 1979 film *10* and Farrah Fawcett during her *Charlie's Angels* period. Similar photographs were purchased and marketed by poster companies such as Athena, the UK company that specialized in highly airbrushed images, which had its heyday in the 1970s and '80s. Posters became big sellers with entire stores devoted to their sale. With the advent of video and the internet, the poster industry eventually died out, but Farrah and Bo remain the poster girls of a generation.

Since the 1970s, most of the world's major fashion models have posed for Pirelli, breaking the unwritten rule about combining 'glamour' modelling with retaining a saleable face for fashion. Gisele Bündchen, Karen Elson and Kate Moss are just some of the biggest names who have recently graced its pages, but the pool of talent has extended to serious A-list actors too, with models that include Hillary Swank and Penelope Cruz. Swimsuit modelling is clearly no longer simply a vehicle for the upwardly mobile wannabe. For now, Pirelli and *Sports Illustrated* occupy a unique position in swimwear image history, proving that after a whole century of pin-ups, there is mileage in the bathing beauty yet.

FAR LEFT: Bo Derek shot to fame in the 1979 film *10* and became a poster pin-up sensation with her braided cornrow hairstyle. Her bikini-clad image graced the cover of March 1980 *Playboy*, which ran a 12-spread feature inside the publication on her and husband John Derek.

LEFT: This iconic poster of sex symbol Farrah Fawcett showed that even a one-piece swimsuit can be red hot. She was America's favourite pin-up in 1976, selling 12 million copies of the poster in that year alone.

BELOW: The babes of *Baywatch* pose on the Malibu beach where the show was filmed. Pamela Anderson had moved on by the time this shot was taken, but she remains the ultimate Californian beach blonde. *Baywatch* was a 1980s phenomenon with unmemorable storylines. No one was following the plot anyway.

chapter eight

LET'S GET PHYSICAL

In many ways, the 1980s fashionable woman stands in direct contrast to the slender, rather boyish figures of the 1970s. In place of the slim hips and smallish breasts that were ideal for the tiniest string bikini came the Amazonian woman – with her firm breasts and muscular body. Fashion's love affair with the athletic body coincided with the regime of body-maintaining gym sessions and fitness classes that we are now all so accustomed to. 'Let's Get Physical' was a 1982 pop chart hit for Olivia Newton John, and her electrifying accompanying video shocked the Western world with the sight of her toned body encased in a high-cut leotard and fluorescent pink tights. In a similar fashion statement, Jane Fonda, queen of the aerobics workout, led the world to 'feel the burn' in her stripy leotard and legwarmers.

Swimwear designers embraced this ideal of the perfect athletic body and drew inspiration from active sportswear and the second-skin silhouettes found in modern dance, gym and aerobics. Even swimming caps found their way back into fashion shoots. Swimwear was intended to show off the new erogenous zones: the sleek, toned upper thighs, the flat washboard stomach and the muscular shoulders. There was little of the decoration associated with 1970s swimwear as the mantra was 'minimal and unadorned' – the body was the star. Sunbathing now had an element of risk attached to it for the new super-sleek goddess, as the truth about the damaging effects of the sun's rays started to become more widely known.

Photographers for the glossy fashion magazines, such as Robert Mapplethorpe and Bruce Weber, were quick to pick up on this physical ideal. Although both are now more known for their Adonis-style male pin-ups, their aesthetic of androgynous beauty set the tone for the decade.

PAGE 236: The swimsuit became a wardrobe essential in the 1980s, when sculptural shapes and physiques dominated fashion. Here, model Pilar Crespi demonstrates her sculpted form for photographer Norman Parkinson in 1980, wearing a typical design at the time – the legs were cut ever higher and the arms ever lower to expose the sides of the body and breast.

LEFT: Priscilla Presley wears a chamois-leather one-piece with Pocahontas-style trimmings. Beads, feathers and fringing were big news in 1980 but lost ground as the decade progressed. Loincloth-style bottoms, cut very high at the sides, were fashionable accompaniments to Native American and cowboy/ prairie looks.

ABOVE: The idle rich at play – the jet-setting Duchess of Feria rolls on a Barbados beach with her stallion, Idle Ruler, in a photograph by Norman Parkinson. Animal print was synonymous with wealth and glamour in the 1980s, hence the one-shouldered zebra-print suit. Luxe gold accessories complete this classic look from 1982.

Sports Styling Made Sexy

It is the New York designer Norma Kamali and her label OMO (On My Own) that can be credited for much of the sports-swimwear crossover. Her swimwear collection took off after Christie Brinkley wore a Kamali swimsuit on the cover of *Cosmopolitan* magazine in 1977, and by the early 1980s it was her vision of gym fanatic, boxer and swimming pool attendant chic that set the pace for swimwear design.

Kamali's signature styles revolved around the one-piece swimsuit – a style of swimwear that had fallen out of favour, relegated to the 'older women' category. Now the one-piece was back, in the form of 'tank suits' (vest-tops), slash-neck suits with cap sleeves or 'wrestling suits' cut low to the waist in the front, which required a T-shirt or bandeau top underneath.

Front necklines were modest; it was the back and shoulders that were in the spotlight. Racerback and T-back shapes borrowed from the athletics track were used for both the one-piece and the cropped top – another key shape of the early 1980s. High-cut polo necks were sensuously cut away to reveal a well-toned shoulders and lower back.

Many of the early decade swimsuits were simply cotton jersey or cotton with Lycra. Textures were smooth or knitted in a rib structure for a sporty feel. To us now, these fabrics would seem rather weighty; the jerseys were certainly sturdy and not ideal for the water, becoming even heavier when wet and drying slowly. In contrast to these matt cottons, Kamali and other directional designers started to use ultra-shiny nylons and nylon/Lycra, plus PVC and neoprene. Much of this swimwear was destined to see more of the disco lights than daylight hours on the beach, such as those in the Norma Kamali's 'Wear Me Don't Wet Me' range.

Over on the West Coast of the USA, the budding surf culture spawned the craze for swimwear made from neoprene, the fabric used for wetsuits. Working for the Californian scuba and surf wetsuit company

LEFT: Grecian-styled swimsuits from Shankara, mid 1980s. Twist-top bandeau tops were often made with two layers of cloth in contrasting colours. With the legline creeping ever higher, the waist also rose and became the focus for decoration.

RIGHT: This wetsuit-styled yellow swimsuit is a 1987 Body Glove design by Californian Robin Piccone. Her sleek silhouettes and bright colours defined the 1980s look and brought the wetsuit label mainstream recognition.

Body Glove, swimwear designer Robin Piccone updated the conventional black neoprene into sexy, curvaceous silhouettes in fluorescent-coloured neoprene trimmed with black. Zip-front one-piece suits were seamed to flatter and cut high on the leg. Crop tops were paired with high-cut briefs decorated with a wide logoed elastic waistbands. A key feature of the Body Glove collection was the figure-hugging coordinates, such as the zip-front miniskirt or scuba top, designed to be worn over a one-piece or bikini.

LEFT: A 1980 trikini by Jantzen made from DuPont Antron nylon and Lycra spandex. Three-piece swimsuits allowed the wearer to remove the maillot component for tanning. This version combines a string bikini with a white lace zip-front see-through maillot.

Carrying the torch forward for sports-influenced swimwear in fashion was Liza Bruce, an American designer who set up her body-conscious swimwear label in 1980s London. Bruce favoured synthetic fabrics, especially nylons with a high Lycra content. Like Kamali's, her designs revolved around the ergonomics of the body and as the decade evolved they became more daring – a deep plunge neckline, a hooded one-piece or cut-away front panels that showed off a totally flat stomach were some of the features of here designs. The most well-known image of Liza Bruce swimwear is the 1980s-defining photographs of bodybuilding champion Lisa Lyons taken by Robert Mapplethorpe. One photograph, taken in 1984 for British *Vogue,* shows the shoulders to upper thigh of the strongwoman in an asymmetric bra and cut-away brief composed of strips of nylon/Lycra.

In Paris, meanwhile, the Tunisian-born designer Azzedine Alaïa was creating a more glamorous version of this stretch-to-fit fashion. He combined traditional corsetry techniques with stretch jerseys to create a new take on the hourglass silhouette. His designs were often multifunctional and could be worn as swimwear, lingerie or partywear. Silhouettes balanced second skin with volume – for example, a body-conscious nylon/Lycra crop top might be worn with woven shorts.

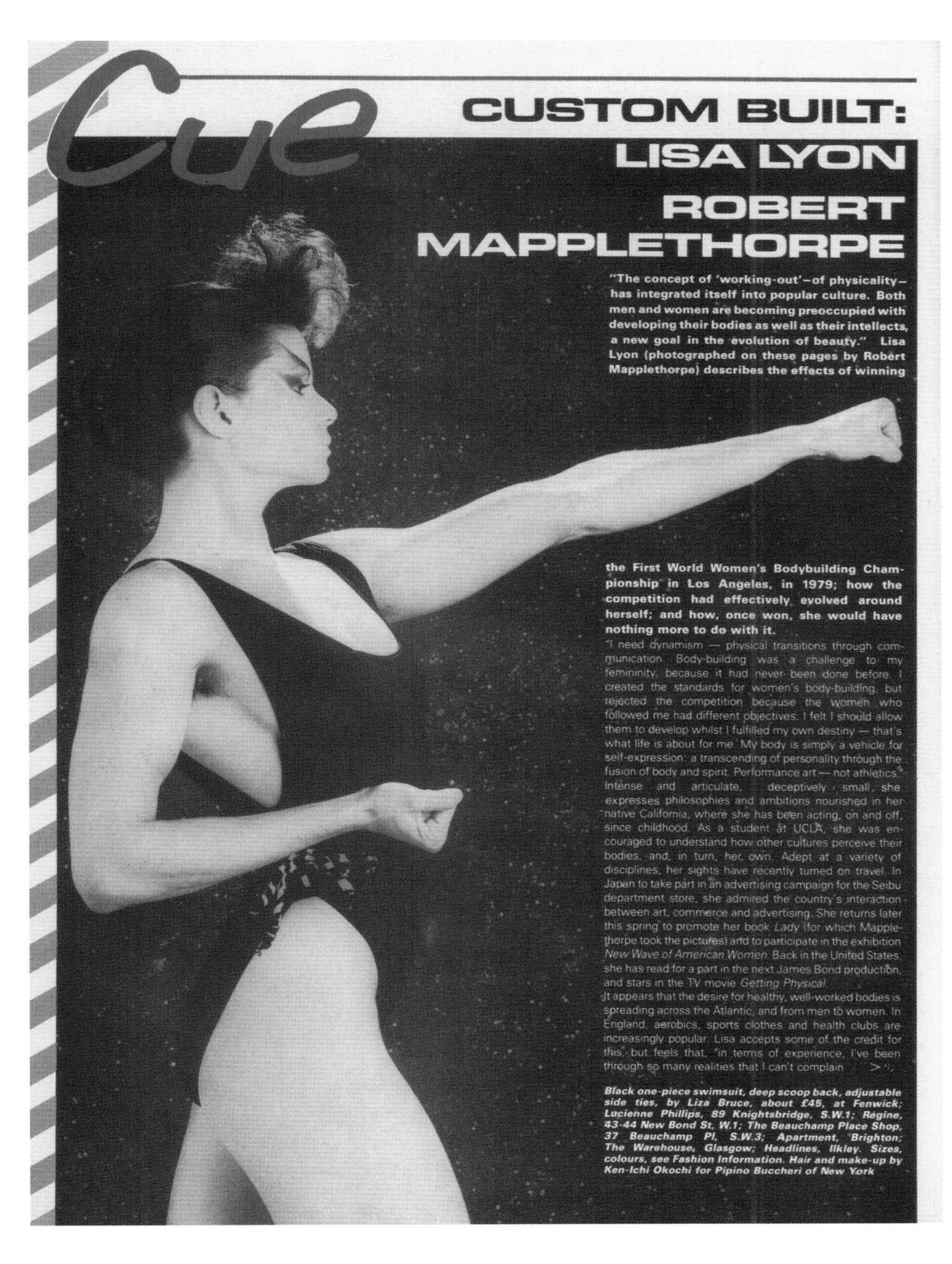

Cue

CUSTOM BUILT: LISA LYON

ROBERT MAPPLETHORPE

"The concept of 'working-out'–of physicality–has integrated itself into popular culture. Both men and women are becoming preoccupied with developing their bodies as well as their intellects, a new goal in the evolution of beauty." Lisa Lyon (photographed on these pages by Robert Mapplethorpe) describes the effects of winning the First World Women's Bodybuilding Championship in Los Angeles, in 1979; how the competition had effectively evolved around herself; and how, once won, she would have nothing more to do with it.

"I need dynamism — physical transitions through communication. Body-building was a challenge to my femininity, because it had never been done before. I created the standards for women's body-building, but rejected the competition because the women who followed me had different objectives. I felt I should allow them to develop whilst I fulfilled my own destiny — that's what life is about for me. My body is simply a vehicle for self-expression: a transcending of personality through the fusion of body and spirit. Performance art — not athletics."

Intense and articulate, deceptively small, she expresses philosophies and ambitions nourished in her native California, where she has been acting, on and off, since childhood. As a student at UCLA, she was encouraged to understand how other cultures perceive their bodies, and, in turn, her own. Adept at a variety of disciplines, her sights have recently turned on travel. In Japan to take part in an advertising campaign for the Seibu department store, she admired the country's interaction between art, commerce and advertising. She returns later this spring to promote her book *Lady* (for which Mapplethorpe took the pictures) and to participate in the exhibition *New Wave of American Women*. Back in the United States, she has read for a part in the next James Bond production, and stars in the TV movie *Getting Physical*.

It appears that the desire for healthy, well-worked bodies is spreading across the Atlantic, and from men to women. In England, aerobics, sports clothes and health clubs are increasingly popular. Lisa accepts some of the credit for this, but feels that, "in terms of experience, I've been through so many realities that I can't complain >

Black one-piece swimsuit, deep scoop back, adjustable side ties, by Liza Bruce, about £45, at Fenwick; Lucienne Phillips, 89 Knightsbridge, S.W.1; Regine, 43-44 New Bond St, W.1; The Beauchamp Place Shop, 37 Beauchamp Pl, S.W.3; Apartment, Brighton; The Warehouse, Glasgow; Headlines, Ilkley. Sizes, colours, see Fashion Information. Hair and make-up by Ken-Ichi Okochi for Pipino Buccheri of New York

FAR LEFT: A late 1980s, early 1990s photograph, taken by the Sicilian photographer Ferdinando Scianna, shows a black cut-away Liza Bruce creation with deep plunging neckline and high-cut legs.

LEFT: A page from *Vogue* magazine in 1984 features the bodybuilder Lisa Lyons, photographed by Robert Mapplethorpe in a black Liza Bruce swimsuit. Lyons embodied the physicality and bold sexuality of Bruce's designs, which were cut away at strategic areas to emphasize musculature.

What about the Bikini?

What had happened to the bikini in the meantime? As mentioned, sporty crop tops were a key look for the younger or more trend-led fashionista. These were designed simply to cover the bust or as a to-the-waist vest top, which could be rolled up for sunbathing (later this would be known as the 'tankini' top).

For the more conventional bikini customer, the strapless bandeau bra top was the shape of the decade. Inspired by the disco boob tube, the bandeau could be a slim band across the breasts or cut deeper to the waist – again for rolling up to catch the sun. The slim bandeau was often ruched in the centre to give the bust some shape, embellished by a fabric bow or loop. More sophisticated versions included draped crossover styles and boned sides for support. This styling also moved over into one-pieces, where the strapless bandeau was the choice for women who wanted a more glamorous style.

As with the tops, bikini bottoms contrasted covered-up versions with the skimpy. In the early 1980s the sporty styles of Norma Kamali and Liza Bruce favoured waist-high shorts or bottoms that could be rolled down to the hip, or those with a belted waistband. Even shortened versions of cycling shorts were introduced. Many of these silhouettes had a 1940s influence; 1980s designers were especially inspired by the style of American Claire McCardell (see pages 121–9), who

popularized sportier shapes for swimwear. Her 'nappy'-style bathing suits and shorts were taken up by designers and reworked in a skimpier loincloth fashion – consisting of a thong, given modesty by a shaped belt of fabric around the hips that could be rolled down. Another of McCardell's influences was the more feminine skirted swimsuit. Bloomers and puffball designs gave feminine alternatives to the sleek, streamlined look of more minimalist styles.

LEFT: In a 1980 photograph taken by Terry O'Neill the supermodel and 1970s icon Marie Helvin wears a classic V-kini swimsuit in silver. The high-sided V-shaped bottoms accentuate her long legs.

BELOW: A model poses in a floral print bikini with a bandeau top and high-sided V-shaped bottoms in Barbados, 1989, for photographer Norman Parkinson. Matching accessories complete the look.

In opposition to this covered-up look for bottoms were the skimpier styles of briefs. As seen on the one-piece swimsuits, bikini bottoms were cut high to make the leg look longer. The waist was scooped down, so creating a deeply curved V-shape silhouette. The front and back panel often had gathered centre seams to accentuate the effect. Adventurous labels produced a tanga back to echo the cut-away front. More sports-influenced brands included a wide elastic waistband with the company's logo included in the design. The gathered thong, adjustable along a casing in the front and the back, was brought over from the beaches in Brazil in the 1970s and continued to be important in the 1980s. Wide thongs that could be pulled up for modesty, or rolled down for sunbathing, were also introduced. These thongs tended to be dramatic in colour or pattern and were often produced from pleated or waffle nylon fabrics that could be dyed brilliant shades or printed in eye-catching designs, such as animal-skin patterns. The gathered thong was worn with a skimpy triangle bra top or 'casually' with a vest or T-shirt.

The body-conscious swimwear silhouettes of this decade were contrasted with voluminous beach coordinates. Oversized full-length terry towelling robes in white, brights or black were the fashion editor's top choice, followed by square-cut chunky-gauge cotton-knit cropped sweaters or colourful batwing tops. Later, these were supplanted by Grecian-style draped jersey dresses, tunic tops and harem or dhoti-style trousers.

LEFT: Christie Brinkley in a tanga X-back by OMO Norma Kamali in a photograph for *Sports Illustrated*, 1981. What it must have lacked in comfort it made up for in looks. By the late 1980s the tanga had evolved into an X-back, as shown here, a V-back and a T-back. Always an innovator, Norma Kamali started her swimwear line after the successful launch of her Pull bikini in 1977, modelled by Christie on the cover of the June issue of *Cosmopolitan* magazine that year.

RIGHT: A 1984 *Sports Illustrated* cover of Paulina Porizkova by Paolo Curto wearing a pink plunge miokini by Ellen Ann Dobrovir.

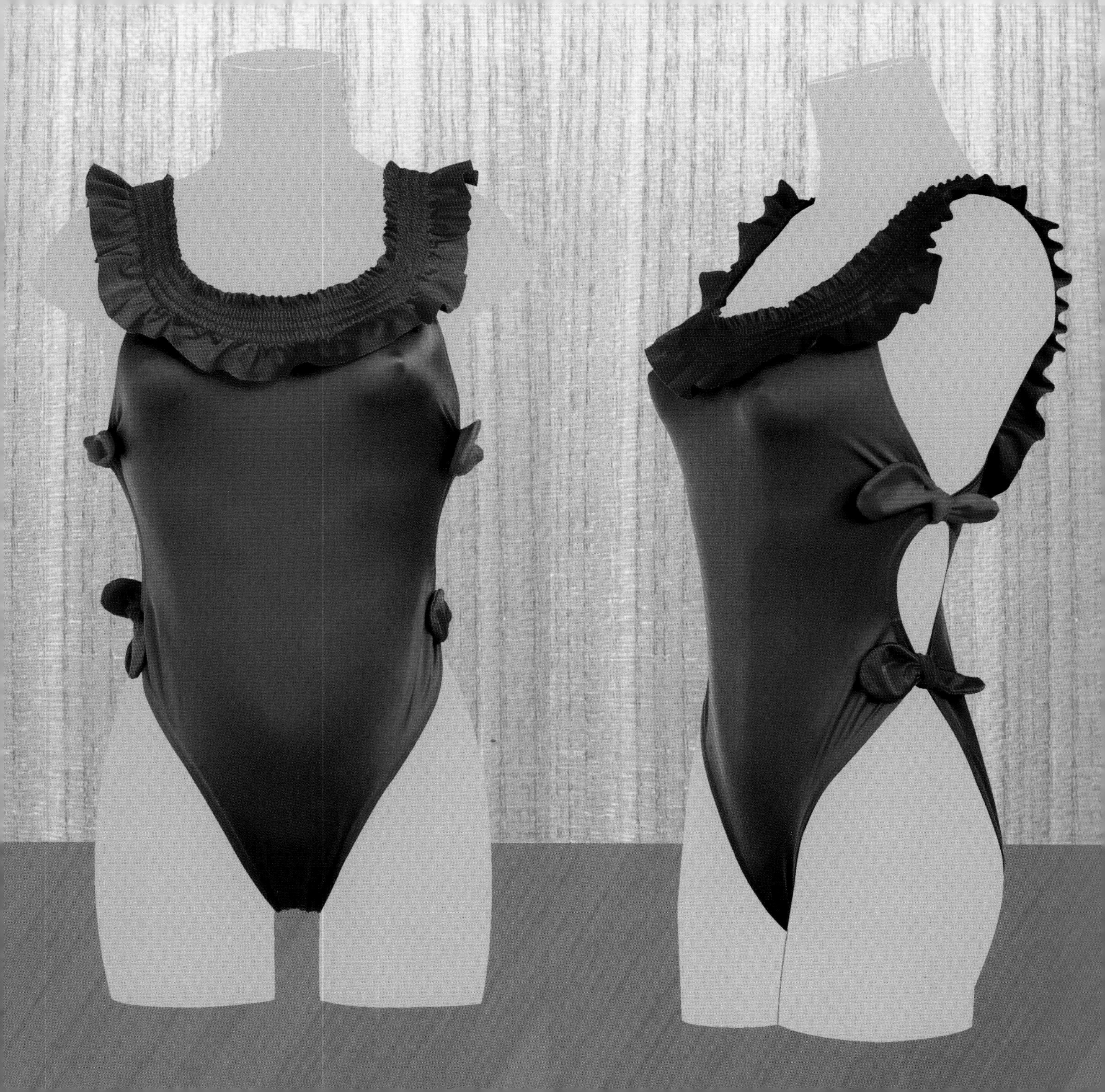

Simple Colour Palettes

During the early part of the decade, the swimwear colour palette was quite simple: black, plus primary red, yellow and blue and classic white. However the dyeing and printing of fluorescent inks was refined in this decade, leading to the increased use of Day-Glo tones, especially lime, pink and yellow, which were often used with black. Colour-blocking and the use of contrasting colour edges and banding were important styling features. Prints had been banished from the high-fashion wardrobe, with the exception of classic bi-colour stripes, especially in red-and-white or navy-and-white combinations. Polka dots and chequerboard diamonds, primarily in black and white, were also popular, often using a mix of scales – from the giant to the tiny. Graphic lettering, in a 1920s Constructivist-style paved the way for the early use of the brand logo. Key labels to use the logo included Norma Kamali, the label Wet designed by Chrissie Walsh and the Italian designer Coveri.

By the second half of the decade, swimwear colours had escaped the primary straightjacket and become more exuberant. Plain fabrics rather than prints, in rich chocolate browns, burnt oranges and nude tones, were used by the sophisticated end of the market, represented by designers such as Calvin Klein and Giorgio Armani. Vibrant shades of emerald green, emperor purple and fuchsia pink allowed swimwear designers to create high-glamour attention-seeking pieces in the more structured silhouettes that defined the later years of the *Dallas* decade.

LEFT: A 1980s swimsuit with a purple frilled neckline and scoop back with a Jerry Hall label. In early 1980s maillots, as shown here, the leg line rose above the pubic bone and the armhole and back deepened so that the curve of the breast could be seen from the side view.

RIGHT: Christie Brinkley models the trend for primary colours in this asymmetrical cheerleader style from 1981. The flattering high-cut leg and frilly decoration demonstrates the return of curves to fashion. This time, however, the curves had to be highly defined and muscular as opposed to the rounded and super-feminine look of earlier times.

Show-Off Luxury

If the first half of the decade was influenced by sportswear, the second half was fascinated by 1940s and 1950s corsetry. Seen in the catwalk collections of European designers such as Dolce & Gabbana or Jean Paul Gaultier, corsetry was taken up by high-end lingerie labels including the Italian company La Perla, which then reinterpreted them in lingerie and swimwear. Padded cups, underwired bras and hidden support had largely disappeared from the swimwear market, kept only for an older clientele. As with lingerie, this revival of vintage silhouettes was not frilly and delicate, but rather hard-edged, like the famous corset that Gaultier designed for Madonna's 'Blond Ambition' tour of 1990. These padded and underwired silhouettes were perfect vehicles for fabrics with more glitz, inspired by the high-octane glamour of American soap stars in shows such as *Dallas* and *Dynasty*.

By now, all swimwear fabrics were nylon- or polyester-based, enabling them to be used for the special finishes and techniques being developed by the swimwear fabric manufacturers, who were, and still are, mainly Italian. Fabrics were high-shine satin, knitted with gold Lurex yarns, given crushed and crinkled finishes, laminated with metallic or covered in sequinned films. Faux chamois suedes and leathers began to be used. Prints reappeared,

LEFT: A 1986 black-and-coral striped miokini by Jantzen with a mitred V-design at the front and back, constructed of Antron nylon and Lycra spandex.

BELOW: A C&A department store advertisement from the early 1980s. C&A, a Brussels-based company, produced affordable sportswear in Britain and Europe throughout most of the twentieth century but eventually closed in the UK in 2000. These Lycra pieces feature typical 1980s styling details, including a twist-tie bandeau top with a central knot and primary-coloured edgings.

BELOW: An 1980s trend that has run and run – the swimsuit and matching sarong. Aqua blue featured in many swimwear collections of the time, and this graphic print by Furstenberg swimwear is Pucci-inspired. The simple lines of the suit and spaghetti straps for better tanning are aimed at a more mature market.

Furstenberg
Manufacturers of
elegant nightwear, housecoats
beach and swimwear.

accented with gold foil. In addition, jewellery details started to decorate swimwear, such as gold coins, chains of pearls and colourful gemstones.

It is no surprise that this return to old-style sophisticated glamour coincided with the rise of the designer label. The catwalk collections from Paris, Milan, New York and London increasingly came to dominate both the glossy magazines and also the rail space of the upmarket department store. Therefore, as the designers grew in importance, they looked to make their mark on other sections of the marketplace. Swimwear was a popular choice and by the late 1980s, it was possible to buy swimsuits from labels such as Gianfranco Ferré, Versace, Moschino, Dior and Armani. These collections were either designed in-house or, more often, organized as a license arrangement with traditional swimwear manufacturers. As the fabric manufacture was primarily based in Italy, swimwear companies sprang up there. Key Italian swimwear labels of this decade included La Perla, Marvel, Parah and Ritratti. Magazines such as *Sports Illustrated* promoted this vision of glamour swimwear, showing the season's best pieces on the decade's influential supermodels, such as Christie Brinkley, Cindy Crawford and Elle Macpherson, on location on exotic beaches.

Competing in the glamour stakes was the Israel-based label Gottex, started by Lea and Armin Gottlieb (see also page 174). By the 1980s, the company had

LEFT: A Gottex swimsuit from their 1985 summer collection, sold in Harrods, the London department store. The huge, clunky costume jewellery is a classic 1980s touch, worn for photographic styling purposes rather than real-life swimming or sunbathing. Graphic black-and-white prints were a hot trend in the mid 1980s.

RIGHT: Supermodel Stephanie Seymour poses in the perfect 1980s bikini shape in a photograph from *Sports Illustrated*, 1988. This cut was enduringly popular – the high cut elongated the legs while the wrapped waist pulled in and disguised any tummy bulges. The top flattered all breast sizes and the whole ensemble suited most shapes.

a reputation for high-end swimwear using dramatic prints and embroideries. In 1984 Gottex introduced the first version of its bestselling '7' suit. Called Nile, the strapless bandeau swimsuit had a wide decorative geometric patterned border running along the top of the bandeau and asymmetrically across the front of the suit, creating a giant colourful figure '7'. Gottex also bucked the trend for non-floral suits, by designing rather abstract tropical leaf or floral designs, often strategically placed on the garment which gave the style a more modern look. A good example is Honolulu, a white plunge-front suit from 1982 decorated with brilliant green leaves printed around the neckline.

Surf Culture

The return of florals and patterned swimwear also came from the opposite end of the spectrum. The surfing culture grew quickly in California, and there was a wide collection of surfwear brands to choose from. Starting initially as menswear labels, these companies reintroduced the baggy knee-length Bermuda shorts, a style not worn since the early 1960s. This 'Bermuda boom' was soon adopted by girls, who would steal their boyfriends' shorts. Quick to spot an opportunity, the brands recognized the purchasing power of the girls and women's markets and began designing swimwear for them with the same surfing

feel, drawing on references from vintage surf florals as well as contemporary graffiti and skateboard imagery.

Quiksilver was a key brand that came out of California. Developed by surfers Bob McKnight and Jeff Hakman, the brand owes its fame to its men's boardshort, designed in a durable lightweight fabric that dries rapidly and is anatomically styled to move with the surfer, with a wide waistband for support. The surfboard labels Rusty, Gotcha and Stüssy also started to develop surfwear and swimwear in 1980s California.

Surfwear was not restricted to California, however. On the other side of the globe in Australia, brands such as Billabong and Rip Curl were well established in their own markets and had started to export to North America and Europe. Others that began in the mid 1970s, such as Seafolly and Sunseeker, went on to developed strong markets in the 1980s. However it was Brian Rochford who really dominated Australian swimwear. Known as the 'king of swim', he built his business with a series of small shops around Australia's coastline, including Surfers Paradise. The tropical prints and vivid colours of the surfer brand designs became some of the more dominant fashion statements of the decade.

LEFT: A tropical-print maillot from 1985 shows typical deep armholes, high-cut legs and deep scooped back. The emphasis has moved from the midriff of the 1970s to the bottom; the high-cut leg extends into the buttocks area to expose them.

RIGHT: A 1980s black-and-white geometric print with pink flowers. The square-cut neckline and bottom straight hem gives a long rectangular bodice area in which the graphic design is framed.

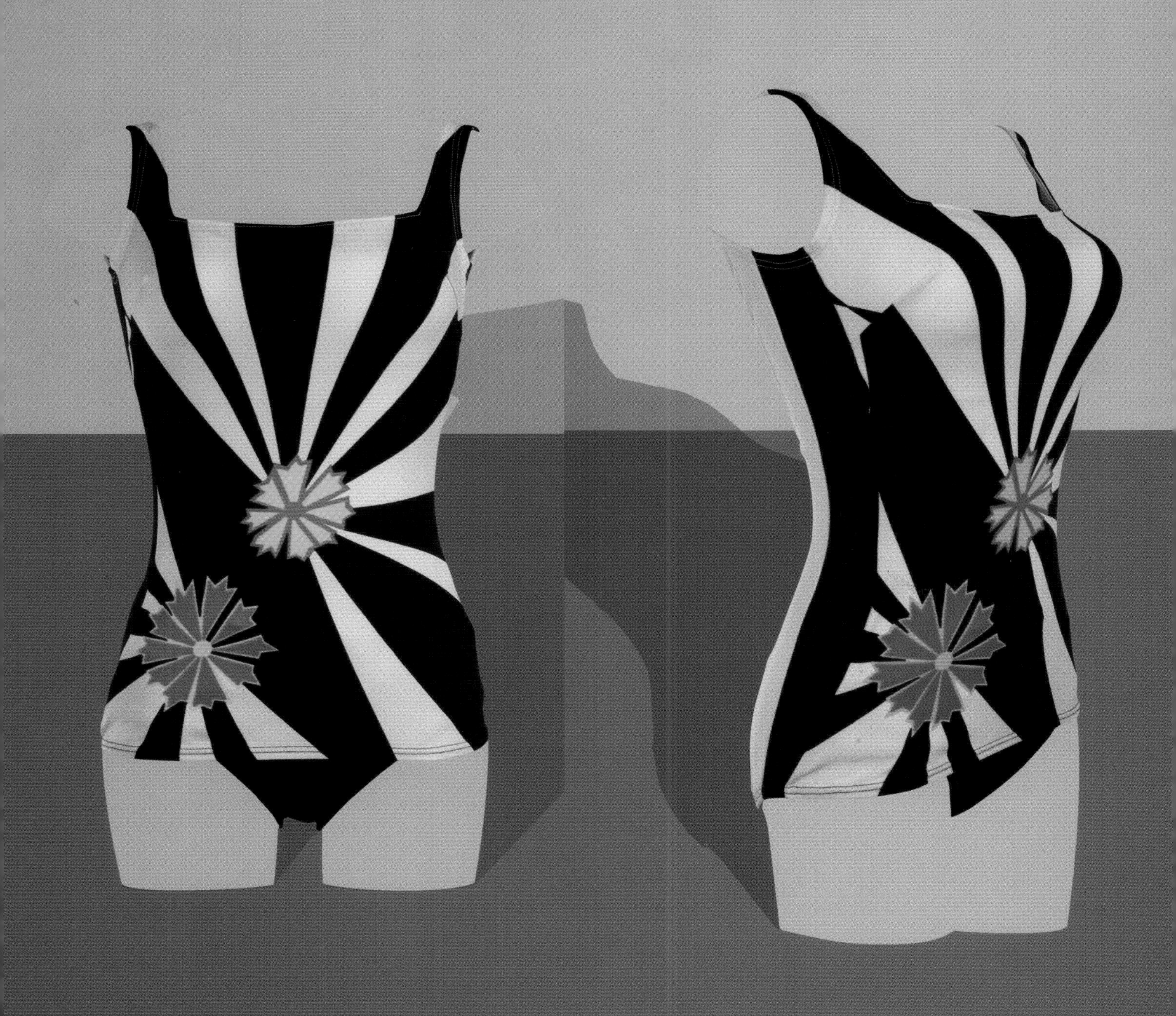

chapter nine

NEW-LUXE NINETIES

PAGE 256: A photograph by Norman Parkinson entitled 'Mermaid's Tale' from the American magazine *Town & Country*, 1990. Gold spandex was *the* swimsuit fabric of 1990 – it was a fantasy element fuelled by the rebirth of hippy styles and spiritual awareness in fashion. After the hard, thrusting glamour of the 1980s, fashion took a more luxurious, pampered turn.

ABOVE: A strapless one-piece swimsuit from 1990 by Liza Bruce, an American designer based in London. Exotic paisley prints, much like the fabric here, were in demand fashion-wise. Note the beaded, moulded breast pieces. This shape was pretty much a Bruce trademark and her flattering designs became jet-setter's favourites.

BY THE START OF THE 1990S, HOLIDAYS IN THE SUN HAD COME WITHIN THE REACH OF A MUCH LARGER PERCENTAGE OF EUROPEAN AND NORTH AMERICAN HOUSEHOLDS. This increase in travel led to a corresponding increase in beachwear, as you needed not only more swimsuits, but a whole beach wardrobe to take you from breakfast on the seafront through to evening cocktails by the pool. With the pressure to acquire a suntan easing and fake tans becoming more sophisticated, women spent more time investigating and planning their holiday destinations.

Beachwear therefore became more closely allied to fashion than ever before, fuelled by the increase in designer swimwear. Most spring/summer catwalk collections were peppered with swimwear – some purely for the photographic opportunities offered by top models wearing very little, others presenting commercial silhouettes aimed at the upscale swimwear buyer.

As swimwear became more fashion-conscious, it is hard to define one overriding 1990s style, as the key silhouette and look would change year by year. In addition, as with fashion generally during this decade, brands sprang up to cater for a wide range of ages, prices and taste levels. To simplify the main trends, though, swimwear can be divided into two opposing camps: ostentatious luxury for posing by the pool and the more exclusive, hidden luxury of the spa and private resort. The decade also saw the return of a 1970s-inspired ethnic influence, feminine styling with a vintage Hawaiian twist, plus 1950s glamour pin-up stories incorporating corsetry techniques.

RIGHT: Eva Herzigova, the original Wonderbra girl, models a winged ensemble featured as part of Alexander McQueen's Givenchy collection in 1997. Luxurious, cream satin and gold brocade complete the dramatic look forming the foundations of the 1990s new extravagance – resortwear.

Global travel returned to everyone's multicultural agenda in the early 1990s, giving rise to huge trends in ethnic fashion and world music. Cheaper than ever, air travel put Africa and Asia firmly on the map. African influences in particular were seen on the hippest trendsetters: dreadlocks, raffia, natural-looking leather accessories, huge prints, beads and vibrant colours were all seen as accents on the leading designer's summer fashion collections. The African influence was great news for the swimsuit, which fashionwise had almost become a highly charged but barely-there neoprene-and-lycra garment for the very fittest only. However, some of the African detailing in fashion went too far, as ethnic prints seldom work well on sleek designer swimsuits – they are often best left for softer, more textured fabrics. Most successful were ethnic shapes in plain colours, or traditional swimsuit styles cut from African prints.

LEFT: A somewhat unusual ensemble by Karl Lagerfeld for Fendi in 1992. Naomi Campbell was the lucky girl sent down the catwalk in this tribal loincloth two-piece. Ethnic looks were explored by various fashion designers, such as Rifat Ozbek in the early years of the decade.

RIGHT: A 1990 simple graphic maillot with matching espadrilles (just out of shot) by Liza Bruce. Interesting prints and fabric designs were trademarks of upmarket swimwear such as this, but affordable brands focused more on plain colours and cut-away, revealing designs.

Ostentatious Luxury

In the late 1980s and into the 1990s, the influence of designer glamour had never been stronger. This was the era of the supermodels such as Christy Turlington, Linda Evangelista and Naomi Campbell, with their manicured beauty. The early 1990s saw the love of luxury manifest itself in swimwear in a major way, through fabric in all shades of gold – from the palest white gold to dramatic bronze tones. Styling ranged from 1950s pin-up glamour girls in underwired, strapless bras and swimsuits with skirts through to softer, more feminine draped halterneck one-piece styles or simple triangle bra tops and tanga briefs. Golds came as high-shine satin, Lurex jerseys and foil prints on white or black. Designers enjoying success with these looks included Gucci, Hermès, Michael Kors, Emporio Armani, Louis Féraud and Moschino. These years were also important for the Israeli brands Gottex, Gideon Oberson and Trulo. At this time, Trulo pioneered an early celebrity tie-up with the model Jerry Hall.

By mid-decade prints had made yet another comeback. Designers such as Gianni Versace revived the statement one-piece suit printed with dramatic placement imagery – classical Italian crests, shells, florals, fruit and even butterflies, all in strong-contrast colour combinations, often black, white and gold. These designs were printed onto high-shine satin for maximum effect.

CHANEL
26 OLD BOND STREET · LONDON W1
31 SLOANE STREET · LONDON SW1

LEFT: Claudia Schiffer became the face of Chanel at the end of the 1980s, just as designer logos began to dominate. Young, rich and sexy was the upmarket vibe many designers were aiming at, and traditional fashion houses began to re-focus their markets away from mature business wives and ladies towards the younger generation.

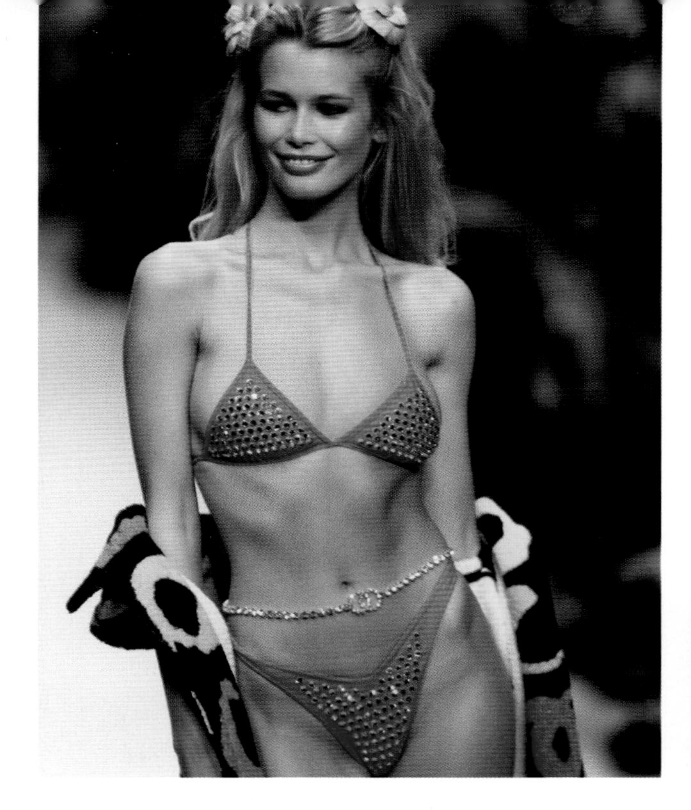

LEFT: Claudia Schiffer demonstrates the luxe accessories that Karl Lagerfeld introduced at Chanel to go with the teeny bikinis the couture house was producing. A diamanté belt is worn around a bare midriff, between two small, mirror-sequinned bikini pieces for a 1995 showing.

BELOW: These 1996 Chanel designs are reminiscent of early 1920s designs, particularly the longer-length briefs. Printed-on pearls reproduce the bejewelled look Coco Chanel loved and which Karl Lagerfeld rekindled.

Luxury designer swimwear moved up a notch with the rise of 'bling' culture. Rooted in the American hip-hop scene, this cult of conspicuous consumption and excessive spending, especially on expensive jewellery and designer clothing, led to the increasing use of designer logos and 'glitter' detailing. Gucci became famous for creating the tiniest, and most expensive, triangle bikinis decorated with interlocking Gs in diamanté. The slim straps on the triangle top and tanga briefs were in leather with tiny buckles. Design houses such as Chanel and Dolce & Gabbana worked with rhinestones, velour, patent faux leathers and suede – these bikinis were only for poolside posing.

Clean Lines

A less flamboyant, but certainly an equally important trend in luxury swimwear came from the growth in spa holidays and spas in upmarket gyms designed for a mix of pampering and keeping in shape. Part of the 'caring decade' trend for wellbeing and a good work/life balance, this swimwear aesthetic followed the purists' love for minimalism, clean lines, neutral colours and tactile materials.

The American designers Calvin Klein and Donna Karen were strong advocates of the trend for plain-dye swimwear, focusing on the flattering one-piece or the simple bikini top with shorts. The one-piece could be a simple tank shape or given flattering bust seaming and a halterneck. Bikini tops were based on the crop top or the bandeau, but were refined with the slimmest straps, expensive understated hardware and often a measure of hidden support. Briefs started the decade cut high on the hips, but by the end of the decade the trend for low-rise jeans and skirts led the bikini brief to become the low-rise boyshort – a good look for the gym-going customer.

In 1997 German-born designer Tomas Maier used the couture experience he had gained in Paris to launch a swimwear line in Miami, Florida. This elegant, luxurious and very expensive swimwear was designed, as Maier explains, for 'time off'. Maier paired his swimwear with ultra-fine cashmere knitwear and a

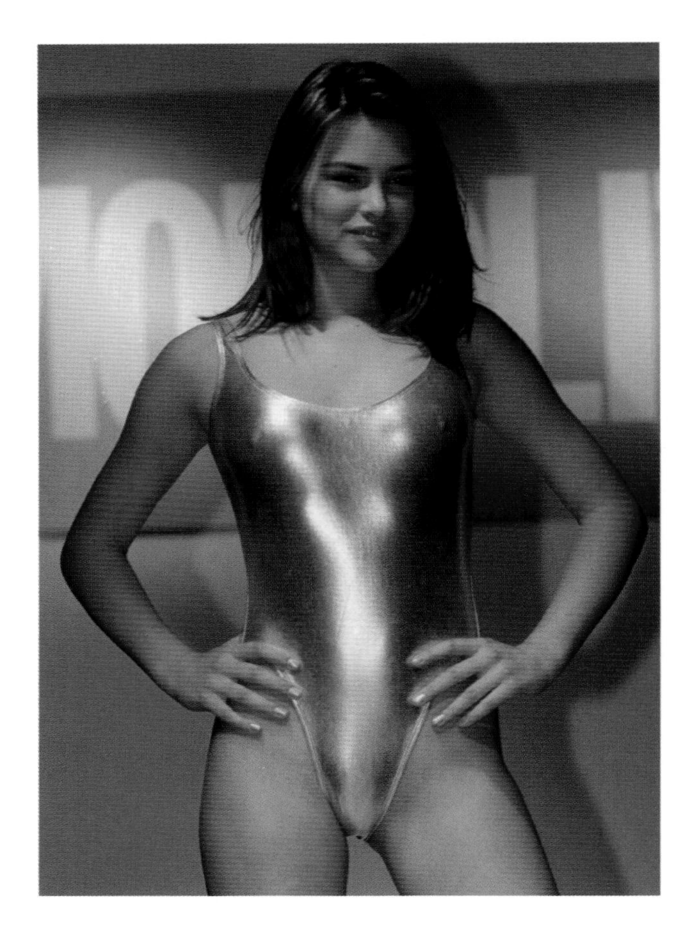

ABOVE: A gold spandex swimsuit by Norma Kamali, from a fashion show launching the swimsuit issue of US *Cosmopolitan* magazine. The May 1990 issue featured over 200 swimsuit looks to help discerning readers choose one for themselves.

RIGHT: The model Manon von Gerkan wearing a silver T-back swimsuit by Darling Rio on Cape Agulhas for the 1996 issue of *Sports Illustrated*. The swimsuit is all about the daring but perfectly simple cut and high-shine metallic fabric.

capsule collection of accessories. The Maier look became highly influential and a favourite in the growing number of upmarket 'lifestyle boutiques'.

Another key designer was the American Malia Mills, who has built her business on allowing customers to buy 'separates'; that is, the tops and bottoms are sold separately to suit individual body shapes. Although this was already common at the lower end of the market, it was relatively rare at the designer level. Mills sources high-quality European fabrics but has her swimwear manufactured in the USA. Her simple, sexy tops, available in a huge range of cup sizes, are marketed as providing a 'swimwear solution' for women, while the bottoms comprise low-rise briefs and shorts.

In Europe the most sought-after subtle-but-luxurious swimwear came from the French label Erès. Designed by Irène Leroux, who took over the family swimwear boutique in Paris's Place de la Madeleine in the late 1960s, the Erès style was made for the understated and modern look. Leroux used the best of the new microfibre nylon/Lycra fabrics that were developed during the decade by both French and Italian manufacturers. These fabrics often had a high Lycra content, allowing the swimsuits to behave rather like modern lingerie shapewear – creating curves in all the right places.

In North America this understated elegance was introduced by the Canadian label Shan, launched in the mid 1980s by Quebec-based Chantal Levesque. As with

ABOVE: A daring cut-away miokini by Givenchy from the spring/summer 1999 collection. Black sequins sparkle on the super-svelte body of Esther Canadas. Double straps give little extra support but provide a decorative detail that draws attention to the bare areas of the body.

Erès, the focus was on the gentle reshaping of the figure and minimizing imperfections through the use of sophisticated cutting techniques and top European fabrics. Levesque also understood the need for equally luxurious coordinates to wear with the swimwear, so all the tunic tops, simple dresses and sarongs came in silk chiffons or fluid microfibre jerseys.

LEFT: A Hervé Léger 1997 design with signature curved lines radiating from the centre of the body to create a glamorous and flattering look. Léger daywear featured similar styling.

ABOVE: A one-piece by resort aficionados Celine, the French company that have worked hard to win over the affluent, mature ladies. This swimsuit is strictly for teeny weenies, with sparkling black Lycra gathered on to a central halterneck strap.

Another contender for the swimsuit budget of the wealthy woman was the French designer Hervé Léger. Léger started by working for Karl Lagerfeld, designing swimwear for Lagerfeld's clients Fendi and Chanel. Famous for his hourglass dresses painstakingly made from narrow strips of elastic, his swimwear, though less dramatic, was equally flattering on the female form. He would use bands of elastic to lift the bust or accentuate the curve of the back.

Cruise Collections

Towards the end of the decade, as more and more wealthy North Europeans and Americans could afford to head for the sun during the cold winter months, upmarket swimwear became an all-year-round business. To meet the new demand designer labels in Europe began to copy their American counterparts and produce resort or cruise collections. These would feature in a designer's own boutique as well as in upmarket department stores around the world,

LEFT: A Hervé Léger 1996 design with a vintage nautical belt over a Y-fronted design. Léger's skin-baring banded swimsuits developed from his signature 'bandage' dresses, which emerged from 1980s body-conscious, stretch fashions, such as those created by Azzedine Alaïa.

RIGHT: This tricolour piece modelled by Naomi Campbell for spring/summer 1997 demonstrates the fashion house of Hermès' natural flair for glamour and their grip on the cruisewear market. A simple gold hoop holds the three pieces together; the sunset orange and yellow looks stunning against dark or tanned skin.

which could now sell these new cruise swimwear collections for all 12 months of the year.

Although some designers are known for their flamboyant style and this was likely to translate into their resortwear, most of the upmarket cruise lines were and continue to be understated, in neutral colours and timeless shapes. Design houses that exemplify the look include Celine, Hermès, Chanel and Calvin Klein. Sold alongside flattering one-piece suits and simple bikinis are thong sandals, beach bags, sunglasses and towels.

Upmarket swimwear designed for all-year-round spas and pools was also a lucrative market. Streamlined swimsuits, vest tops and shorts (tankinis) and crop tops with shorts came from the newly created sports lines of major design houses, such as Prada Sport, La Perla Sport and Polo Sport from Ralph Lauren. Best known for swimsuits for serious swimmers, Speedo brought out a revolutionary fabric in 1995 called Endurance. The fabric has the same stretch and recovery as a swimsuit in nylon with elastane (elastane is the generic name for elastomeric fibres – the most well-known brand name being Lycra), but it actually contains no elastane. The elastane in the fabric is the reason why swimsuits so often perish, as it is destroyed by the high chlorine content in modern swimming pools. For the water athlete Speedo went on to develop Aquablade in 1996, and Fastskin, a fabric created to mimic the technical qualities of shark's skin that enable it to glide effortlessly through water, in the year 2000.

Hippy Chic Returns

This lust for travel affected not only the new jet set, but also a younger generation who wanted to explore the globe. Turning their back on the materialism of the previous 20 years, they chose to seek out the hippy haunts of the 1960s and 1970s, such as Goa on the west coast of India, the island of Ibiza in the Mediterranean and the sun-soaked beaches of South America. A hedonistic party scene evolved in these resorts, from the mystic raves of Goa to the highly organized mega-clubs of Ibiza Town.

The 1970s string bikini, consisting of triangle top and low-rise hipster tanga brief sold in small boutiques in these resorts, was often highly decorated, translating traditional handcrafted beading and embroidery techniques on to skimpy triangles of nylon or cotton fabrics. As these beach resorts became more heavily publicized and attracted a greater number of young people, so the swimwear began to get noticed, too.

In the late 1990s, British designer Matthew Williamson took these hippy Indian influences and

LEFT: Mismatched styling became a signature of the Ibiza 'hippy chic' look in the 1990s, as this Roberto Cavalli design from 1999 shows. A one-designer ensemble outfit of swimwear, sarong, matching shoes and bag would never be worn by this island's elite. Swimwear Ibiza style still required the right labels, as long as they were all worn at once.

began to create his now-famous signature collections of hand-embroidered and beaded dresses and tunics based on the neon colours and vibrant motifs of Asia, but updated for the new bohemian girl about town, such as Helena Christensen, Jade Jagger and Kate Moss, who all modelled for his first catwalk collection in 1997. This trend for bohemian luxury, or boho luxe, had a strong influence on swimwear, with Williamson pairing a floaty chiffon tunic top embroidered with exotic blooms with a tiny hot-pink sequinned tanga brief with long dangling tie-sides, and a skimpy sequinned bandeau top with an embroidered sarong skirt. Stella McCartney, who started designing for the French label Chloé in 1997, was totally in tune with this boho vibe of the late 1990s. For her swimwear, she took motifs from the 1970s, such as sunsets, rainbows and seagulls, and printed them on to minuscule triangle tops and tanga briefs.

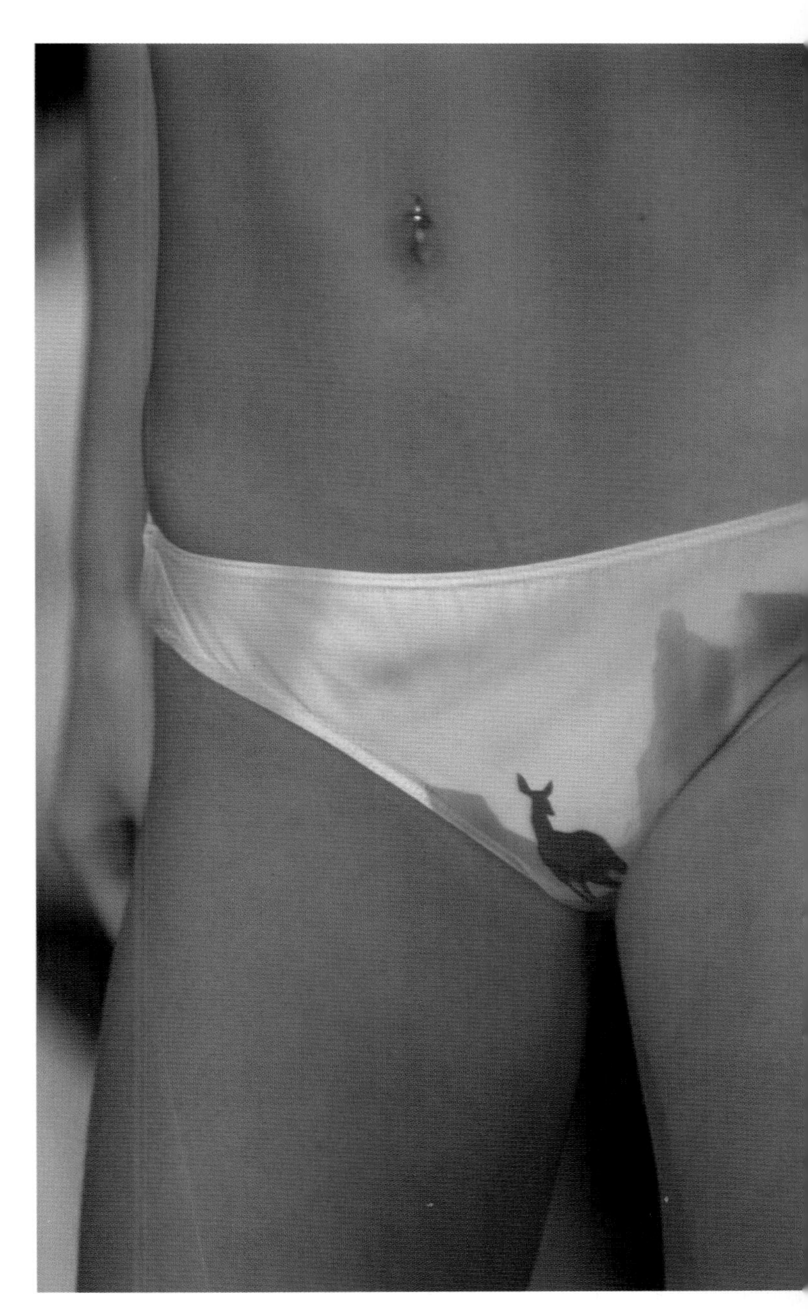

RIGHT: A Stella McCartney design for the fashion house Chloé, featuring a desert pony scene, on a model with a fashionably pierced belly button. This design is from Chloé's 1999 collection, a year when hippy chicks and rich girls crossed over style-wise and body piercing enjoyed a high-fashion sojourn.

One important resort area captivated by the bohemian trend was California and the original home of hippydom, San Francisco, though the flashier city of Los Angeles also took this look to heart, having the weather to sustain a beach lifestyle all year round. It was in California where Brazilian swimwear labels took off in a big way. Late 1990s brands such as OndadeMar and Vix were developed to satisfy a market eager for this hippy-chic swimwear.

Vix was launched in 1998 by the Brazilian designer Paula Hermanny, who decided to create her own line when she could not find any stylish swimwear in the USA during her years studying in California. Vix, short for her home town of Vitoria, took Brazilian-cut swimwear and adapted it for the American market – so that women could choose to have the skimpy Brazilian back to their briefs or more classic covered styles. The new labels, designed by Brazilians who had lived in the USA and knew its swimwear market, took advantage of the fashion for handcrafted products that formed

LEFT: By the end of the 1990s Brazilian swimwear was finally getting international attention. Here Brazilian model Fernanda Tavares wears Rosa Chá, one of Brazil's most important swimwear labels, in 2000. The two-piece features a brown bandeau top with a small boy's brief in hibiscus print. The stretchy purple skirt over the top is silk.

part of the boho trend and the brands embellished their swimsuits and bikinis with fabric appliqués and corsages, macramé, seashells, glass beading and a variety of exotic stones such as aquamarine.

No discussion on Brazilian swimwear would be complete without mentioning the designer label Rosa Chá. Started in 1988 by Amir Slama, the label shot to fame in the late 1990s when it entered the US market. Rosa Chá is known for its bright colours, vibrant patterns and dramatic sexy cut-outs. With two collections a year, the range encompasses a whole beach lifestyle wardrobe, from bikinis to dresses and tunic tops through to handbags and sandals. Slama is heavily influenced by Brazilian culture, using local legends and personalities to enliven his designs, which can include unexpected fabrics such as frog or fish skins. Swimwear is now a key part of both the Rio de Janeiro and São Paulo spring/summer fashion weeks held in June and features Rosa Chá, of course, plus Lenny, Blue Man, Sais, Poko Pano and Água de Coco.

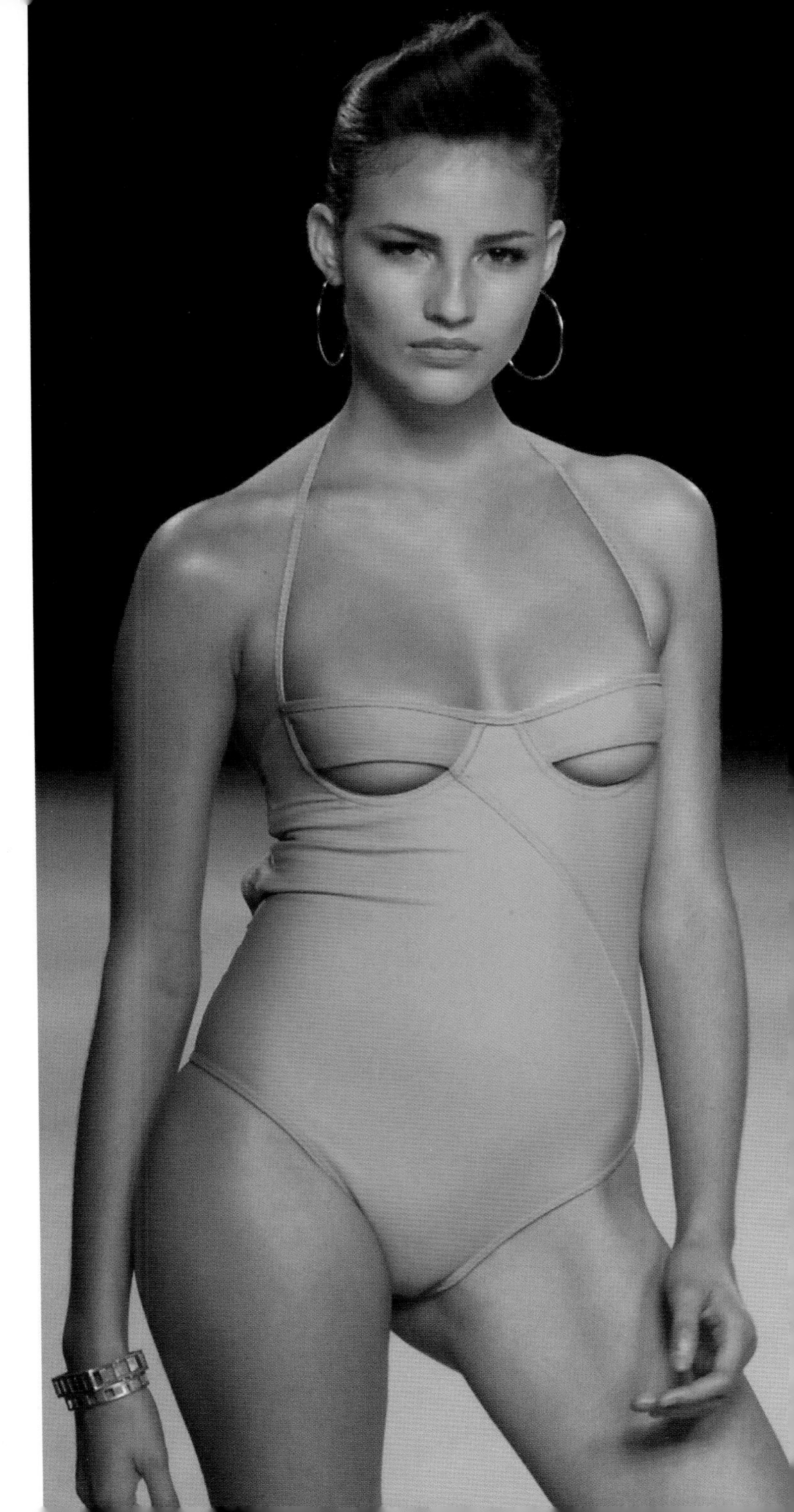

RIGHT: A daring look straight from Copacabana Beach for the year 2000. Rosa Chá's aquamarine one-piece demonstrates some unusual cutting and panelling. Peek-a-boo takes on a whole new meaning but one assumes the stretch in the fabric means that the panels will stay in place.

It is through the Brazilian swimwear brands that the trend for jewellery trinkets worn on bikinis has evolved. Good-luck charms and friendship ribbons were attached to the side of tanga briefs or between the breasts on a triangle bra in many South American swimwear designs. The Brazilian influence also led to the revival of the crochet bikini, handmade using the traditional macramé patterns normally used to decorate tablecloths and bedlinen. The labels aimed at the younger market, such as Sais (a division of Rosa Chá) and Salinas (which began in 1997), adopted a more feminine girlie look, with the introduction of character prints, ruffles, frills and skirted briefs, known as skirtinis.

Retro Surf Style

By the late 1990s, the teenage and girls' labels that were developed by the now-global surf brands also became more feminine and fashion-led, and often expanded their women's lines into several different labels. Quiksilver launched the women's swimwear line Roxy in 1990, designing boardshorts especially for girls in 1993. Quiksilver has also developed Raisins, a fashion-led beach lifestyle brand and also Radio Fiji for a sexier look. In 1994 Roxy began to sponsor well-known female surfers and this quickly developed into the Roxy-sponsored women's surf competitions that are

key events today. The Roxy brand spawned Roxy Girl, a line for seven to 16-year-old girls and also Teenie Wahine, a children's line. These labels concentrate on prints, especially from the nostalgic golden era of the 1970s. Hawaiian hibiscus prints are reworked into a never-ending selection of new colours and patterns, while 1960s and 1970s florals are hugely popular.

In Europe swimwear labels to take up this California-influenced surfer style include Banana Moon, which has been based in Monaco since the late 1980s. Combining Hawaiian prints with sports influences, Banana Moon gives the West Coast beach style a sophisticated French spin. The brand now has more than 20 boutiques, including a string along the coastline of the South of France, in resorts such as St Tropez and Cannes.

Spain, too, has become a hotspot for swimwear design, usually as a development from the lingerie sector, and such names as André Sardá, Guillermina Baeza, Totón Comella of TCN, Dolores Cortés, Rosa Ferrer, Agatha Ruiz de la Prada and Vives Vidal (under labels Belcor and Majestic) dominate.

LEFT: This exuberant, original and fun-looking bikini by hot Brazilian label Sais features ultra-low-cut briefs and heart-shaped motifs on the fabric and between the bra cups. The label produces vibrant girly styles.

RIGHT: Spanish model Veronica Blume wears a flowered halterneck bikini by Spanish swimwear queen Guillermina Baeza at the 2002 Pasarela Gaudi show in Barcelona. Baeza's Lola Escobar line is aimed at a younger market. Like many designers, she believes swimsuits should be considered as important outerwear pieces.

The New Australians

Just when the European designer labels thought that they had the monopoly on glamorous fashion-forward swimwear, along came a whole range of Australian designers. The climate in Sydney and Melbourne, where designers develop their lines, is perfect for swimwear most of the year, so fashion designers have always included swimwear in their collections. They have to keep it fresh and new for Australian women, who wear and buy swimwear far more often than their European counterparts.

The label Jets was bought and relaunched by Jessika and Adrian Allen in 2001. Jets swimwear is as luxurious and elegant as a top European swimwear label, but with a more contemporary 'Australian edge' that is less fussy. Styles are designed to flatter, borrowing style details from a host of decades, from the 1940s through to the 1970s. Dramatic prints, such as peacock feathers, are a signature look and the prints are then worked into a wide range of beach and lifestyle coordinates.

Zimmermann Swimwear, founded and run by sisters Nicole and Simone Zimmermann, began in 1991. The label mixes swimwear with resort pieces to create a sophisticated feminine look using original prints, often in unexpected colour combinations. The designer Lisa Ho is also renowned for her swimwear, with the prints based on her passion for vintage textiles. A recent licensing deal with Bondi has enabled her to market her collection worldwide. Brands such as Seafolly are also capturing a lot of the mid-market swimwear business in Europe, thanks to their mix-and-match separates, usually not available at a higher price level. Other notable designer brands from Australia include Serjeant, TC Swimwear, Baku, Watersun, Anna & Boy, Bond-eye and MaraJoara.

LEFT: A fashionable leopard print and floral pattern on an easy cotton/Lycra lime-green bikini from Zimmermann in 1999. The Australian brand is known for their bold silhouettes, original prints and unexpected colourways.

RIGHT: Australian sportswear brand Speedo goes luxe in this 1992 design. A standard, high-cut Speedo maillot shape is updated with shocking pink Lycra and a sequinned front panel.

chapter ten

POST-MILLENNIUM TRENDS

SINCE THE MILLENNIUM, SWIMWEAR MANUFACTURERS HAVE BEEN TAPPING MORE INTO THE PSYCHE OF THE SWIMSUIT-BUYING WOMAN WHO TAKES HER CUE FROM CELEBRITY SPREADS IN MAGAZINES BUT ALSO FROM HER OWN DESIRES AND NEEDS. In the twenty-first century the woman wears the swimsuit, rather than the other way round, and it is hard to convince her through one glossy advertisement that a certain brand is best. To win business, companies are adopting a friendlier, more holistic 'suits you' approach that promotes individuality and expression.

Post-millennium, ordinary women have taken the swimsuit into their own hands to dictate the shapes and styles they want to buy by voting with their wallets. In ready-to-wear the story remains the same as with every other genre – skinny is where it is at, but clever manufacturers are bridging the high-fashion/ high-street gap with celebrity ranges and styles to suit all body shapes. Reflecting this, mix-and-match swimwear and bikinis are big news; it would have been inconceivable in the past to try to buy different sizes of bikini tops and bottoms. Also, despite attempts by the fashion industry to regulate sizing, there are still huge variations from store to store, so mix-and-match is a godsend. Women can now pop into a multitude of stores or visit the countless online websites, to choose tops and bottoms that fit them well.

PAGE 278: A 2006 showpiece from Australian label Hallican Boodie. Ultra-luxe, feminine 'cossies' make a huge comeback in the early 2000s, and Halle and Savannah Purcell, the designers behind the label, take inspiration from the curvy silhouettes of yesteryear.

LEFT: New York's hardbody take on the swimsuit in 2005. From left the designs are: Roberto Cavalli, Wolford, an Erès Acapulco suit and Wolford's Hibiscus bikini.

ABOVE: An advertisement for Dolce & Gabbana's Union Jack string bikini. Simple shapes, long straight hair and low-cut hipsters are all reminiscent of the 1960s and made a return to style in the early 2000s.

Swimsuits that Slim?

Although some designers embrace the curvy female form, being thin is still in, with underweight models and 00 sizing being debates of the decade. Cosmetic surgery numbers are at an all-time high and although this may not be totally positive news for women in general, it does impact on the swimsuit industry. In the twenty-first century, some women are prepared to pay the highest prices financially and personally to look good naked and nearly naked. Beauty treatments to achieve a groomed swimsuit look, such as tanning and waxing, are easier to do than ever before. For those women who still feel self-conscious and in need of extra help to ensure that their bodies look as good as possible on the beach, there are new options in the swimwear market in the form of Miraclesuit and Magicsuit, which claim to make a woman look 10 lbs (4.5 kg) lighter. Like the 1950s predecessors, these are costumes with inner 'scaffolding' in the form of tough elastic straps, panels and plastic boning. Some versions feature highly flattering wrap designs or ruching, crafted in a creative and effective way to enhance he female physique. Other flattering style features include deep V-necks, scoop necks and central panels that are slightly rucked or ruched to disguise bulges. There are also styles with built-in bra underwiring and flattering simple shapes with mesh cut-outs to draw the eye away from lumps and bumps.

Designer Resortwear

Despite the body fascism of recent years, beach holidays are as popular as ever, though modern sunseekers increasingly want something exclusive and special. The trend for more exotic holiday destinations has been fantastic news for the swimwear industry, which seizes every opportunity to convince consumers that they need another swimsuit, or two, or three.

Resort holidays, whether upscale or downmarket, mean swimsuits and related accessories are must-have fashion items. No longer the reserve of celebrities or the aristocratic elite of the 1920s and 1930s, these lines are developed for those who want to look smart and chic on their expensive beach holiday, on the deck of a cruiseliner or even when enjoying city breaks to 'hotspots' such as Las Vegas. The core market are those looking for the style and comfort of traditional summer clothes but in a very upmarket way that will distinguish them from the average holidaymaker. No longer for the older demographic, the lines now appeal to all ages. Resortwear is usually based on breathable, lightweight and light-textured fabrics that are easy to pack. Not only do the collections feature the usual combinations of swimsuits and bikinis with matching kaftans, sarongs, tops, skirts and accessories, but they also include pyjamas and eveningwear for all-occasion, head-to-toe looks.

Upmarket ranges by Italian designers, in particular Gucci, Versace, Dolce & Gabbana, Roberto Cavalli and Missoni, cater for the higher end of the resort market. Other international designers who have all shown recent ready-to-wear collections for their resort lines are Vera Wang, Matthew Williamson, Michael Kors, John Galliano and Oscar de la Renta. Williamson's 2001 Nu-topia collection catered directly for the hippy-chic crowd, and in 2006 he became creative director at Pucci, a long-time innovator of resortwear. Vera Wang's line is a natural extension from her bridal wear, while Michael Kors has developed the 'swimdress' and long-line tankini, offering conservative but stylish coverage.

LEFT TOP: A bling-tastic gold-and-sequin offering from Gucci in 2003, strictly for adorning the deck of a billionaire playboy's yacht. Taut body, super-tanned skin and perfect hair are optional but necessary extras for the super-glam.

ABOVE: A softly gathered, sophisticated take on the swimsuit from Gottex in 2005. Almost sheer jersey in muted greens gathered on to a tropical flower makes for a more grown-up catwalk look, but may have proved a touch too revealing in real life. The new millennium saw Gottex reinforcing its reputation as a prestige brand.

LEFT BOTTOM: The most expensive swimsuit in the world from the 2005 spring/summer collection by Gottex, photographed during New York fashion week. The swimsuit is adorned with over $18 million dollars worth of diamonds surrounding the 103-carat, pear-shaped Golconda Diamond, one of the rarest and most valuable in the world.

RIGHT: The high-necked halter look of this 2005 Gottex design is offset by dramatic geographic cut-aways at the midriff, a vibrant chevron pattern and a floaty, layered chiffon wrap. By this point Gottex had enlisted the aid of one-time rival Gideon Oberson, and his influence can clearly be seen here.

Specialist resortwear brands have emerged to cater for the fact that the average vacationer feels a need for several changes of clothing. After all, who wants to appear at breakfast in the same swimsuit and sarong for a week or more? Instead of taking 'one wet, one dry' swimsuit, most women find they need more. This, coupled with the sociable aspect of such trips, means women want swimwear that flatters and fits to perfection but also want styles that are smart and versatile enough to go from a pool-side lounger to a drink at an elegant beach bar. As the passion for travel increases, newly rich consumers in countries such as Russia are also starting to get a taste for luxurious holidays and the 'must-have' beach wardrobe to go with it. The Asian market is developing, especially in Japan and China, where younger consumers are less self-conscious than their parents about appearing in swimwear in public. Swimwear labels have never had so many consumers to sell to and, accordingly, there have never been so many swimwear brands to choose from.

LEFT: The Miami Sound comes to life in this vivid blue, cut-out suit from the Miami swimsuit shows, 2005. The be-legged design and matching bag is by Gideon Oberson. It was designed to complement a range of sunglasses for a special show, rather than as an everyday swimwear look.

RIGHT: Another Gideon Oberson design that features a bandeau bikini in fashionable multicolour stripes with detachable leggings. Leggings, boob tubes, midriff bands, arm bands and leg warmers are add-ons that became increasingly fashionable with swimsuits, all in matching fabrics, of course.

MISSONI

Retro and Brazilian Styling

In the early years of the new century, the desire for maximum luxury led to a revival of prints. The rejuvenation of two Italian fashion houses famous for their prints, Emilio Pucci and Roberto Cavalli, instigated a fashion for 'top-to-toe dressing'. Simple bikinis with triangle tops and the now-trendy hipster tanga brief, or cut-away one-piece suits, were accessorized with handbags and high-heeled sandals. Pucci's swirling 1960s and 1970s prints were recoloured on silk jersey or fine woven satin, while Cavalli is best known for his rock-chic mix of animal skins and romantic florals, Pop-Art motifs, snakeskins and patent leather. These years also saw Missoni, the house so firmly associated with the 1970s, rework many of its gorgeous archive prints.

The fashion trend for reworking the classic silk scarf with elaborate borders further fuelled this craze for prints. Pucci, especially, found ways to engineer a border design along the slimmest of triangle bras. Vintage-inspired scenic scarf prints of the South of France or the Italian Amalfi coast were restyled into bikinis, pareo skirts and featherlight chiffon kaftans.

LEFT: The ultimate twenty-first-century swimsuit girl, Brazilian Gisele Bündchen poses in a 2003 Missoni swimsuit. Missoni's 1970s styling is enjoying a huge revival. The suit in this picture features three key aspects: a halterneck, closely knitted multicolour weave and the all-important front lace-up detail.

RIGHT: The fashion house Pucci continues to create exciting swimwear from their gorgeous, trademark prints. This 2005 offering perhaps attempts to combine too many features all at once, from string and asymmetrical to 1950s bustier and 1970s crisscross fastening, but does so in a stunningly sexy way.

Currently, superstylish ranges, including Heidi Klein, Chloé, Rosa Chá and brands OndadeMar and Lenny, feature strong 1970s colour palettes and styling reminiscent of the late 1960s and early 1970s editions of *The Pirelli Calendar*. Creams, brown, black, white and aqua colours in thick, stretchy Lycra come with halternecks, deep-cut bottoms, thongs, lace-up styles on the fronts and sides of bikini tops, hoops and belt or buckle details. Straps are thick or string-thin on halters. Fringing has also made a big comeback at Dolce & Gabbana, with detailing running around the edging on bikinis and swimsuits. Latin America's influence on swimwear fashions continues unabated, notably with the derrière becoming the dominant emphasis in the cut and styling of swimwear bottoms. The Latin influence is also apparent in the vibrant patterns, detailing, embroidery and placement designs making their way into the collections of both the standard-bearers of ready-to-wear and boutique brands.

ABOVE LEFT: Brazilian beach styles continue to dominate the swimwear fashion spectrum. New looks include these boy-style pants with Japanese-style print and the model's tattoo peeking above, from designer Amir Slama for Sais in 2006.

ABOVE: Bling rules supreme in this luxury bikini by Rosa Chá, photographed during Sao Paulo fashion week in July 2002. The stunning bikini was manufactured as a one-off with pieces of white gold attached to a mesh base.

Despite the obviously youthful overtones of a string bikini, women have more or less worn similar types of swimwear across the age ranges since the 1960s. Body-wise, curves are battling it out with the waifs and look likely to triumph because, apart from up on the catwalks, size zero women are relatively few.

Retro styling going back even further in time is set to become big news over the next few years. Forecasts point to a return of the ladylike look on the beach. Recent designer day- and eveningwear fashions already reflect this new, elegant mood: waists have made a welcome return with the cinch-in belt and hourglass-shaped dresses. And swimwear brands are taking note. In a rebranding of their traditional image, Jantzen debuted a range of swim- and resortwear for 2007 that is timelessly elegant, yet contemporary and fresh.

Designer previews looking ahead are featuring 1950s styling including more coverage from bikini tops, bigger shapes and vampish ruching. The American brand Nicolita is reviving the styles of Hollywood's old favourites including Catalina, with polka dots, florals and ruched bikinis in midnight black or scarlet.

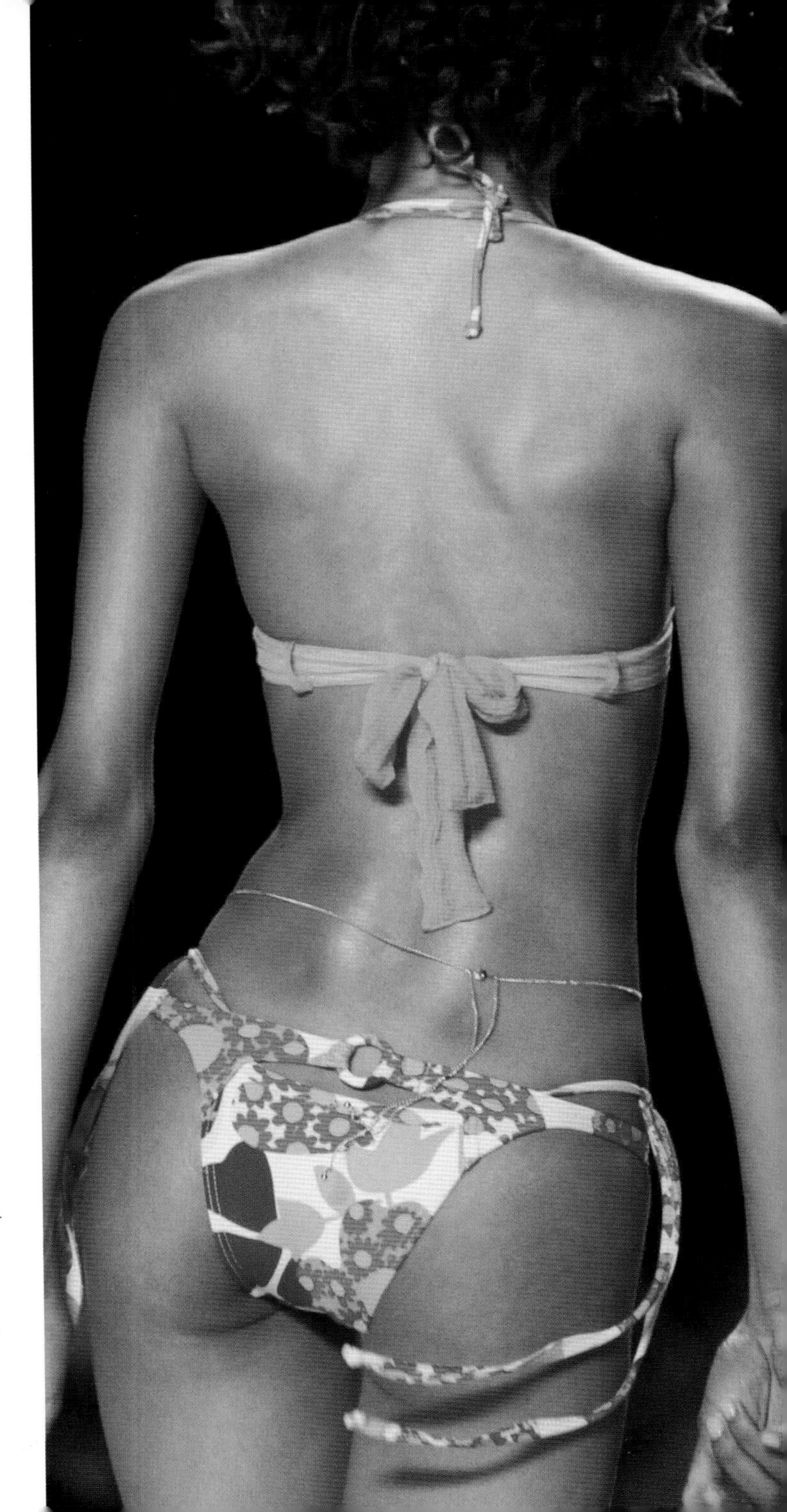

RIGHT: Fun styling details and a chain belt give a youthful vibe to this bikini by Rosa Chá, the stronger-than-ever Brazilian brand, here modelled at the 2005 spring/summer fashion week in New York. The hoops, ties and buttock-baring cut are elements sure to carry over to mainstream labels and copycat retailers.

Boutiques and Brands

Swimwear sections in department stores have a traditionally off-putting ambience. Too much choice, too bright lights and not enough advice mean that many women dash in and out, buying the first thing they see or worse don't buy anything at all after suffering 'changing room shock'. The upshot of this is that women have been voting with their feet and many stores on both sides of the Atlantic have felt the pinch as women shop from mail-order catalogues, small boutiques and online.

Heidi Klein is a British-based company currently expanding internationally. The founders, Heidi Gosman and Penny Klein, have realized the dream of a woman buying an entire holiday outfit package at once. At Heidi Klein's flagship shop in London, it is possible to buy not just swimsuits, but accessories, shoes, summer clothes and beauty treatments to compliment your beach 'look'. Hugely successful, the brand has recognized that many women need to see the bigger holiday 'picture' before buying a swimsuit, and that

LEFT: A 2005 chocolate-brown, sequined and crochet halterneck one-piece by Melissa Odabash, one of the most sought-after swimwear designers today. Odabash combines the latest trends, such as hippy styling as seen here, with the best swimsuit technology. Her suits are sexy, chic and comfortable.

it is actually easier to make a decision in a small, friendly environment where you can discuss just how much bikini waxing will or won't be necessary for your swimsuit to look its best! The brand offers women the opportunity to face their swimsuit fears, and buy one and wear it anyway, thus putting the power of fashion back into the consumer's hands.

Melissa Odabash is another designer that has become a celebrity favourite but who produces styles that look fabulous on real women. Inspired by Italian designers, she chooses high-quality fabrics and embellishes her sexy swimwear with beading and hoop details. Support is achieved through the use of such innovative technical wizadry as twisted elastic fibres, rather than traditional wiring or padding. Like Roberto Cavalli, Odabash has a fondness for animal prints. Other imaginative newcomers include the Columbian brand OndadeMar, who create bright printed and polka-dotted styles with a distinctive Latin flair, and the Hawaiian-based Letarte, with fun, flirty and highly decorated designs.

BELOW: A Heidi Klein swimsuit with a central cut-out and a halterneck tie, part of the brand's beachside line for 2005. The dedicated Heidi Klein shops, complete with spray-tanning and waxing treatments, cater for the whole look.

Celebrity Trends

Celebrities are making their presence felt within the industry, too. In the UK Elizabeth Hurley has led the way with her sell-out range of high-quality, flattering swimwear. The upmarket feel of Hurley's range has brought the 'jet-set' feel within the grasp of ordinary women who are seeking more adventurous and glamorous holidays. In the USA, swimwear offerings are available from Jennifer Lopez and Mariah Carey.

Although the paparazzi undoubtedly pester some stars too much, we cannot help being grateful to them for showing us what the rich and famous really wear on the beach. It is an interesting mix. The good news is that many celebrities take a more practical, less formal look to the beach. Cameron Diaz, a California beach babe known for her surfing skills as well as her acting, is often photographed in a string bikini or wetsuit heading out into the surf. Pamela Anderson was born to wear a bikini, and although her ample assets and all-round glamour set her apart, she has also forged a practical style of sorts: over her bikini base she mixes fleeces, Ugg boots and denim cut-offs, depending on the weather.

Pamela Anderson may be busty and blonde, but she's no airhead, says Simon Hattenstone in The Guardian. Take reading, for example. People expect her to be illiterate, but she's always got a book or two on the go. "Even as a kid I read Jung – *Reflections* and *Individuation in Fairy Tales* – all the inner circle of Jung was a real huge thing for me." And if you go to her Twitter page, you'll see she's also a fan of European arthouse cinema. As for claims that she is entirely plastic, she had her breasts enhanced within two weeks of arriving in California as a Playboy model, but that's all. "There was one quote saying if I stood next to a radiator I'd melt. My mother cried over that one." The 43-year-old former *Baywatch* star, who now lives with her two sons in a trailer park in Malibu, says her ambition is to age gracefully. These days, she refuses to talk about her cleavage ("That's very 1999"), preferring to discuss her campaigns, for hepatitis C charities (she is a sufferer) and animal rights. Anderson recently rescued 50 dogs from a Louisiana shelter, put them on a tour bus and found them new homes. She adopted two herself. "Now I have four dogs in the trailer. I am turning into the person I knew I would. Sometimes I look at myself and say: 'Be careful what you wish for', because the floppy hat, the sunscreen, the knitting, the dogs – it's happening."

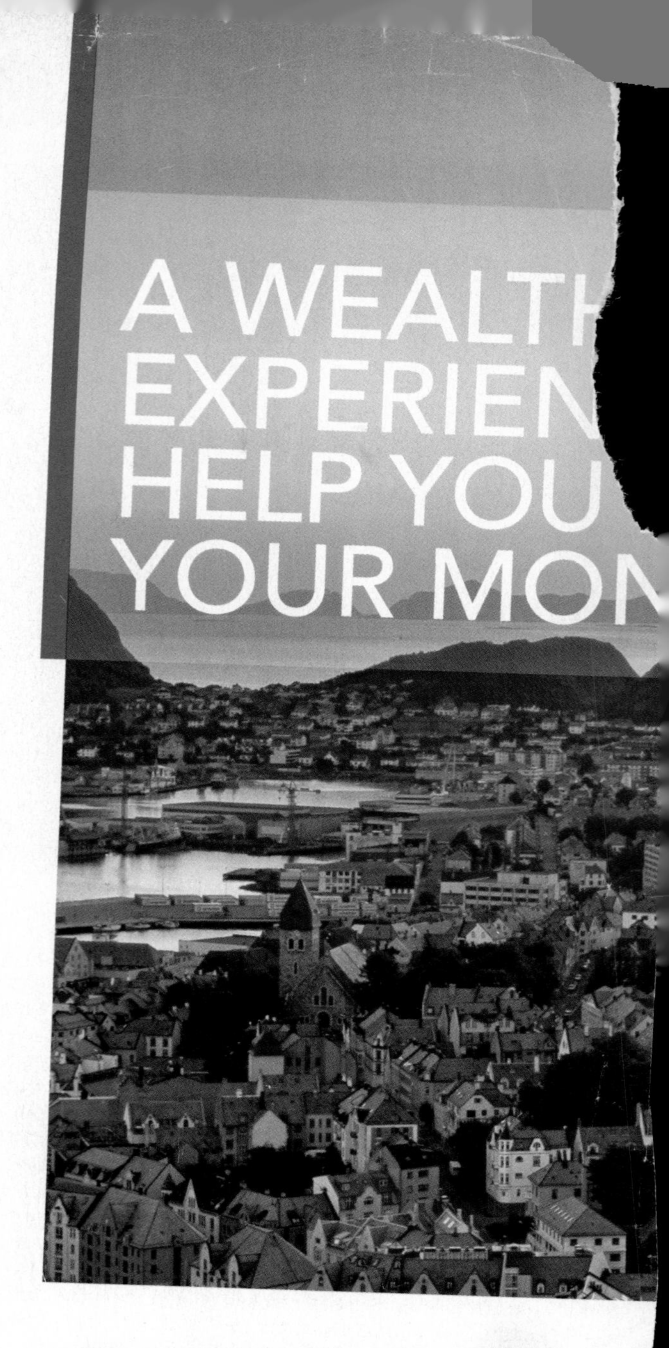

A WEALT
EXPERIEN
HELP YOU
YOUR MON

Sports stars and models have also influenced swimwear, some signing endorsement contracts, others branching out with their own lines and still others simply by being photographed wearing a certain designer. The fashionable Ibiza set have their own swimsuit-wearing stars in Kate Moss and Jade Jagger. Frolicking on this Balearic island is a far more casual affair than it is on the billionaire yachts cruising by. The local market sells crochet and denim 1970s-style bikinis and an 'adorned' beach look owes more to African tribes than Italian designers. The one-piece swimsuit has barely made it to Ibiza, as this is Bikini Island. Even in the Ibiza's nightclubs, a top or pair of shorts slung on over a bikini is considered 'formal' wear, and near-nudity is the order of the day. In the 1960s and 1970s many fashion designers were predicting full beach nudity by the end of the twentieth century, and Ibiza is one of the few places in the world where this might be considered to be happening. Thankfully the rest of the world is happy to indulge in the many innovative styles on the market.

LEFT: Model and actress Elizabeth Hurley designed this range of bikinis and one-pieces for her debut swimwear collection in 2006. As a model, Hurley certainly knows how to work a bikini and swimwear manufacturers are now cashing in on an opportunity to combine celebrity glamour with commercial savvy.

RIGHT: A model wears J.Lo Swim, designed by actress and singer Jennifer Lopez, at the Miami Beach fashion show in 2005. Lopez's line of swimwear includes a lot of the detail decoration found in Brazilian-influenced designs and is ideal for women with curves.

Designers and Brands

Agua de Coco
Founded in 1986 and led by Liana Thomáz, this Brazilian brand produces beachwear, sportswear and accessories. In July 2002 Agua de Coco made its debut at the Sao Paulo Fashion World – the largest fashion event in Latin America.

Louella Ballerino
In the late 1930s Louella Ballerino (1900–78) began designing for custom shops and wholesalers, having first studied with MGM costume designer Andre Ani. Drawing on library research into Native American, Latin American and African heritage, and later European and Oriental design, Ballerino used unusual motifs and lines as a focal point around which she designed her Californian leisure clothes. For two to three years, starting in 1946, she produced a successful range of themed beach sets in bright printed fabrics for Jantzen. Early sets, using Bates fabrics, were not credited to her, but from 1947 Ballerino's name was included on the label.

Banana Moon
In 1986, Daniel Flachaire, his wife Véronique and Bernard Donati met Nat Maori, a French designer living in the US and set up Banana Moon. Inspired by the vitality and colours of California, this feminine sunwear label has boutiques throughout France.

Billabong Girls
Billabong is a surf, skate, snowboard and wakeboard clothing company started up in Australia in 1973 by Gordon Merchant. The Girls label produces cool swimwear in surfer prints for young women.

Tom Brigance
The well-known Parsons-trained American fashion designer Tom Brigance (1913–90) specialized in women's swimsuits and sportswear, as well as day- and eveningwear. Brigance, who worked for the New York department store Lord & Taylor before joining the US Army, helped develop the American sportswear style during the 1940s, which was in contrast to the boned and corseted two-piece bathing suits of the day. He cut his swimwear from colourful cottons in stripes, large prints and polka dots. Brigance also designed swimwear for Gabar and Waterclothes, working up until the late 1970s.

Liza Bruce
After attracting attention with the sophisticated swimwear she designed for herself and her friends, innovative designer Liza Bruce (1955–) set up her company in New York in 1981. She expanded her collection to include minimalist daywear, which reflected her swimsuit and bikini designs, with their body-hugging silhouettes and extensive use of Lycra, mixed with crepe, silk and mohair. With textile specialist Rosemary Moore, she developed a 'crinkle' crepe fabric that was widely copied in the swimwear business.

Catalina
One of the oldest clothing manufacturers in California, Catalina was founded in 1907 by John C Bentz and was among the first to create the knitted swimsuit. Like many West Coast swimwear manufacturers, the company began as a knitting mill, originally named Bentz after its founder. The company founded the Miss USA and Miss Universe pageants as promotion tools for their swimwear (which sported the flying fish logo), which gave it access to a wide audience. Their styles largely appealed to the 'girl next door' and her mother; although at one stage it enlisted the services of motion-picture wardrobe designers including Orry Kelly and Edith Head.

Chanel
Gabrielle 'Coco' Chanel (1883–1971) was one of the most enduring and influential designers of women's fashions. In 1916 she began to make clothes from jersey, a cheap fabric previously only used for underwear. In 1924 Chanel's costume designs for the Ballet Russes' performance of *Le Train Bleue* included jersey bathing costumes and cardigan suits, similar to those seen in her collections. Today Chanel brand continues to produce swimwear lines for their spring/summer and cruisewear collections.

Cole of California
The swimwear company was formed by silent film actor Fred Cole via his family's knitwear firm in Los Angeles, California, in 1923. He began collaborating with Hollywood costume designer Margit Fellegi in 1936 and the company lays claim to many 'firsts' in swimwear, including the backless and strapless swimsuits, the short overskirt and the boy short. In the 1950s Cole secured the services of famous swimming beauty Esther Williams to promote his designs. The company is still producing swimwear, and the sister company, Anne Cole, is designed by Fred Cole's daughter.

Danskin
Ballet dancers of the late 1800s motivated the Danskin family to go into the business of quality dancewear making better tights and dancewear than was available at the time, and the company has been in operation since 1882. Known for its fitness, dance and yoga wear, Danskin began marketing swimwear in 1976, becoming noted for their use of a nylon-spandex mix in their fabric.

Mary Ann DeWeese
After heading design at Catalina, Mary Ann DeWeese went on to form her own company, DeWeese Design, specializing in swimsuits and sundresses in the 1950s and 1960s.

Dolce & Gabbana
Italian designers Domenico Dolce and Stefano Gabbana formed their fashion consulting studio in 1982. They showed their first womenswear collection three years later in Milan, and became one of Italy's most important and successful ready-to-wear companies in the 1990s, with highly established swimwear and resort lines.

Eres
Established in 1968 in Paris, France, when Irène Leroux took over her parents' lingerie business and expanded it to include swimwear, Eres was the first in France to stock swimwear all year round. Irène Leroux continues to create comfortable, supportive, durable swimwear with an emphasis on designer ready-to-wear collections rather than basic swimwear.

Margit Fellegi
Head designer at Cole of California from 1936, Margit Fellegi was responsible for many innovations in the swimwear industry, such as the use of Lastex fabric, nylon and spandex. She was also known for her creative use of fabrics, cut-out and side-lacing styles, cross-backs, and tennis dresses with lace panties. Credited with creating pedal pushers (because her trousers kept getting caught in the wheels of her bicycle), she created clothing that allowed an easy transition from the beach or pool to dinner, such as sundresses and tie-tops.

Rudi Gernreich
In 1964 futurist designer Rudi Gernreich (1922–85) daringly unveiled his bare-breasted bathing suit. Called the monokini, it caused the Vatican to denounce the topless garb, but an unrepentant Gernreich sold more than 3,000

suits in less than a season in Europe, though they were illegal on most public beaches around the world. Defending his creation, he said, 'Sex is in the person, not in what she puts on.' Gernreich continued with his body-baring designs throughout the early 1970s.

Gottex
The leading Israeli swimwear company established by Leah and Ermine Gottlieb in 1949 was purchased by Africa Israel in 1997. The company achieved success and international recognition for its unique, durable and original fabrics and styles, and has been a leader in its field since its inception, developing its own innovative ultra-light materials.

Gucci
Guccio Gucci (1881–1953) started with a saddlery shop in Florence, Italy, taking traditional leather accessories and redesigning them using equestrian motifs. By the 1950s the Gucci double-G intertwined trademark was firmly established as a status favourite. Purchased by an investment firm in 1993, a year later the American designer Tom Ford became its design director and created an exciting ready-to-wear collection, which continues today under its current creative team.

Jacques Heim
Having designed for and later inherited his family's fur business, Jacques Heim (1899–1967) opened his own couture house in Paris in 1930 and sportswear boutiques in Biarritz and Cannes in the 1937. Many credit his 1947 'Atome' two-piece, rather than Louis Réard's design, as the official first-ever bikini.

Hermès
The company dates from 1837 when Thierry Hermès opened a shop in Paris selling moneybelts. He added silk scarves, jewellery and boots and the first boutique opened in Paris in the 1930s. The company was known for handcrafted leather goods and its equestrian motif headscarves. In 2004 Jean Paul Gaultier became head designer, and Hermès moved into ready-to-wear.

Izod
In the early 1900s Jack Izod was a British tailor, who sold his name to an American dressmaker's, David Crystal. It became one of the greatest brand names in America for knit shirts, making upmarket casual clothing that included swimwear along with sports clothes. In 1952, Rene 'The Crocodile' Lacoste partnered with Crystal, the owner of both Izod and Haymaker, to make Lacoste shirts in the US. Thus began the Izod Lacoste line and its later ubiquitous green crocodile logo.

Jaeger
A British fashion house founded in London in 1884 by Lewis Tomalin, Jaeger was based on the principles of Dr Gustav Jaeger who believed in wearing wool next to the skin. Tomalin began manufacturing 100 per cent wool sanitary underwear, but by the early 1930s had became known for the quality and durability of its clothing, designing everything from cardigans and coats to swimsuits and daywear.

Jantzen
Founded by John A Zehntbauer and Carl C Jantzen as Portland Knitting Company in 1910 in Portland, Oregon, the company began as a knitwear manufacturer. In 1913 they launched a rib-stitched rowing suit and the company expanded into swimwear, becoming Jantzen Knitting Mills in 1918. Sun Clothes, an active sportswear line, began in 1940 and the company also manufactured intimate apparel until the late 1970s. Today, Jantzen is the leading brand of swimwear in over 100 countries.

Norma Kamali
Born in New York, Norma Kamali (1945–) studied fashion illustration before opening a boutique with her husband in 1967 and launching swimwear in 1974. Her one-piece swimsuits from the 1980s were remarkable for their cut-out sections, intricate tie constructs and strong colours. Her swimsuit designs continue to be hugely influential in the industry.

Donna Karan
After a period designing sportswear for Anne Klein, Donna Karan (1948–) set up her own label in 1984. In sympathy with women whose body shapes were difficult to dress, she used fabrics that draped and flattered, and created bodysuits of Lycra. DKNY swimwear was launched in 1999.

Calvin Klein
For many years Calvin Klein (1942–) specialized in designing suits and coats, but during the mid 1970s he became known for the softly tailored, clean lines of his sportswear collections and, in the 1980s, for his intimate apparel. Klein favours linen, silks and linen fabrics, without too much superficial detail.

Koret of California
Founded in 1939 by Stephanie and Joe Koret, the company's first product, the Trikskirt, used a drawstring and a series of stitched pleats to create an adjustable skirt. They developed a full range of sportswear, sun clothes and swimwear, and were known for a special no-iron fabric they developed, Koratron.

La Perla
Founded in 1954 by Ada Masotti, the La Perla brand began as a small corsetry manufacturer in Florence, Italy. Taken over by his son in the 1960s, today La Perla Group is a market leader in the underwear and swimwear sectors. His wife Olga is head designer of swimwear.

Hervé Léger
After assisting Karl Lagerfeld and working at Chanel, Hervé Léger (1957–) opened his own company in 1985. His famous 'bandage dresses' are made of elasticized wool, silk or Lycra, woven horizontally around the body and emphasizing it natural shape – a technique he carries through in his swimwear.

Lucien Lelong
Known for his couture fashions for women in the 1920s and 1930s, Lucien Lelong's (1889–1958) sportswear and swimwear were based on the classic silhouettes of the time. A contemporary of Chanel, Molyneux and Patou, he employed many young designers, including Christian Dior and Pierre Balmain.

Tina Leser
In 1935 American Tina Leser (1910–86) opened a shop in Honolulu, Hawaii, where she designed sportswear and daywear using Hawaiian and Filipino fabrics. After a move to New York City in 1940 she worked for Edwin H Foreman sportswear and developed her signature American style that incorporated international ethnic influences from her travels abroad. She utilized Hawaiian shapes – the sarong and the wrap skirt – to create an innovative bathing suit that had just one strap, but it was not just swimsuits she was designing – it was a new way of wearing them. The cover-ups, skirts, matching shorts and wraps worn with the swimsuits created complete ensembles.

Florence Lustig
A New York designer of upscale clothes that were coveted by socialites and celebrities from the 1940s to the 1960s, Florence Lustig's also designed costumes for the movies in the 1950s.

Mabs of Hollywood
Founded by Mabs Barnes, a former ballet dancer, as an intimate apparel and bathing suit company, Mabs of Hollywood began to produce swimwear from Lastex, a woven satin-finish elastic and silk material first used for girdle manufacture, in the 1930s. Hollywood stars Joan Crawford, Loretta Young and Jean Harlow promoted the brand.

Claire McCardell
Often considered the inventor of American women's sportswear, designer Claire McCardell (1905–58) redefined women's fashion in America. While couture designers were perfecting the New Look, McCardell designed garments that were as comfortable and easy to wear as they were stylish. She launched many groundbreaking fashions, including her nappy- (diaper-) style swimsuit in 1943.

Addie Masters
One of the successful California designers of the 1940s and 1950s, Addie Masters was known for her 'hostess pants', but also designed swimsuits and casual clothes that were in keeping with the laidback California lifestyle.

Marjorie Montgomery
In 1926 Marjorie Montgomery began designing pretty dresses and casual play clothes that typified the West Coast lifestyle. Her casual line was called Marjorie's Things. In the mid 1930s, Montgomery joined with other California designers, including Louella Ballerino and Addie Masters, to form the Affiliated Fashionists of California.

Edward Molyneux
Working primary in black, navy blue, beige and grey, and in slim elegant silhouettes, Captain Edward Molyneux (1891–1974) created swimwear for the international jet-set in the 1920s and 1930s.

Ocean Pacific
Originally a California surfboard label founded by Jim Jenks in 1968, Ocean Pacific began producing apparel in 1972. The corduroy surf short was introduced and the brand diversified into male and female attire for a range of sports.

O'Neill
Beginning as a northern Californian surf and wetsuit shop set up by Jack O'Neill in 1952, by 1980 the brand had developed into a highly successful international surf label.

Jean Patou
Successful in both France and the USA, Jean Patou (1880–1936) opened his first design house in 1912. His clothes were sporty and youthful, and he became noted for his tennis dresses and bathing suits.

Emilio Pucci
During the 1950s Italian designer Emilio Pucci (1914–92) gained a reputation as a designer of sportswear and relaxed daywear. The swirling patterns and fluid fabrics he used became internationally recognized, and he also designed ranges of underwear and swimwear for such American designers as Rose Marie Reid.

Quiksilver
An Australian-based company founded in 1969, Quiksilver is one of the world's largest manufacturers of surfwear and other boardsport-related equipment. The company also markets a line of apparel for young girls and women, under the brand Roxy, named after the daughter of one of the founders.

Louis Réard
Credited with having introduced the bikini in 1946, engineer Louis Réard (1897–1984) began in fashion by running his mother's lingerie business. Reard's bikini caused a stir internationally and in the USA it was described it as a 'two-piece bathing suit that reveals everything about a girl except her mother's maiden name.'

Rose Marie Reid
The Canadian-born American designer Rose Marie Reid went into the swimsuit business in 1937 when she couldn't find a suit that met her needs as a swimmer. Her suits were sculpted, much in the manner of evening dresses of the era, with elaborate cuts that incorporated draping, tucks, pleats and shirring. In 1951 she launched her famous 'hourglass' maillot.

Elsa Schiaparelli
An undisputed luminary in the world of couture, Elsa Schiaparelli (1890–1973) launched her career in 1928 in Paris and produced practical, ingeniously designed attire for tennis, golf, swimming and other sports.

Carolyn Schnurer
In 1940 Carolyn Schnurer (1908–98) began designing sportswear for her husband's bathing suit company, Bert Schnurer Cabana, which became Carolyn Schnurer Inc. in 1946. An inexpensive sportswear label, making mainly sundresses with clever cover-ups, swimsuits and casual party dresses, Schnurer produced some evening wear. A world traveller, she based many of her collections on exotic locales, and was noted for work with textile manufacturers. The label closed in the late 1950s.

Alfred Shaheen
Best known for his work in the 1950s, Alfred Shaheen (1922–85) was a Hawaiian garment and textile designer. His handprinted textiles were based on the flora and fauna of the Hawaiian Islands, along with Hawaiian traditions and authentic tapa cloth designs. Shaheen was known for sarong dresses and swimsuits, Hawaiian shirts and halter dresses, especially under the Surf 'n Sand label.

Slix
Founded in 1937 in the UK, Slix concentrated on the enhancement of the female figure and produced form-fitting styles that were especially popular during the 1940s to the 1960s. The company continues to manufacture swimwear, catering mainly for the mature woman.

Speedo
Founded on Bondi Beach in Sydney, Australia, in 1928, Speedo began when MacRae Hosiery, established by Alexander MacRae in 1914, extended the manufacture of underwear to swimwear and became MacRae Knitting Mills. Building on the nation's active beach lifestyle and the growing acceptance of swimming as a competitive sport, the company produced a racer-back costume for men and women. In 1960, Speedo America was born and the brand is at the forefront of athletic swimwear.

Tiktiner
Founded in 1949 by Henri and Dina Tiktiner Viterbo in Nice, France, Tiktiner became known for high-style beachwear and sportswear that was casual but chic.

Emily Wilkins
Starting by producing clothing for the children of Hollywood stars, Emily Wilkins (1920–2000) would base her individual designs on the personality of the little girl, rejecting the notion that children should be dressed like their mothers, and sew the garment herself. In 1943, she started Young Originals to manufacture girl's clothing, which were often adjustable to fit as the girl grew. Her clothing and sportswear was feminine and nostalgic.

INDEX Figures in italics indicate illustrations.

Acalpulco, Mexico 194
Adidas 226
Afghanistan 213
African influence 260
Água de Coco 273
Alaïa, Azzedine 242, *268*
Allen, Carol *139*
Allen, Jessika and Adrian 276
Allen & Cole *192*
Amateur Swimming Association (ASA) *22*, 38
American Association of Park Superintendents 148
'American Look' 103, 121
American Rubber Company 8
Amies, Hardy 103
And God Created Woman (film) 10, 137, *137*, *163*
Anderson, Pamela *235*, 292
Andress, Ursula 6, 138, *138*
Anna & Boy *276*
Antibes 34, *35*, *49*
Aquablade 11, 269
Arena 11, 206, 226, *227*
Ariel *225*
Armani, Emporio 262
Armani, Giorgio 249, 251
Armstrong, Rolf 229, 230
    'Sunny Skies' *229*
Army & Navy stores, London 84
Art Deco *55*, 60, *84*
Ashby, Vera 229
Asia 260, 271, 284
Astaire, Fred 83
Athena 234
Atlantic City, New Jersey *36*, *37*, *90*
Atlantic coast, USA 14
Atlantic French label *74*
Austen, Jane 18
    Persuasion 18
Australia 254, 276, *277*, *281*
Avalon, Frankie 137, *185*

Bacall, Lauren 103
backless swimsuit 8
Baeza, Guillermina *275*, *275*
    Lola Escobar *275*
Baker, Josephine *57*
Baku *276*
Balearic Islands 194
Ballerino, Louella *122*
Baltrik 193
Banana Moon *275*
'bandage' dresses *268*
bandeau tops *108*, *113*, *117*, *126*, 141, 153, 240, *241*, 244, *245*, *250*, 264, 271, *272*, *284*
Bara, Theda 31
Barbados *239*, *245*
Barbier, Georges: *At the Lido 61*
Barclay, McClelland *104*
Bardot, Brigitte 6, 10, 137–8, *137*, 147, *156*, *163*, 182, 190
Barondess, Barbara 68
Barribal, William *40*
Bates disciplined fabric *148*
Bath 16, 21
Bath Assembly Rooms 18
bathing beauty boom 228–9, *228*
Bathing Beauty (film) 108
'Bathing Belles' 6, *30*, 31, 90
Bathing Suit Day fashion show, Madison Square Garden, New York 8, 90
batwing tops 246
Baywatch 235
beach bags *55*, *79*
Beach Blanket Bingo (film) 137
beach capes 53
beach coats *176*
beach cover-ups 50
beach holidays 6, 15, 34
Beach Party (film) *137*
beach pyjamas 45, *45*, *79*, *194*
beach suits *81*
beach volleyball 11
beach wraps *52*, *53*, *79*, *167*, *194*
beachrobes *53*, *55*
beauty pageants 90–99
Beckwith, Agnes *22*, 23
Belcor *275*
belts *35*, *50*, 53, *56*, 110, 130, *220*, *263*, *268*, 288, 289
    sash-tie *107*
    tie-belts 29
Bennet, Eliza 23
Berenson, Marisa *194*
Bergasol 210
Berkeley, Busby 158
Berlei 110, 152
Bernardini, Micheline 135, *135*
Berry, Halle 138, *138*
Bert Schnurer Cabana 129
Betbeze, Yolande 9, 160
Bianchini-Ferier 53
Biarritz, France 15, 34, 49, 53
bikini bra top *187*
bikini waxing 220, 291
bikinis
    adjustable *143*
    'apron' style *164*
    banned from contests 9, 95, *95*
    considered too risqué 153, *154*
    crochet *140*
    fashions 10
    forerunner of 8, *76*, 122
    fur 138, *139*
    halterneck 11
    hipster *200*
    launch of 9, 114, 134–9
    liberated 142–3
    mink 9, *139*, 156
    readmitted to contests *99*
    string 98, 141, 143, *143*, *189*, 206, 208, *210*, *218*, 219, *222*, 238, *241*, 270, *281*, 289, 292
    and teenagers 181
    thong 11
    topless 10, 141
Billabong 254
Bimba *88*
Blass, Bill *196*
'bling' culture 263
Blondell, Joan *67*
Bloomer, Amelia 23, *23*
bloomers 19, *23*, 24, 26, *167*, 168, 245
    ankle-length 18
    below-knee *25*
    knee-length *19*
    Princess suit 24, *25*
Blue Book modelling agency *135*
Blue Man *273*
Blume, Veronica *275*
boardshorts *182*, *274*
bodices, lace-up front 198
Body Glove 9, 240–41
Boeck, Doris 183
bohemian luxury (boho luxe) 271
Bond, Lillian 68
Bond-eye *276*
Bondi *276*
bonnets 18, *30*
bootlace cords 193
botanical prints *55*
bottoms
    'classic' 140
    high-waisted *113*, *117*, *163*
    hip-slung *140*
    hipster *162*
    loincloth-style *239*
    low-waisted *200*
    modesty *114*
    'nappy'-style 129, *130*
    V-shaped *245*
bouclé 49
Boudin, Eugène 21
Bourne & Hollingsworth, London 84
Bournemouth, Dorset 119
Bow, Clara *66*
Boyd, Duke 183
brassieres *57*, 108
    brassiere-top tie *129*
    California *167*
    cantilever wiring 152
    'floating' *72*
    'no-bra bra' 201
    shelf bra top *116*
    two-piece bra top *113*
    underwired *162*, 250, 262, 281
Brazil *196*, *218*, 219, 246, 272–4, *272*, *273*, *274*, *288*, *289*, *293*
Brazilian 219
breast moulds *74*
breeches *17*
Bri-Nylon 9, 142, 173, 186–7, *186*, 217
briefs 241, *263*, 264, *272*, *275*
    tanga 262, 263, 271, 274, 287
Brigance, Tom 83, *87*, *110*, 198
Brighton, Sussex 14, *14*, *34*, *35*, 119
Brinkley, Christie 10, 206, *206*, 223, *225*, 232, 240, *247*, *249*, 251
British Nylon Spinners 9
brocade *259*
Brooks, Louise 49
Brown and Bigelow *229*
Bruce, Liza 11, 242, *243*, 244, *258*, *260*
Brunet, Luiza *143*
buckles 53, 98, *206*, 214, 263, 288
Bündchen, Gisele 235, *287*
Burns, Lucille 91
buttons 29, 53, *72*, *108*, 110, *116*, 118, *119*, *121*, *124*, 130, *172*, *186*, *193*, *203*
BVD *71*
Bystander, The magazine *40*

C&A department store *250*
Cagney, James *161*
calendar girls 228, 229, 230
calendars
  Hollywood calendars 230–31
  Pirelli Calendar 10, 223, 228, 231
  Playboy Playmate Calendar 232
calico 122
California 14, 31, *71*, 90, 182–5, 253, 254, 272, 275
California Stylist magazine 168
callottes de bain 40
Caltex 135
'cami-top' 140
Campbell, Naomi *260*, 262, *268*
Canados, Esther *266*
Cannes 34, 49, 53, 275
  Film Festival *137*
Cap Ferrat, South of France 34, *227*
caps 19, *28*, *35*, *102*, *175*, 238
  see also hats
cardigans 50, *171*
Cardin, Pierre *196*, 197
Cardinale, Claudia *147*, 156, 194
Carey, Mariah 292
Caron, Leslie *175*
Carver, Sonora *37*
Cassini, Oleg 197–8
Catalina 6, 9, 28, 67, 71, 92, *147*, 160, *160*, *180*, 183, 187, 289
Cavalli, Roberto 143, *270*, *281*, 283, *287*, 291
celebrity trends 292–3, *293*
Celine *267*, 269
Chagall, Marc 170
chainmail 142
chamois leather *239*
Champs Elysées lido, Paris *61*
Chanel, Gabrielle 'Coco 6, 15, 45, 48–9, *48*, *50*, *52*, 53, 54, 79, 104, 121, 170, 174, *262*, 263, *263*, 268, 269
  'eyepatch' bikini *143*
changing cabins 14, *14*, 19, *20*, 21, *21*, *24*, *119*, 125
Charisse, Cyd *154*, *167*
Charlie's Angels (television show) 223, 234
cheesecloth 213
Chicago 38
chiffon 271, *283*
  silk *267*
China 284
Chloé 271, 288
Christensen, Helena 271
chromspun acetate 148, 168
Clark, Frank *43*, *72*, *76*
Clark, Hilda 229
cleavage *16*, 54, 65, *108*, *114*, *133*, 142, 148, 152, 153, *172*, *189*, *227*, *233*
Coca-Cola 228–9
Cocteau, Jean 48
Coffin, Clifford *102*
Cole, Fred 42, 158–9, *158*, *159*, *160*, 174, 176, 203
Cole of California 8, 9, 11, 28, 42, 67, 71, *102*, 110, 135, 141, *154*, 158, 159, 160, 167, *186*, *209*
  'Esther Williams' swimsuit 108, 158, *159*
  Scandal 159
  Swoon 159
College (film) *30*
colour palette 249, *249*
Columbia Studio 68
combinations 15, 21
Comella, Totón 275
Condé Nast *147*
Constructivism 249
Continental Hotel, Hollywood *203*
Coombs, Lyn *98*
Cooper, Lady Diana 67
Copacabana Beach, Brazil *218*, *273*
Coppertone 95, *210*
corselettes, strapless 152
corset, corsetry 21, 24, *57*, *82*, 93, 103, 110, 125, *147*, 148, 152, 180, *180*, *189*, 206, 242, 250, 259
corset-lacing *108*
Cortés, Dolores 275
Cortesca label *56*
Cosmopolitan magazine 240, *247*, *264*
Côte d'Azur, France 37, 48, *48*
cotton 10, 21, 23, *108*, 118, *119*, 126, 130, 135, 136, 148, *157*, *187*, 190, *190*, *200*, 240, 246, *277*
  drill 18, 42
  fishnet *222*
  jersey 240
  poplin *172*, *176*
  sateen *88*, 130
  seersucker *87*
  serge *19*
  velvet 122
Courrèges, André 142, *197*
Cover Girl (film) 108
Coveri 249
Coward, Noel 67
Cox, Willard *70*
Coyle, Rose Veronica *90*
Cozumel, Mexico *188*
Crawford, Cindy 251
Crawford, Joan 54, *67*
Crespi, Pilar *239*
crochet *140*, 142, 190, *190*, *192*, 213, 274
crop tops 240, 241, 244, 264, 269
Crosby, Bing *68*, *229*
cruise collections 268–9
cruisewear *82*
Cruz, Penelope 235
Cubism 53
Curto, Paolo *247*
Cypress Gardens, Florida 183

Dacron 88, 132
d'Ahetze, Jean *62*
Daily Mail 60
Daily Sketch 230
Dali, Salvador *52*
Dallas (television series) 249, 250
Dan River Fortel *190*
Daniels, Bebe *30*
Danskin *227*, *227*
Danube River *19*, *27*
Dassler, Horst 226
Daughter of the Gods (film) 27
Day, Doris 165, 185
De Carlo, Yvonne *231*
De Dienes, André *135*
de Gay, Sylvia *198*
de la Prada, Agatha Ruiz 275
de la Renta, Oscar 283
Deauville, France 15, 21, 34, 48, 49, 53, *53*, 54
Debenham & Freebody 133
Debenhams, Oxford Street, London 140
Dee, Sandra 137, *164*, 165, *165*, 185
Delaunay, Sonia 53
denim 122, 126, *156*, 190, 206
Dennys, Joyce *56*
Derek, Bo 232, 234, *235*
Derek, John *235*
Dereta 173
designer resortwear 282–5
DeWeese, Mary Ann 68, 160
Diaghilev, Sergei 48, *48*
'diaper' swimsuit 8, *119*, 121, 170
Diaz, Cameron 292
Die Another Day (film) 138, *138*
diet pills *57*, 80, 83
Dietrich, Marlene 67, 68
Dior, Christian 6, 9, *50*, 159, 174, *176*, *176*, 197, *220*, 251
  New Look collection 9, 103, 121, 155, 173, 176
Diplomat Hotel, Florida *171*
disco boob tube 244
disco influences 220, *220*
disco-style swimsuit *97*, 240
Disney, Walt *185*
Diving Girl 43
Do Not Disturb (film) 185
Dobrovir, Ellen Ann *247*
Dolce & Gabbana 143, 250, 263, 283, 288
  Union Jack string bikini *281*
Dolly Sisters 49
Donahue, Troy 165
Dors, Diana 9, *139*, 156
Dr No (film) 138, *138*
dresses *17*, 18, 21, 23, 50, 54, 68
  'bandage' *268*
  coat *23*
  halterneck 168
  hourglass 268, 289
  jersey 246
  and knickerbocker-combos 45
  Princess suit 24, *25*
dressmaker styles *76*
Drilon 173, *187*
Dunlop rubber company *71*
DuPont 6, 10, 88, 132, *132*, 173
DuPont Antron nylon *241*
DuPont Fibersilk Company 88
Durbin, Deanna *67*
Dynasty (television series) 250

Earl, Robert *138*
Eastbourne, East Sussex 119
Eastman, Ruth *43*
elastane 269
Elgin, Illinois 91
Elizabeth I, Queen 16
Elon *225*
Elson, Karen 235
Endurance 269
English, Kay *66*
English Channel 14, *27*
Erabnit, Merlin: 'All Clear' *230*
Erès 266, *267*
  Acapulco suit *281*
Eugenie, Empress 34

Evans, Muriel *66*
'everfloat' safety swimsuit *161*

faille 9
'Fall Frolic' festival (Atlantic City) 91
Fanssagrives, Mia *198*
Fastskin 11, 269
Fath, Jacques 174
faux chamois suede 250
faux leather 250, 263
Fawcett, Farrah 223, 232, 234, *235*
Fellegi, Margit 9, 159
feminism 201, 206, 214
Fendi 268
Féraud, Louis 262
Feria, Duchess of *239*
Ferré, Gianfranco 251
Ferrer, Rosa *275*
First World War 15, 38, 61
Fisher, Carrie 138, *139*
fishnet 142, *222*
flappers 31, 45, 50, *57*, 65, *67*
Flexees 138
Floral Parade (California) 90
Fogarty, Anne 198
Fonda, Jane 238
Fonssagrieves, Lisa *110*
Forestier, Amédée *24*
Forma label *77*
Fosporter *25*
foundation garments 146
Foxtone News 31
French Riviera 34, *34*, *35*, 48, 49, 53, *53*, 54, *55*, 64, 141, 194, 201
fringing *200*, 214, *239*, 288
fruit prints *45*
Funicello, Annette 137, *185*
Furstenberg swimwear *251*

G-string 219
Gail, Pam *187*
Galliano, John 283
Gantner-Mattern 72
Garbo, Greta *67*
Gardner, Ava *108*, *114*, *116*, 230
Gaultier, Jean Paul 250
Gawthorn, Henry George *34*
Gazette du Bon Ton magazine *51*
Gentlemen Prefer Blondes (film) *154*, 155
geometric prints *52*, *210*, *254*
George IV, King 14
Gerkan, Manon von *264*
Gernreich, Rudi 10, 11, 141, 143, 201–3, *203*, 218
Giacobetti, Francis 223, 232
Gibson, Charles Dana 229
Gibson girl 229
Gideon Oberson 262, *283*, *284*
Gidget (film) *164*
Gilda (film) 108
gingham 10, 118, 126, *163*, *164*, *190*
girdles 110, 180
Givenchy *259*, *266*
glamour girls 154–63
Goa 270
Golconda diamond *283*
gold lamé 146, *148*
gold Lurex 250
gold spandex *258*
Gorringes department store, London *40*
Gosman, Heidi 290
Gossard *186*
Gotcha 254
Gottex 11, 174, 206, *209*, *217*, 251, *252*, 253, 262, *283*
  Honolulu 253
  Nile 253
Gottlieb, Lea and Armin 174, 251
Grable, Betty 103, *114*, *116*, 230, *231*
graphic prints *46*, *53*, *252*, *254*
Greek Islands 194
Greig, Evelyn *72*
Gruau, René *153*
Gucci, Guccio 262, 263, 283, *283*

Hakansson, Kerstin 'Kiki' *95*
Hakman, Jeff 254
Hall, Jerry 208, *209*, *214*, *249*, 252
Hall, Pat *164*
Hallican Boodie *281*
halternecks 11, *76*, *79*, 84, 98, *105*, 110, *110*, *114*, *117*, 129, 130, 143, 152, *167*, 168, 176, *176*, *200*, 214, 262, *275*, *287*, 288, *290*
Hang Ten 183
Harlow, Jean 155, 230
Harrods department store, London 140, *252*
Hartnell, Norman *167*
hats 21, *55*, *79*, *167*
  bobble *43*
  helmet-style *18*
  sunhats *190*
  see also caps
Have Designs *225*
Hawaii 183
Hawaiian Tropic 95
Hawley, Pete *102*, *104*, *148*, *152*
Hays Code 65, 68, *68*, 219
Hayworth, Rita 6, 103, 106, 108, 133, 230
Head, Edith 68, 160
Hefner, Hugh 224, 231
Heim, Jacques 9, *136*, 140
  'Atome' 134
Helvin, Marie *245*
Hemingway, Margaux 208
Hepburn, Audrey 182
Hermès, Thierry 262, 269
Herzigova, Eva *259*
hippies, hippy styles 213–14, *258*, 270, *290*
  hippy chic 270–72, 283
Hollywood calendars 230–31
Hong Kong 194
hoops 98, *196*,*197*, 214, *268*, 288, *289*, 291
Hope, Bob *68*, *229*
Horst, Horst P. *72*, *85*, *110*
Hot Tuna 185
Houdini, Harry *37*
hourglass silhouette 9, 54, 121, 133, 146, *146*, *171*, *233*, 242
How to Stuff a Wild Bikini (film) 137
Hoyningen-Huene, George *64*
Hucksters, The (film) 230
Hughes, Howard 108
Huie de Caldée 54
Hurley, Elizabeth 292, *293*
Hyland, Brian 10

Ibiza 270, 293
Ibiza set 293
Ibiza Town 270
Illustrated London News 24
Illustrazione, L' 72
Imports International *171*
India 213
Inter City Beauties Showmen's Variety Jubilee Pageant, Atlantic City *93*
Inter-City Beauty Contest, Atlantic City, New Jersey 8, *93*
International Festival of Beauty (Long Beach, California) 92
Ireland, Kathy 232
Irwill, Jane *129*
  Baby Bloomer swimwear *129*
  'Knitticisms' knitwear *129*
Italian Riviera *175*, 194
'Itsy Bitsy Teenie Weenie Yellow Polka Dot Bikini' (pop song) 10
Izod swimsuits *85*

jackets, bolero *45*
Jaeger *65*, *81*, 83, 133, 173
  Bathing Suits for Men, Women, Boys and Girls; Pure Wool Suits 38
  Beachwear ladies' catalogue *107*
  Swimwear, Shorts and Slacks 78
Jagger, Jade 271, 293
Jantzen 6, 8, 11, 28, *28*, 31, *43*, *64*, *67–8*, *70*, 71, *71*, *102*, *113*, 135, 143, *153*, 160, *160*, 161, *167*, *180*, 183, *250*
  Aquarius *214*
  Bashful bikini *185*, *190*
  Bold Violets *190*
  Bra-Lift swimsuit *70*
  Coquette *102*
  Double Dare swimsuit 110
  'Heat Lightning' *210*
  Miss Photo Splash *148*
  Molded-Fit swimsuits *70*, *72*
  Nylastic quick-dry swimming suits *152*
  Petty Girl *104*
  Shouldaire *76*, *76*
  Shy Violets *185*
  Summer Siren *148*
  Sun-suit *72*
  Water Star *148*
Jantzen, Carl 202–3
Jantzen Smile Girls *182*
Japan 284
JerSea 193, *213*, *217*
jersey 15, *17*, 42, 48, *50*, *64*, 121, 122, *122*, 126, *206*, 240, 242, 246, *283*
  Celanese *87*, *122*
  cotton 240
  microfibre *267*
  rayon 173, *187*
  silk *287*
  wool 122
jerseyette *81*
Jet Set 194–9, 206, *254*
J.Lo Swim *293*
Joao, Maria *218*
John, Olivia Newton 238
Juan-les-Pins, France *49*
June, Mildred *30*
Jungle Princess, The (film) 68, *68*

Kamali, Norma 240, 242, 244, *247*, 249, *264*
Pull bikini *247*
'Wear Me Don't Wet Me' range 240
Karan, Donna 126, 208, 264
Kearney, Georgina *98*
Kellerman, Annette 8, 26–*7*, *27*, 31, *36*, *37*
Kelly, Grace 174, 182
Kennedy, Jackie (later Onassis) 174, 185, 194, 198
Keystone Kops 31
Klein, Calvin 208, 249, 264, 269
Klein, Heidi 288, 290–91, *291*
Klein, Penny 290
Kleinert 87
knickers *39*
knitted costumes 6, *14*, 15, *19*, 27, *27*, 28–9, *28*, *29*, 34, *35*, *36*, 38, *39*, *43*, 45, 48–9, *58*, *59*, 64, *65*, *66*, 71, 72, *74*, *75*, *77*, 84, 87, *122*, 125, *136*, 229, 240, *287*
Kors, Michael 262, 283

La Baule *49*
La Perla *138*, 250, 251
La Perla Sport 269
lace 190, *241*
Ladies' Jaeger Swim and Sun Suits catalogue *84*
Lagerfeld, Karl *260*, *263*, 268
Lamour, Dorothy 68, *68*, *229*
Lanvin, Jeanne 45, 53
Lapape, Georges *51*
Las Vegas 282
Lastex 8, *68*, *71*, 72, 84, 87, 110, 125, 136, 148, *148*, 203, *233*
latex 10, 158
Latin influence 288
Lauren, Ralph 269
leather, chamois *239*
Léger, Fernand 170
Léger, Hervé *267*, 268, *268*
Leia bikini 138
Lelong, Lucien *50*
Lenglen, Suzanne 49
Lenny 273
Leroux, Irène 266, 288
Leser, Tina 103, 121, 126, *126*, *129*, 167
Letarte 291
'Let's Get Physical' 238
Levesque, Chantal 266
lidos 60–61, *61*, 118
Life magazine *43*, 170
loincloth beachware *121*
Lollobrigida, Gina 156
London 251
Long Beach, California 92, 183
Long Island, New York *37*
Lopez, Jennifer 292, *293*
Lord & Taylor 132
Loren, Sophia 147, 156
Los Angeles 272
Love Finds Andy Hardy (film) 108
Loy, Myrna *68*
Lurex jerseys 262
Lyceum Ballroom, London *95*
Lycra 6, 10, 88, 132, *173*, 190, *209*, *217*, 220, *220*, *222*, 226, 240, *241*, 242, *250*, 260, *267*, 269, *277*, 288
Lycra elastomeric lace 190
Lyons, Lisa 11, 242, *243*

Mabs of Hollywood 8, 28, 71, 110, 135, 160–61
McCardell, Claire 8, 103, 121, *121*, 122, *124*, *129*, 167, 170–71, 244–5
'Art' collection 171
McCartney, Stella 271
McKinney, Florine *66*
McKnight, Bob 254
Macpherson, Elle 251
McQueen, Alexander *259*
MacRae Knitting Mills (later Speedo) 8, 28
macramé 142, 274
McWilliams, Rose *203*
Madonna: 'Blond Ambition' tour 250
Madras plaid 126
Magicsuit 281
Maidenform 148
Maier, Tomas 264, 266
maillot 8, 34, 38, 45, 48, *50*, 54, 62, *76*, 122, 190, *198*, *209*, 217, 220, *225*, *227*, *241*, *249*, *254*, *260*, *277*
cut-out 8, *56*
hourglass 168
Majestic *275*
Majors, Lee 223
Makaha, Hawaii 185
Malibu, California *235*
Malignon, Jacques *209*
Manina, la fille sans voile (*The Girl in the Bikini*; *The Lighthouse*) *137*
Mansfield, Jayne 152, *154*, 156
Mapplethorpe, Robert 11, 238, 242, *243*
MaraJoara 276
March, Babette *188*
Marcus, Stanley 104, 121
Marineland Oceanarium, Florida *87*
Marks & Spencer 133, *173*
Marrakesh 206, 208
Marvel 251
Matletex 8, 110, 132, 136
Maxim's, Paris *198*
Mayo, Virginia 103, 160, *161*
Meistrell, Bob and Bill 9
Melbourne 276
Olympics 10
MGM *66*
Miami, Florida 194, 264, *284*
Miami Beach fashion show *293*
midriffs (1960s) *202*
Milan 251
Million Dollar Mermaid (film) *27*, 158, *158*
Mills, Malia 266
miniskirts, zip-front 241
miokini (maillot-bikini) *214*, 217, *218*, *247*, *250*, *266*
Miraclesuit 281
Miss America pageant 8, 9, 90–91, *90*, *93*, *94*, 98, 160, 201
Miss Great Britain 93
Miss Hawaiian Tropic 183
Miss Ladybird *217*
Miss Tourism Queen International Pageant *99*
Miss United Kingdom *98*
Miss Universe beauty contest 9, 92, 95, 160, *160*
Miss USA pageant 160
Miss World Contest 9, 95, *95*, 97, *97*, 98, 99, 214
Missoni 143, 283, *287*
Modern art 171
Modernism *52*, *53*, *59*

modesty *14*, 15, 18, 24, *25*, 29, *36*, *71*, *74*, 92, *105*, *130*, 141, 148, 183, 245, 246
modesty/decency laws 15, 24, *27*, 29, 38
skirt *59*, *72*, 92
wardens 24, 68
Molyneux, Edward 53, 54, *64*, *79*, 103, 229
Monaco *275*
Monet, Claude 21
Monika *225*
monokini 6, 10, 141, 202, *203*, 218, 219
Monroe, Marilyn 6, *117*, *135*, 139, 147, 152, *154*, 155, 164, 168, 230, 232, *233*
Monte Carlo 34, 49
Montreal Olympics (1976) 11, *227*
Morecambe, Lancashire 93
Morgan, Helen *97*
Morley, Eric 95
Morocco 194, 213
Morris, William *55*
Moschino, Franco 143, 251, 252
Moss, Kate 235, 271, 293
most expensive swimsuit 11, *283*
Mountbatten, Lady Edwina *53*
Munro, Caroline *222*
Munsingwear 198
Munsters, The (television show) *231*
Murray, Ken *94*
Muscle Beach Party (film) *185*
muslin 18

necklines
gathered 24
high *65*, 83
plunging 217, *218*, 242, *243*
polo 240
scoop *27*, *30*, 53, 54, 155, 187, 281
square 53, 187, *254*
turn-over cuffed 110
turtleneck *167*
U-shaped 42
V-necks *39*, 50, 54, *74*, 281
Neiman Marcus department stores 104
Nelbarden International *206*, 217, *217*
neoprene 9, 240, 241, 260
'Neptune' beachware *142*
'Neptune's Daughter' ensemble *39*
Neptune's Daughter (film) 108
Neves, Vivien *206*
New York fashion week *283*, *289*
Newton, Helmut 223, 224
Nice 34
Nicolita 289
Nijinsky, Vaslav *48*
nitrocellulose 88
Normand, Mabel *30*
nudity 219, 293
nylon 10, 88, 103, 104, 110, 122, 125, 130, 148, 152, 160, *167*, 173, 185, *187*, *189*, 208, *213*, 227, 240, 242, 246, 269
Antron *241*, *250*
crocheted 190
nylon/Lycra 240, 242, 266
piqué 140, 186
satin *159*

Odabash, Melissa *290*, 291
Olympics 10, 11, *29*, 226, *227*

OMO (On My Own) 240
OMO Norma Kamali, New York 10, *247*
OndadeMar 272, 288, 291
One Million Years BC (film) 138, *139*
O'Neill 9
O'Neill, Robert and Jack 9
O'Neill, Terry *245*
organdy *142*
Orlon 132
Outlaw, The (film) 108
overskirts *72*
Ozbek, Rifat *260*

paisley *187, 215, 258*
'palazzo' design *45*
Palermo, Sicily *175*
Palm Beach, Florida *37*
pantaloons 21, 23, *23*, 24
pants
    boy-style *288*
    shorts-style 187
pantsuits *46, 47*
Parah 251
parasols *55*
Paris *40*, 45, *47*, 48, 54, 104, 121, 134, 135, 167, 170, 197, 229, 230, 251
Parkinson, Norman *206*, 224, *239, 245*
    'Mermaid's Tale' *258*
Pasarela Gaudi show, Barcelona *275*
Patou, Jean 15, *35*, 45, 49, 50, *51*, 53, 54, *64, 79*
Patou, Madeleine 50
'peekaboo' swimwear 142
Petty, George *71, 104*, 229
Picasso, Pablo 48, *52*, 170
    The Bathers, Biarritz 21
Piccone, Robin 241, *241*
Pickford, Mary 31
Pictorial Review 229
Picturegoer Film Annual 1953–4 155
Pierrot image *47*
pin-ups 228–9, *229, 231*, 232, 235, *235*, 262
piqué 140, 186
Pirelli 228, 232, 235
Pirelli Calendar 10, 223, 228, 231, 288
Piscine Molitar, Paris 60, 135
Playboy magazine 224, 230–31, 232, *233, 235*
Playboy Playmate Calendar 232
playsuits *79, 82*, 92, *122*, 125, 126, *130, 163, 164, 167*, 170
Playtex 110
Plummer, Penelope *97*
Poiret 53
Poko Pano 273
Polo Sport 269
polyester *190*, 250
Pop Art 387
Porizkova, Paulina *247*
pornography 224, 231
Portland Knitting Company, Oregon 28
Portland Rowing Club, Oregon 8, 28
posters 234, *235*
Potter, Clare *129*, 167
Powerskin 11, 226–7
Prada Sport 269
Presley, Elvis 137
Presley, Priscilla *239*
'pretzel' 141
Princess suits *17*, 23–4, *25*, 26, *30, 56, 90, 129*
'Prohibition Swimsuit' 42
psychedelic prints 193, *193, 215*
Pucci, Emilio 168, 193, 194, *194, 215, 251*, 283, 287, *287*
puffball designs 245
Purcell, Halle and Savannah *281*
PVC 240

Quiksilver 185, 254
    Radio Fiji 274
    Raisins 274
    Roxy 274–5

Rabanne, Paco 142, 197
Rational Clothing movement 23
Rawlings, John *121*
rayon *57*, 71, 88, *122, 126, 132, 167*
    jersey 173, 187
RCA *229*
Réard, Louis 9, 134, 135, *135, 136*, 140
Reece, Gabrielle 11
Regny, Jane *64*
Reid, Rose Marie 167, *167*, 168, *168, 187, 188*
    Enchantress 168
    Rave Notice 168
Reid Holiday Togs 168
resortwear 174, *259*, 269
    designer 282–5
retro 287–9
    surf style 274–5
Return of the Jedi (film) 138, *139*
Revere Beach, near Boston 27
rio 219
Rio de Janeiro, Brazil 194, 218, *218*, 273
Rip Curl 254
Ritratti 251
Rizzo, Alberto *227*
Road To... series (films) *68*
Roberta (musical) 83
Rochas, Marcel *45*
    Lido collection *45*
Rochford, Nrian 254
Rodgers, Aggie Guerard 138
Rogers, Ginger *67*, 68, 83
Rosa Chá *272*, 273, *273*, 274, 288, *288, 289*
Rowan & Martin's Laugh-In 139
Roxy
    Roxy Girl 275
    Teenie Wahine 275
Royal Crown Cola 160, *161*
rubber *35*, 68, *78*, 87, *87*, 123, 132, 159, 173
    latex 10
Ruber-Staier, Eva *97*
Russell, Jane 106, 108, 133, 147, 152
Russia 284
Russo, Rene 208
Rusty 254

Sabine *121, 122*
safety issues 26, *27*
St Laurent, Yves: 'Eve au Paradis' 142
St Leonards-on-Sea, East Sussex *21*
St Michael 173
St Tropez, France 34, *49*, 181, 198, 201, *275*
Sais 273, 274, *275, 288*
Saks Fifth Avenue 133, 198
Salome, Where She Danced (film) *231*
San Francisco 202, 272
Sant'Angelo, Giorgio di 10, 142, *206*
São Paulo, Brazil 273
    fashion week *288*
Sardá, André 275
sashes 122
satin *87, 108, 116*, 146, 206, *259*, 262, 287
    delustred *190*
    nylon *159*
Satin-Knit 71
Saturday Evening Post 70
Scandal swimsuit 10
scarves 18, *124*, 167
Schiaparelli, Elsa 8, *52*, 53, *79–80*, 167
Schiffer, Claudia *262, 263*
Schnurer, Carolyn *105*, 121, 129–30, *129, 130*, 170
Schnurer-Cabana *171*
Scianna, Ferdinando *243*
Scott, Ken *194*
scuba tops 241
Seafolly 254, 276
Seberg, Jean 190
Second World War 61, 103–119, 155, 230
seersucker *87*, 118, 122, 126
Seine River *27*
Sennett, Mack *30*, 31, 90
'separates' 266, 276
serge 18, 21, 23, *40*, 42
Serjeant 276
Seymour, Stephanie *252*
Shan 266–7
Shankara *241*
'shape insurance' *148*
sheath swimsuits *180*
shifts 18
shoes 19, *25, 79*
shorts *30, 35*, 42, 50, *72, 79*, 83, *142, 180*, 183, *187*, 264, 269
    baggy *14*
    Bermuda 253
    cycling 244
    shorts-style swimsuits *107*
    shorts-suits *122*
shot 18
Shrimpton, Jean 141
Silhouette 206, *214*
silk *36, 57, 66*, 110, 122
    artificial 88, 130
    chiffon *267*
    jersey *287*
    stockinette 42
Simpson's of Piccadilly 83
Sinatra, Frank 155
Sinclair and Gabar 198
Siren of the Sea (film) 27
Sketch magazine *40, 56, 146*
skin cancer 210, *210*
skirtinis 274
skirts 24, *35*, 38, *39*, 42, 50, *76, 167, 272*
    modesty *59, 116*, 174, *213*
    wrap-around 129
Skirts Ahoy! (film) 158, *158*
Slama, Amir 273, *288*
Sleeper, Martha *66*, 68
sleeve bands *176*
slimming swimsuits 281

'slingshot' 141
Slix *172*, 187, *206*
Sloan, Robert *198*
Sommer, Elke *200*
Sonny & Cher Show 139
South America 270
'space age' fabrics *196*, *197*
Spain 194, *275*
spandex *114*, 132, 136, 146, *189*, *220*, *225*, *227*, *241*, *250*, *258*, *264*
Speedo 6, 8, 10, 11, 28, *29*, 206, 226, 227, 269, *277*
sports brands 226–7
Sports Corner 50
Sports Illustrated 10, 206, *206*, *218*, *222*, 223, 224, *225*, 235, *247*, 251, *252*, *264*
sports-swimwear crossover 240–43
Stevenson, Janet *122*, *129*
stockings *17*, 18, 21, *25*, *27*, *27*, *36*, 88, *90*, 104, 180
strapless swimsuits *121*, *146*, *163*, *167*, 253, *258*
straps 130, 180, *189*, 288
  button-down *76*
  crossover back *59*, *107*, *124*
  double *266*
  halterneck *267*
  tie-back *77*
Stratten, Dorothy *233*
Stüssy 254
suede 263
  faux chamois 250
  suede effect 187
Suedette *71*
suncream 54, 95, *210*
sunlamps *57*
Sunseeker 254
suntan 15, 18, *18*, 34, 54, *57*, *58*, 61, *72*, *102*, 210, *210*, 213, 214, *283*
  fake 213, 258
  frowned on 18
  strap-free tanning 8, *76*, *76*
  and topless sunbathing 202
supermodels 209, *245*, 251, *252*
surf culture 253–4
surf style, retro 274–5
Surfers Paradise, Asutralia 254
surfing *182*, 183, 185, *189*, 240
Swank, Hillary 235
Swanson, Gloria *30*, *54*
'swimdress' 283
Swimfit website 11
swimming pools 108, 147, 269
  public 60, 118
swimsuit timeline 8–11
Swing Time (musical) 83
Sydney 276
  Olympic Games (2000) 11
Sylvander, Yvette and Yvonne *225*

T-back swimsuit *264*
T-shirts *14*, 64, 158, 240, 246
taffeta 9, *40*, *110*
taking the waters 16, 26
tanga 10, 141, 142, 143, *143*, *206*, 217, 218, 219, 246, *247*, 270
  briefs 262, 263, 271, *274*, *287*
'tank suits' 240
tankini 140, *140*, *214*, 244, 269, 283
tassels *192*, 214
Tate, Sharon *196*
Tatler magazine *78*, *180*
Tavares, Fernanda *272*
Taylor, Elizabeth *113*, 139, 194, *198*
TC Swimwear 276
TCN 275
'tease sets' 190
10 (film) 234, *235*
They Won't Forget (film) 108
Thiel, Rita *187*
thongs *213*, 219, 245, 246, 288
three-piece swimsuits *241*
tie-waists *18*, 121, *130*
Tiegs, Cheryl 206, *222*, 223, 232, 234
Tiel, Vicki *198*
ties *116*, *289*
  crossover back *129*
  front-lacing *214*
  halter *175*
  narrow *76*
  thong *217*
tights *14*, 28
timeline 8–11
Toms, Carl 138, *139*
Top Secret swimsuite 11
'top-to-toe dressing' *287*
topless bikinis 10, 141, 202, *203*
towelling (terrycloth) 80, 122, 126, *167*, *171*, 174, 193, 246
Town & Country magazine *258*
Train Bleu, Le (ballet) 48, *48*, 170
tricot bathing suit *64*
trikini 10, 142, *241*
Triumph 152
trousers 48, *79*, 246
Trouville, France 21
Trulo 262
trunks *64*, 206
tunic tops 271
Tunisia 194, 213
Turkey 213
Turlington, Christy 262
Turner, Lana 106, 108, 133, *147*
Twentieth Century-Fox *135*, *154*
Twiggy (Lesley Hornby) 141, 200
twinsets 50
two-pieces *76*, 84, *108*, *113*, 114, *114*, *116*, 129, *129*, 130, *133*, 134, 139, 153, *162*, 170
  halter-tie *163*
  sarong-style *129*

underpants 24, *27*
underwear 21, *88*, 110, 121, 180, 201
underwiring 93
unitards *19*, *20*, *27*, *27*, *124*
United States influence 167–8
upholstery 80
US Rubber 6, 68, *87*, 132

V-back *247*
V-kini 143, *245*
V-string 219
Vadim, Roger 137
Van Doren, Mamie 156, 182
Vargas, Alberto *104*, 229
Vela, Rosy 208
Velva-Lure *71*, *102*
velvets 9, *71*, *117*, 146
  cotton 122
Venice 49
  Film Festival 9, 156
  Lido 60, *61*
Versace, Gianni 251, 252, 283
Veruschka *194*, *196*
vests 24, 27, *27*, 246
Victoria, Queen 18, 26
Vidal, Vives 275
Villeneuve, Justin de 200
vinyl *198*
Vionnet, Madeleine *51*, 121
Vix 272
Vogel, Lucien *51*
Vogue 64, *121*, *206*, 242, *243*
  Coronation Issue (1953) 9, *43*
Von Ravenstein, Apollonia *206*
Voyage to the Planet of the Pre-Historic Women (film) 182

Walford *281*
  Hibiscus bikini *281*
Walker, Joset *129*
Walsh, Chrissie 249
Wang, Vera 283
Warner's 110, 152, 201
Waterclothes 198
Watersun 276
Weber, Bruce 238
Welch, Raquel 138, *139*
West Coast Knitting Mills 42, 159
Wet 249
White Heat (film) *161*
Wilkens, Emily *122*
Williams, Esther 9, 27, 108, *108*, 158, *158*, *159*
Williams, Vanessa *97*
Williamson, Matthew 270–71, 283
  Nu-topia collection 283
Wolsey Knits *75*
Wonderbra girl *259*
wooden swimsuit 42
wool 10, *14*, 15, 18, 21, *25*, 28, 29, 42, *64*, *66*, 87, 104, *105*, 118, 122, 125, 130, 170, 190
  jersey 122
Woolworths 84
Worth, Charles 21
'wrestling suits' 240
Wright, Nikki *98*

X-back 10, *247*

Young, Loretta *67*
Yrande, Helene 54, *64*, 83

Ziegfeld Follies (film) 108
Zimmermann, Nicole and Simone 276
Zimmermann Swimwear 276, *277*
zips 80, *113*, 148, *163*, *186*, 187, *189*, 241, *241*

Bibliography and Further Reading

Bathing Beauties, Michael Colmer, Sphere Books, 1977.

The Bikini, Pedro Silmon, Diadem Books, 1986.

The Bikini: A Cultural History, Patrick Alac, Parkstone Press Ltd, 2002.

Blondes, Paula Yates, Michael Joseph, 1983

California Fashion: From the Old West to New Hollywood, Marian Hall, Marjorie Carne and Sylvia Sheppard, Harry N Abrams, 2002.

Costumi da Bago (Swimsuits), Doretta Davanza Poli, Zanfi Editori, 1995.

'Girls Who Arouse Dangerous Passions': women and bathing, 1900–39, Catherine Horwood, *Women's History Review*, Vol 9. 4, 2000.

Gottex: Swimwear Haute Couture, Hélène Schouman, Assouline, 2006.

In Fashion: Dress in the Twentieth Century, Prudence Glynn with Madeline Ginsburg, Oxford University Press, 1978.

Making Waves: Swimsuits and the Undressing of America, Lena Lencek and Gideon Bosker, Chronicle Books, 1989

Model Girl, Charles Castle, David & Charles, 1977.

Nova 1965–1975, David Hillman and Harri Peccinotti, editor David Gibbs, Pavilion Books, 1993.

Nylon: The Manmade Fashion Revolution, Susannah Handley, Bloomsbury, 1999.

Splash! A History of Swimwear, Richard Martin and Harold Koda, Rizzoli, 1990.

Sports Illustrated Knockouts: Five Decades of Swimsuit Photography, editor Steve Hoffman, Sports Illustrated Books, 2003.

Twentieth-Century Fashion, Linda Watson, Carlton Books, 2003.

Twentieth-Century Fashion: The Complete Sourcebook, John Peacock and Christian Lacroix, Thames & Hudson, 1993.

Women in Wartime: The Role of Women's Magazines 1939–45, Jane Waller and Michael Vaughan-Rees, Optima Books, 1987.

Picture Credits

Front jacket cover: A 1942 Jantzen Peekay Print swimsuit, worn by a model standing inside an exercise ring and photographed by John Rawlings. The red-and-white two-piece is a soft and light knit piqué with Lastex yarn in a poppy leaf print. It was also available in blue and green.

Back jacket cover and spine: The iconic Jantzen logo – the red Diving Girl – first appeared on the cover of a 1920 swimwear catalogue. The image here is taken from an advertisement that ran with the slogan 'The Suit that Changed Bathing to Swimming' and the words 'Jantzen: The Nation's Swimming Suit'.

The publishers would like to thank the following sources for their kind permission to reproduce the photographs in this book.

Key: t=Top, b=Bottom, c=Centre, l=Left and r=Right

Image Courtesy of The Advertising Archive: 132, 150, 160t&b, 161b, 173, 180r, 181, 186t&b, 211, 213, 214t, 217t&b, 221, 240, 250b, 251, 262, 281, 286; ; /Images Courtesy of Jantzen Apparel, LLC. @2007 All copyrights & trademarks in the Images expressly reserved to Jantzen Apparel, LLC: 70, 71, 104, 153b
Aquarius Collection: /©Hammer: 139l
British Library: ©British Library Board. All Rights Reserved. (EVAN.339): 22
©Brown & Bigelow, Inc., Saint Paul, Minnesota: 229
Camera Press London: /Photograph by Ullstein: 61, 66, 68
Corbis: /©Archivo Iconografico, S.A: 49; /© Michel Arnaud: 263t; /©Caetano Barreira/Reuters: 288l; /©Carlos Barria/Reuters: 285; /©Bettmann: 16, 18, 37, 39, 133, 155r, 161t, 164l, 200l, 203b, 231l, 233; /©Blue Lantern Studio: 228; /©Petre Buzolanu: 282b, 283t; /©Cinema Photo: 115, 196, 197, 198; /Condé Nast Archive: 7, 32, 50, 51r, 52l, 55, 62, 64, 72, 85, 86, 87, 100, 102, 110, 111, 120, 121, 123, 124, 126, 127, 130, 140, 144, 147, 169, 170, 171, 174, 176, 177, 178, 183, 192, 194, 195, 197, 198, 208, 209, 224, 226; /©Corbis Sygma: 143b; /©Corbis Sygma/Julio Donoso: 260; /©Corbis Sygma/Orban Thierry: 266, 271; /©Corbis Sygma/Vauthey Pierre: 259, 263b; /©Neville Elder: 280; /©David Gray/Reuters: 278; /©Hulton-Deutsch Collection: 191; /©Nancy Kaszerman/Zuma: 283b, 289; /©John Springer Collection: 158; /©K.J.Historical: 36; /©Douglas Kirkland: 249, 254; /©Genevieve Naylor: 122, 128, 131, 159b, 169; /©Stefano Rellandini/Reuters: 287; /©Reuters: 272, 273, 288r; /©Herb Schmitz: 220; /©Marc Serota/Reuters: 284; /Stapleton Collection: 60; /Stapleton Collection/ Henry George Gawthorne: 34; /©Sunset Boulevard: 134, 154, 155l
Culture Archive: 51l
Empics: /AP: 142, 187l; /PA: 95; /PA/Ian West: 292
Getty Images: /2005 China Photos: 99; /AFP: 135; /American Stock: 90; /Eric Carpenter/John Kobal Foundation: 114; /Central Press/Stringer: 98b; / Evening Standard/Stringer: 97r; /FPG/Hulton Archive: 12; /General Photographic Agency: 27; /Hulton Archive: 14, 21t, 30, 31, 48, 53, 67, 167r, 184, 199, 207, 223, 238; /Hulton Archive/Terry O'Neill: 244; /Hulton Archive/Stringer: 91, 92–93, 167r; /Imagno: 19; /Harold M. Lambert/ Lambert: 17; /ND/Roger Viollet: 20; /George Rose: 241r; /Clarence Sinclair Bull/John Kobal Foundation: 108; /Time Life Pictures; 94, 159t
Image Courtesy of Heidi Klein: 291
Illustrated London News Picture Library: 1, 24, 40, 41l&r, 56, 78l, 89, 146, 180l, 230
Images Courtesy of Jantzen Apparel, LLC. @2007 All copyrights & trademarks in the Images expressly reserved to Jantzen Apparel, LLC: 28, 42, 43, 76, 103, 148, 149, 152, 153t, 182, 185, 190t&b, 210, 214b, 241l, 250t

Jupiter Images: /Comstock: 4
Magnum: /Bruno Barbey: 218t; /Guy Le Querrec: 227; /Ferdinando Scianna: 242, 258, 261
Mary Evans Picture Library: 15, 23, 44, 113; ; /Image Courtesy of Jantzen Apparel, LLC. @2007 All copyrights & trademarks in the Image expressly reserved to Jantzen Apparel, LLC: 73
Image Courtesy of Norman Parkinson Archive: 204, 236, 239, 245, 256
Offside: /Sports Illustrated: 188, 206, 219, 225, 246, 247, 253, 265
Photos12.Com: /ARJ-©Succession Picasso/DACS 2007: 21b
Picture Desk/The Kobal Collection: /20th Century Fox/Powolny, Frank: 231r; /20th Century Fox/Reisfeld, Bert: 232; /Baywatch Co/Tower 12 Prods: 235; /Columbia: 164r; /Lucas Film/20th Century Fox/Nelson, Ralph Jr: 139r; /MGM/EON/Hamshere, Keith: 138; /Orion/Warner Bros/MC Broom, Bruce: 234l; /Paramount: 69
Reuters: /Mark Baker: 276; /Jack Dabaghian: 267l&r, 268, 269; /Albert Gea: 275; /Peter Morgan: 264; /Paulo Whitaker: 274
Rex Features: 98t, 141; /Peter Brooker: 252; /Everett Collection: 109, 222, 234r; /Michael Friedel: 143t, 218b; /News Group: 277; /Reset: 282t; /Robert Hunt Library: 156; /Sipa Press: 136, 137; /SNAP: 165; /Steve Wood: 270; /Bill Zygmant: 96, 97l
Speedo: /Sputnik Communications: 29
Topfoto.co.uk: 26; /Ray Roberts: 35
Victoria & Albert Museum: 88l&r
Vinmag Archive Ltd: /Mapplethorpe: 243
WireImage.com: /Thomas Concordia: 293; /Ferdaus Shamim: 290
Westminster City Archives: 38t&b, 65, 78r, 79t&b, 80, 81, 84l&r, 106, 107

Every effort has been made to acknowledge correctly and contact the source and/or copyright holder of each picture and Carlton Books Limited apologizes for any unintentional errors or omissions, which will be corrected in future editions of this book.

Author's Acknowledgements

This book is dedicated to my mother, my sister and my Aunty Jen. With special thanks to Jane W. Kellock for help, advice and inspiration and thanks also to Julie Cooper for brilliant brainstorming. Extra-special thanks to Gail Gubbins for absolutely everything else.

Publisher's Acknowledgements

The publishers would especially like to thank the Jantzen Apparel, LLC for providing advertisements and vintage swimsuits from their archives, and supplying caption information. The brand's revolutionary advances in swimwear mark them as pioneers and one of the most recognized names in swimwear history, while their iconic Diving Girl logo – featured on their bathing suits and in their advertising campaigns – is recognized nationally and internationally as a symbol of quality and innovation.

The History of the Jantzen Diving Girl

In 1920 the Portland, Oregon-based Jantzen Knitting Mills released a catalogue of their bathing suits, which featured an illustration by Frank and Florenz Clark of a diving woman, clad in a daring red suit complete with stockings and cap. Some of her many admirers cut out the Diving Girl and pasted it on the windscreens of their automobiles, in classic pin-up fashion. The fad spread beyond the West Coast when Jantzen officials pasted the images on the windows of a train en route to a Shriners convention in Washington, DC. A national advertising campaign followed, with millions of Diving Girl decals produced. The Diving Girl craze became so intense that Massachusetts authorities insisted that the stickers be removed from automobile windshields in the interest of public safety. In 1931 an independent brand survey revealed that she was the seventh most recognized symbol in the USA.

She first appeared on Jantzen suits in 1923. Her classic outfit of red-and-white stripes exhibited one of Jantzen's early knitting technologies. As Jantzen gained world-wide acclaim the Diving Girl became an international symbol, at one time reigning over 17 Jantzen design studios around the globe. Since 1920, the red Diving Girl has graced Jantzen advertising, billboards and the company's Learn to Swim and Clean Water campaigns. She has been embroidered on Jantzen swimsuits for decades and was the splash heard around the world. Over the years she has been modified and updated. The stocking cap and stockings gradually disappeared and in 1948 she went strapless. In the 1980s she was revised again. She is still visible today as an integral part of the company logo. True to her iconic past, she continues to lead and revitalize the brand in the current national advertising campaign and in glamorous swim collections inspired by Jantzen's rich heritage. The Diving Girl, one of the longest-lived apparel icons, remains eternally timeless.

For more information and historical background on both the Jantzen company and the Diving Girl, visit www.jantzen.com. Store locations and customer information are also available.

JANTZEN